Fishing in Bermuda

Graham Faiella

To David
with love from
John & Cill

MACMILLAN
CARIBBEAN

Macmillan Education
Between Towns Road, Oxford OX4 3PP
A division of Macmillan Publishers Limited
Companies and representatives throughout the world

www.macmillan-caribbean.com

ISBN 0 333 96707 0

Designed by Gary Fielder at AC Design
Cover design by Gary Fielder at AC Design
Cover photographs by Bermuda News Bureau/Captain Keith Winter (front)
and Flybridge Tackle (back)

Printed and bound in Malaysia

2007 2006 2005 2004 2003
10 9 8 7 6 5 4 3 2 1

Contents

Appendices

Acknowledgements

Among the many people who, wittingly or unwittingly, helped me to write this book, with their knowledge and information about, and experience of, fishing in Bermuda, I'm particularly grateful to the following: Captain Billy McCallum, commercial fisherman; Captain Andrew Card, commercial fisherman; Captain Eugene (Gene) Barnes, commercial fisherman; Captain Allen DeSilva, charter fisherman; Captain Keith Winter, charter fisherman; Captain Milton Pitman, ex-charter fisherman; Sean Ingham, Pathfinder Fisheries Ltd; Ellen Jane Hollis, Bermuda National Library; Penny Hill, Librarian, Department of Agriculture, Fisheries and Parks; Dr Brian Luckhurst, Senior Fisheries Officer, Norbert Simmons, Fisheries Officer/Extension, Sarah Manuel, Fisheries Biologist, Tammy Trott, Fisheries Technician, and Pamela Wade, Administrative Assistant, Division of Fisheries, Department of Agriculture and Fisheries; Dr Raoul Andersen, Memorial University of Newfoundland, St John's, NF; Dr Gene Barrett, St Mary's University, Halifax, NS; 'Pete' Perinchief; Duncan McDowall, author of *Another World: Bermuda and the Rise of Modern Tourism*; Bobby Rego, Fly Bridge Tackle; Sue McCarty; John Faiella; Debbie Faiella; and Jill Jarnow.

Grateful thanks also to Kat Cruickshank, whose original watercolour paintings of fishes from around Bermuda illuminate the plate section of this book with their radiant vitality and beauty.

Most of all I'd like to thank my brother, Peter, who first thought of the idea for this book while chumming one day with his half digested breakfast off Hugh Conyers' boat on the South Shore.

Notwithstanding the acknowledgements above, any errors committed or opinions expressed in this book are mine alone for which I take sole responsibility.

Disclaimer

While I have tried to be as accurate and as objective as possible in this book, Nature and fishermen prove as many exceptions to the rules as there are rules to be proved. Fish, for as much as is known about them, which is little enough, have not been advised of the laws of man. Fishermen, too, by their character, and in imitation of their prey, more obediently obey Nature's inclinations than man's dispositions.

Wherever in this book, therefore, a statement about fishing may be construed as fact, as often as not an equal and opposite statement may be inferred to contradict the fact, as and when Nature, or fishermen, may dictate.

Consequently, in this book I make no claim whatsoever to the absolute truth of its statements and observations. I merely offer them in so far as they may generally reflect conditions as I understand them – imperfectly – with respectful admiration for the far greater knowledge of Bermuda's fishermen, and recognizing the infinite capacity for Nature to do what she damn well pleases.

Glossary of Common Fishing and Fisheries Terms

Bag Limit: Fixed maximum number of fish that each boat or fisherman can land, usually per day. Mainly applied to recreational fishermen.

Bycatch: Fish and/or other marine life caught incidentally along with targeted catch species. Most bycatch is discarded at sea.

Carrying Capacity: The maximum population size that a given area or ecosystem can support indefinitely under a given set of environmental conditions.

Catch Per Unit Effort (CPUE): A measure of the amount of fish caught related to the effort expended to catch that amount of fish. With reliable data, CPUE may be used to compare the availability of a species over a number of years. Example (from *Bermuda's Commercial Line Fishery for Wahoo and Dolphinfish 1987–97: Landings, Seasonality and Catch Per Unit Effort Trends;* Luckhurst, B. and Trott, T.):

The catch per unit effort (CPUE) index for wahoo demonstrates marked consistency over the eleven year period. The index, calculated as kilograms per hour trolling, varies only from 2.2 to 3.5 kg. The standard deviations about the means broadly overlap, suggesting that there are no significant differences in the CPUE index values during this period. If CPUE is used as an index of population abundance, then these results suggest that there has not been a significant change in the abundance of wahoo in Bermuda's waters over this 11 year period. This finding, in conjunction with the increased landings over this same period, appears to confirm that these landings increases are probably related to increased fishing effort for pelagics.

Chum/Chumming: The use of whole, cut, or ground fish or other baits thrown into the water to attract fish, and the practice of fishing by this method.

Closed Areas/Seasons: The closure of certain fishing areas, and during certain periods of the year, to protect a particular spawning habitat, or spawning season, or other critical life stage of a fish population.

Coastal Pelagic: Open ocean (pelagic) fish that live near the surface and relatively near the coast.

Commercial Extinction: The depletion of a fish population to the extent that fishermen cannot catch enough to be economically worth while.

Commercial Fisherman: An individual whose primary income is derived from catching and selling fish and/or other marine species (e.g. shellfish, molluscs, crustaceans, etc.).

Crustaceans: Invertebrates (animals without a backbone), including lobsters, crabs, and shrimps.

Demersal: Fish that live on or near the bottom. Often also called benthic, groundfish, or bottom fish.

Effort: A term used to indicate the degree of fishing activity, measured by the number of hours or days spent fishing, the number of vessels within the fishery, the effectiveness of gear used, or a combination of any such quantifications of fishing activity.

Exclusive Economic Zone (EEZ): The concept of an EEZ derives from the Third United Nations Conference on the Law of The Sea (UNCLOS

III) in 1982, the successor to UNCLOS I in 1958 and UNCLOS II in 1960. The EEZ comprises all the ocean waters around the coast of a country extending out to (usually) 200 nautical miles which are the responsibility of that state within the context of UNCLOS obligations.

Fathom: Equal to six feet. Used to express depths (soundings) mainly in ocean or coastal environments but also in rivers and other inland waters. On charts a whole fathom is expressed as a single number (eg. 100). In shallow waters, depths may be expressed in fathoms and feet for greater accuracy (e.g. 5_3 is five fathoms and three feet, i.e. 33 feet).

Fishery: The combination of fish and fishermen in a particular region, fishing for a similar or the same types of fish, with similar or the same types of gear. (In Bermuda there is a pelagic offshore fishery, a mainly demersal reef/inshore fishery, and a lobster fishery.)

Landings: The amount of fish caught and brought back to shore and marketed. Landings may refer to the catch of a single vessel, a fleet of vessels, an entire fishery, or several fisheries combined.

Limited Access/Limited Entry: A general term for fisheries management programmes that reduce or restrict the number of participants in a fishery, mainly by regulatory mechanisms.

Lines: Fishing lines may either be: *handlines* thrown out and retrieved manually; *rod and reel lines* (used with any type of rod and reel combination); *trolling lines* rigged from a boat (usually, though not necessarily, by rod and reel) and towed as *flatlines* from the stern or side, or from *outriggers* deployed and extended outwards from both sides of the boat.

Longline: A main fishing line rigged with a number of branch lines, each of which has a baited hook.

Maximum Sustainable Yield (MSY): The largest annual catch that fishermen can take continuously from a fishery stock without overfishing it under average environmental conditions. MSY is used as one factor to determine the optimum yield of a fishery.

Metric Tonne: One metric tonne equals 1000 kilograms, or 2205 pounds.

Nautical Mile: Equal to 1.15 statute miles, or 6080 feet, or 1852 metres. (A nautical mile is one minute of arc of a meridian of longitude; 60 nautical miles (minutes of arc) equals one degree of longitude; 21,600 nautical miles equals 360 degrees of longitude (the circumference of the Earth through both poles).)

Open Access: A fishery which is open to anyone. If licences or permits are required, it is still open access if there are no restrictions on the number of licences, or if there are no individual quota restrictions or other barriers to entry.

Optimum Yield (OY): Refers to the optimum catch from a particular fishery that will provide the maximum benefit to the community dependent on that fishery. OY is determined by the maximum sustainable yield from the fishery, as conditioned by any relevant social, environmental, economic, or ecological factors.

Pelagic/Pelagic Species: On or near the surface of the open ocean, and therefore fish that inhabit this part of the ocean. (Known in Bermuda as *floating fish*, albeit a rather old fashioned term.)

Recreational Fishermen: Individuals who fish primarily for their own enjoyment. In Bermuda, charter boat operators (who take other people fishing for recreation) are licensed *commercial fishermen*.

Sustainability: Related to fisheries, the term implies the use of ecosystems and their resources to satisfy current needs without compromising the needs or options of future generations.

Trolling: Towing a number of fishing lines behind a boat at moderate speed (usually 4–8 mph in Bermuda waters), primarily to catch pelagic species offshore.

List of Charts and Graphs

Introduction

For most Bermudians 'going fishing' means taking a spool of line, or a lightweight rod and reel, a handful of hooks, some lead weights, and a few pieces of bait down to the rocks or a public dock, to catch grunts, bream, and snappers. At most it means taking a small boat out to bottom fish around the reefs in shallow water, 30 or 40 feet deep.

Walk down to any public dock in Bermuda any time of the year and almost certainly someone will be there hanging a line out, fishing. Look out over the South Shore, the Great Sound, Mangrove Bay, Castle Harbour, in fact, almost anywhere in Bermuda's inshore waters: more often than not you'll see a small boat either anchored or drifting, fishing.

Relatively few Bermudians go fishing in the deeper waters off the edge of the Bermuda Platform, or on the two offshore banks, Challenger and Argus, 15 and 20 miles to the southwest of Bermuda.

Gamefishing on the edge of the deep or on the banks out of sight of land is limited to those with a good sized boat and engine, and with more sophisticated tackle than most Bermudians ordinarily have. Since the 1960s, however, deep sea gamefishing has become increasingly popular as the local population has become more affluent, with the growth of tourism to the island.

Commercial Fishing

Commercial fishing has existed in Bermuda since the original colonization of the island in the early 1600s. Generations of Bermudian fishermen have provided a catch of mainly bottom fish such as groupers and snappers for the local market. Fresh local fish has been complemented by imported dry cured fish, mainly salted codfish. To this day, codfish, potatoes, and bananas continues to be a traditional Sunday morning breakfast in Bermuda.

There has, however, never been a successful long-term *integrated* commercial fishing industry in Bermuda, extending to industrial processing of local fish caught by local commercial fishermen. The few initiatives undertaken to date have been short-term failures.

High costs of labour, fuel, tackle, and maintenance, and the inevitable small-scale nature of an industrial operation in Bermuda, make it difficult for a local integrated fishing industry to be competitive with fish imported into Bermuda from, for example, the United States.

The small-scale commercial fishery in Bermuda catches, but does not industrially process, local fish. Licensed fishermen sell their fish fresh or frozen directly to the public, or wholesale to hotels, restaurants, and retailers in Bermuda.

Although the technology of this trade has changed markedly, it is essentially the same type of small-scale local trade that Bermudian fishermen have practised for generations. It has survived because it remains a small-scale activity attuned to a local market, serving a demand for fresh, local fish.

The experience of fishing in Bermuda embraces the casual amateur tossing a line off a dock or from the rocks as an occasional pastime, the small boat fisherman scuttling around inshore waters, the gamefish enthusiast trolling the deep waters out to the banks, and the several hundred commercial fishermen in Bermuda for whom fishing is their main source of income.

All have in common that they want to catch fish, that they use variations of the same means of catching the fish, and that they enjoy fishing. Critically, too, they all exploit the same vulnerable natural marine resource around Bermuda, and especially around the shallow reef platform, which needs to be managed with responsibility, intelligence, imagination, and cooperation.

Fisheries conservation in Bermuda goes back over 300 years. The first legislation to protect fish stocks was in 1687. The first order to ban fish pots was enacted in 1791, 200 years before the benchmark 1990 ban that, more than 10 years on, still arouses heated controversy today.

Fishing in Bermuda is a way of life, an occasional pastime, an ecological issue, a political quagmire. And, just as farming is not about simply harvesting, 'catching fish is not the whole of fishing'.

Catching fish in Bermuda is the everyday denouement of a more complex story, a plot of twists and turns, of scene changes, characters coming and going, outside influences, background noise, and audience participation.

As much as anything else, fishing in Bermuda is about the story of Bermuda itself: its people, its visitors, its politics, its character, its environment.

And its fish.

A cooler full of Jacks for sale by commercial fisherman on the roadside.

A summer day, a small boat, a hat, and turquoise water: Fishing in Bermuda!

The Marine Environment of Bermuda

The Bermudas are a group of what are said to be 365 islands . . . in north latitude 32 degrees and west longitude 64 degrees . . . Strung together, they have the form of a fishhook, with the stem pointed to the northeast and the curve of the hook to the southwest. From the northeast end to the point of the hook, you can piece out a curving drive 22 or 23 miles long, and the width of land from sea to sea . . . will hardly average a mile. The superficial area of the whole group is $19\frac{1}{2}$ miles.

The Islands of Bermuda, by William Howard Taft,
The National Geographic Magazine, **January 1922**

The land area of Bermuda is 55.6 km², about the same size as the island of Manhattan, or London's Heathrow Airport. The mid-Atlantic seamount which includes the islands as well as the surrounding shallow water reef plateau, the Bermuda Platform (also known as the Bermuda Pedestal), extends over an area of 775 km².

Just off the Platform lie two smaller seamounts, Challenger and Argus Banks, 15 and 20 miles, respectively, to the southwest. Argus is also known as, less commonly, Plantagenet Bank. In old writings about Bermuda it was sometimes called Columbine Bank. The combined area of the two banks totals 175 km².

The area of all the shallow fishing grounds around Bermuda (less than 50 fathoms) totals 895 km², divided between: the reef flats, 665.4 km²; inshore basins of water, 54.3 km² (about the same size as the islands themselves); and the offlying banks, 175 km².

The availability and proximity of inshore waters, shallow reef areas, shelving edges from shallow to deep water, and offlying shallow banks affords fishermen in Bermuda the opportunity to pursue a wide range of types of fishing: simple handline or light tackle fishing from the rocky shore; light tackle fishing in the surf or around the sandy flats close to shore; boat fishing in inshore waters and over the reef areas, using handlines or light tackle; and a range of light to sophisticated heavy tackle for fishing the outer edges and banks.

Occasionally there is some commercial fishing in the deeper waters well off Bermuda by locally based boats. The main commercial ventures have involved longline fishing to catch deep water pelagic fish such as albacore tuna and swordfish.

Fishing over the reefs and around inshore waters is mainly for demersal species *(bottom fishing)*. The outer banks are considered deep sea gamefishing areas for pelagic species *(floating fish)*, although bottom fishing from anchored boats is equally common.

The perimeter around the Bermuda Platform shelves off steeply into deep water, equivalent to a continental shelf on a much smaller scale. This *edge of the deep* (roughly between the 20 and 50 fathom contour) is commonly fished as a convergence zone of shallow and deep water where upwellings and currents distribute abundant nutrients to feed a wide range of pelagic, epipelagic (mid-water), and demersal species. All the deep water around the Bermuda Platform and banks is also fished, but mainly as an occasional adjunct to fishing the banks or along the edge.

The Reef Flats

The reef flats around Bermuda are divided between three areas: the North Lagoon over the northern part of the reefs, with an area of 416 km²; the Western Flats covering the west and southwest of the reef lagoon, 205.3 km²; and the South Shore, the narrow strip of reefs parallel with the south coast of Bermuda, 44 km².

The immediate Platform area around the islands extends to the north as shallows, flats, and reefs to a maximum distance of 10 miles parallel with the southwest to northeast axis of the islands themselves. Most of this shallow area is up to just five or six fathoms deep, with shallower water around coral heads.

In many places along the northern outer fringing reef, the depth of water shoals to less than a few fathoms. In even very moderate sea conditions, breakers commonly appear along the outer ledge, marking the boundary between shallow and deep offshore water.

The shallow water along the South Shore of Bermuda, up to the 100 fathom contour line, extends just a mile or two on average out from the coast, becoming increasingly distant from shore towards the south-west and approaching closest to the shoreline to the northeast of Hungry Bay. The inner reefs along the South Shore, up to the five fathom contour line, extend just half a mile or so from the coast.

It is important to note, from the perspective of fishing conditions, that the north coast of Bermuda is primarily rocky, indented by numerous small bays but with few beaches, and extending as shallow water to the outer edge of the reefs. Because of the extensive area of shallow flats, and the predominantly southern winds in the main fishing months, the waters along the north shore are much calmer than the more exposed south shore waters of Bermuda.

The south shore is interspersed by beaches and rocky coast. Shallow, reef strewn water slopes into deep water quite close to land. The string of breakers along this edge, the more turbulent sea conditions, the generally sandy coralline bottom, and the rocky nature of the coast, with only a few small navigable bays, make it often difficult, or at least uncomfortable, to fish the shallow waters off the South Shore. Fishing here is mainly along the edge of the deep.

The Banks

Offshore, Challenger and Argus Banks are separated from the main Bermuda Platform by deep water. At its mid point Challenger lies 15 miles due southwest of the islands. Argus Bank is another 5 miles southwest of Challenger. Both are approximately 85 km² in area, and roughly circular in shape.

The depth of water over both Challenger and Argus Banks averages 25–30 fathoms, although Argus is, if anything, slightly deeper. Around the edge of both banks the water averages 30–35 fathoms, shallowing to a 'crown' of 22–25 fathoms in the middle of the banks.

There used to be a steel tower rising to about 40 feet above water on the southeast edge of Argus (Argus Tower, constructed by the US military). This was demolished years ago and is now officially an underwater obstruction lying some 15 fathoms below the surface. For fishing folk, however, it is a fortuitously sited Fish Attraction Device (FAD) where columns of fish congregate in great numbers close to the tower.

On charts there appears to be a very small additional seamount or bank just off the northeast edge of Challenger where the deep water rises to a surveyed depth of 35 fathoms in an area no more than 1 km². Another shallow seamount of 29 fathoms appears near the southeast edge of Challenger.

Commercial fishermen claim not to have found these adjacent shallow banks. They may be errors from earlier surveys, or extensions of the main banks. The sea area around the Western Atlantic is pocked by seamounts thrown up by magmatic activity through vents in the sea floor, or by the activity of plate tectonics. Bermuda and its banks are surviving seamounts, but many more may never be surveyed, or may have subsided relatively soon after their appearance. Consider this report from the last century:

Sandbank between Halifax and Bermuda

On the 22nd August, 1827, the Brig *Joseph Hume* on her passage from Mobil [Alabama] to Liverpool, discovered a sand bank in Lat. 39 N. & Long. 64.20 W. As the vessel passed within a quarter mile of the danger, the white sand was seen above water, and sounding at that distance was obtained in 20 fathoms water, sandy bottom – the extent of the bank was estimated at not more than half a mile or three quarters at most. This dangerous bank is situated North of the Bermudas, about 387 miles, and should be surveyed by a vessel of war and its exact site determined. July 6th, 1830

Deep Water

The deep water around the Bermuda Platform averages 1750–2250 fathoms. The depths between the southwest corner of Bermuda and Challenger Bank, and between Challenger and Argus, are 600–750 fathoms.

Twenty-two miles to the northeast of Bermuda lies another bank, Bowditch Seamount, where the water 'shallows' to 600–750 fathoms. The relatively deep water over Bowditch, however, and the proximity of the two shallow fishing grounds to the southwest, Challenger and Argus Banks, effectively rule it out as a destination for most local fishermen.

Generally speaking local fishermen do not reliably depend on the deep waters off Bermuda for fishing. Boats heading out to the banks at high speed may troll lines, with a chance of catching fast pelagics such as wahoo and marlin, or they may fish just off the banks or beyond the edge as an alternative to those grounds if the fishing is poor. But the deeper waters around Bermuda are not usually considered prime fishing areas (except for occasional experimentation by longliners or as scientific expeditions to see what species inhabit the depths).

Inshore Waters

For the purposes of boat safety and navigation regulations, the inshore waters of Bermuda include all enclosed waters south of a line between Commissioner's Point (the end of Dockyard) and Cobbler's Cut (Spanish Point), and including: Mangrove Bay, Ely's Harbour, Harrington Sound, Flatt's Inlet, Castle Harbour, Ferry Reach, St George's Harbour, Coot Pond, Burchall's Cove, Devonshire Bay, and Hungry Bay.

The four main bodies of water are: the Great Sound (including Port Royal Bay) and Hamilton Harbour; St George's Harbour; Castle Harbour; and Harrington Sound. Indented along the perimeters of these bodies of water are numerous small bays and inlets, cliffs, as well as bridges linking the main islands.

The Great Sound

The largest of the inshore bodies of water, the Great Sound and Hamilton Harbour, is approximately 35 km² in area. It extends south from Grassy Bay between Ireland Island and Spanish Point, to Port Royal Bay, and from the shores of Somerset Island to the west as far as Hamilton Harbour to the east.

Within the perimeters of the Great Sound are some 50 small islands, only a few of which have small permanent or seasonal populations. Hinson's Island, off Granaway Deep, is the largest of these, with a year-round population. The group of islands and narrow channels among them to the north of Granaway Deep (Long Is., Perot Is., Marshall Is., etc.) are colloquially known as Paradise Pond.

Darrell's Island, less than a half mile from the Southampton shore, was the site of Bermuda's first commercial airport for seaplanes (1937–1946) until the civil air terminal on St David's was completed towards the end of the Second World War. Darrell's is one of the largest islands in the Great Sound (and, in fact, one of the largest in the Bermuda islands group, excluding those comprising the mainland).

The entry to the Great Sound from seaward is Dundonald Channel, halfway between Spanish Point and Ireland Island. Dundonald Channel is the entry point of large vessels entering or leaving Hamilton Harbour from or to the main ship channel along the North Shore. Depths in this northern part of the Great Sound average four to five fathoms.

In mid-Sound, bounded by Somerset Island, the ex-US Naval Base peninsula, and the islands north of Granaway Deep, the water deepens to a maximum of 10 to 12 fathoms. In Port Royal Bay, between the ex-US Naval Base and the Southampton shore, the water shallows to an average five or six fathoms. Hamilton Harbour's waters are about the same depth (five to six fathoms).

St George's Harbour

At the east end, St George's Harbour is Bermuda's smallest inshore body of water. From the seaward entry, Town Cut Channel, extending west to Ferry Reach, north to the town of St George's, and east past Smith's Island, the area covers approximately 2.7 km².

Although in the middle of the harbour the water deepens to as much as 10 fathoms, the average is less than five fathoms.

At The Causeway bridge (half a mile long) linking St David's Island with the Bermuda main island, the water shallows to less than 10 feet on the Ferry Reach side but deepens to almost 10 fathoms on the Castle Harbour side at the swing bridge.

Castle Harbour

Castle Harbour, with an area of 11.6 km², is bounded on the north by the airport and St David's Island, by The Causeway to the west, Tucker's Town to the south, and a string of small islands (Nonsuch, Castle, Southampton) to the southeast. It is thought to be the remnant of an ancient volcanic caldera (crater), according to a study of the Bermuda marine environment by The Bermuda Biological Station (Special Publication number 15, September 1977).

One of the notable features of Castle Harbour's topography is that it is peppered with shoals and coral heads just a fathom or less deep. Otherwise the average depth of water in this almost circular body of water is five fathoms or so. To the east, the waters around Nonsuch and Southampton Islands are just around 10 feet deep.

Harrington Sound

Harrington Sound, to the southwest of Castle Harbour, is an almost completely landlocked 'water filled interdunal depression' (The Bermuda Biological Station, Special Publication number 15, September 1977) and not, apparently, a sink-hole, as it was for many years thought to be, or a collapsed cave, which it is still popularly thought to be.

Harrington Sound covers an area of 4.8 km². The average depth of water, at seven to ten fathoms, is greater than in Castle Harbour.

Trunk Island lies around three-quarters of a mile from My Lord's Bay on the western perimeter. The smaller Halls Island is about half a mile north of Shark Hole at the northeast edge of the Sound.

A spectacular feature of Harrington Sound is its tidal drainage to the sea at Flatts' Bridge through Flatts' Inlet and into the sea off the North Shore. The flow of water from and into Harrington Sound under the narrow bridge can reach a maximum speed of four or five knots at full flood and ebb. The strong tidal current at the bridge is partly responsible for thriving coral and algal growth just under and near the bridge.

Bermuda's Exclusive Economic Zone (EEZ)

Bermuda has had a 200 mile Exclusive Economic Zone (EEZ) around the islands since 1977 (although it was called an Exclusive Fishing Zone (EFZ) between 1977 and 1996 when the United Kingdom finally recognized the concept of an EEZ). The concept of an EEZ derives from the Third United Nations Conference on the Law of the Sea (UNCLOS III) in 1982, the successor to UNCLOS I in 1958 and UNCLOS II in 1960. The EEZ differs from sovereign rights over a 'territorial sea' (extending out to 12 miles from the shoreline), and from 200 mile exclusive fishing zones claimed by some countries.

Before the introduction of EEZs, a country or territory could exercise sovereign rights over its coastal 12 mile 'territorial sea' boundary. Beyond the 12 mile limit, international rights and the sovereignty of freedom of the seas predominated. The 12 mile limit was the boundary between the sovereignty of the state in question and the freedom of the open sea.

The introduction of the EEZ concept removed that strict delineation by subordinating the rights of the coastal state to obligations specified in the UN Convention (UNCLOS III).

Among the requirements of a state claiming an EEZ are included its obligation to maintain statutory management of marine resources within its 200 mile zone in respect of its fisheries jurisdiction, including *inter alia*: the determination of allowable catches; conservation of harvested species to produce maximum sustainable yields; and protection against overexploitation.

Bermuda issues licences to foreign fishing vessels to allow them to fish in the outer 125 mile perimeter of its 200 mile radius EEZ jurisdiction. By keeping foreign vessels at least 75 miles away from the islands, the most important shallow water fishing areas around Bermuda, including the nearby banks, are nominally protected for local fishing.

In 1990 13 licences were conceded to foreign fishing vessels, mainly Taiwanese longliners fishing for albacore. Between 1991 and 1994 10 licences each year were granted (although two were revoked in 1993 because the vessels violated their terms and conditions of use).

In 1994 a licence was granted to the Canadian exempt company Scotia Bermuda Ltd, which operated the fishing vessel *Stephen B* out of St George's. The vessel was subsequently arrested in international waters, because of a change in Canadian law, which terminated its fishing operations in Bermuda waters.

After 1994 the number of licences granted to foreign vessels to fish in Bermuda's EEZ declined. In 1995 three licences were granted to US flag vessels which never actually fished in Bermuda waters. No licences were granted in the years 1996–1999.

Foreign vessels do fish regularly in Bermuda's EEZ, whether licensed to do so or not. The extent of their influence on local fishing cannot be accurately measured, not least because they cannot usually be identified. Whatever effect they may have on local conditions, Bermuda is clearly unable to police their activity under the terms of its statutory obligations to manage the marine resources within its EEZ.

Given its modest resources of a few small skiffs piloted by a handful of 35 hour-a-week civil servant wardens, it is difficult enough for the Fisheries Division to monitor fishing activity and enforce regulations in the immediate 900 km^2 of the Bermuda Platform (1600 km^2, counting from the 100 fathom contour line). Patrolling *250,000 km^2* of open sea up to the 200 mile limit (an area not much smaller than the United Kingdom) is clearly not only infeasible but patently impossible. There will, therefore, inevitably be unenforceable illegal foreign fishing activity within Bermuda's EEZ, sometimes approaching even as close as the nearby banks.

Punt used to catch bait by net.

The Fishing Environment of Bermuda

Few things are more evident than the fact that what a fish will eat or strike at in one area will not succeed at all in another. This makes it a bit difficult to prescribe the best procedure in attempting to catch a particular species of fish. However, one thing usually holds true, and that is that if the bait used is similar to that on which a fish usually feeds, or a lure resembles it fairly closely success will usually result.

Observations on Fishing, a Guide to the Reef,
Shore and Game Fish of Bermuda
Louis S. Mowbray

Next to procreation, eating is the most important activity in the otherwise banal life of a fish. Fish go where they find food. It is the instinctive driving force behind their daily routine existence. It is more or less the *only* reason for their daily routine existence. No food, no fish.

Where and how fish feed is the most important thing for a fisherman to understand about catching fish. There is no point in a fisherman trying to catch fish where there is little or no food to support the fish population because, without food, there will be no fish.

Understanding the food chain of fish species is one of the keys to locating good fishing grounds. Different species of fish feed in different locations and eat different food. A fisherman looks for specific species of fish according to where their usual feeding grounds are. The feeding grounds of fish are the fishing grounds of fishermen.

The first objectives for a fisherman are, therefore, to discover *where* fish habitually feed, and to understand *how* they feed. Knowing *where* fish feed will lead a fisherman to the fish. Knowing *how* they feed will help the fisherman to catch the fish.

Observation is the critical faculty needed by fishermen to discern where and how to catch fish: observation of the behaviour of the fish, of the immediate marine environment, the weather, tides, currents, moon phases, time of day, state of the sea, and of the behaviour of other fishermen in the area.

Even if a fisherman is told that fish are always to be found in a particular location, he needs to observe at the time and on the spot to see if the fish are there and feeding, and how. If the fish are not there, or are not feeding, the fisherman moves to another location.

If the fish are there, and feeding, and feeding consistently on the fisherman's bait, but not being *caught* by the fisherman, that, of course, is another problem altogether.

These general observations on the nature of fish and fishing apply in all waters of the world. Fishermen observe where and how fish feed. They then aim to catch the fish by offering them food or imitations of food by means that approximate the fish's natural feeding behaviour.

Such are the nuts and bolts of fishing. And, just as nuts and bolts vary by size, material, and use, so fishing techniques vary according to the nature of the particular fishing environment.

Bermuda's Marine Environment

Fishing in Bermuda is exclusively a saltwater pursuit. The art, finesse, and culture of freshwater fly fishing are foreign to the Bermuda fishing experience.

- Freshwater fishing is an art: highbrow or lowbrow, but an art none the less.
- Saltwater fishing is a skill: not too much art, but a lot of technique.

Fishing in Bermuda ranges from the most basic hook, line, and sinker technique, to sophisticated skills of deep sea gamefishing. But the nature of all types of fishing in Bermuda is a consequence of the island's location in the open ocean of the North Atlantic, flanked by the warming waters of the Gulf Stream to the west, and forming the epicentre of the mid-Atlantic pool of water known as the Sargasso Sea.

The climate of the islands and surrounding waters is conditioned by the vagaries of North Atlantic weather patterns, influenced most importantly by the movement of the so-called Bermuda-Azores High, and the flow of the Gulf Stream between Bermuda and North America.

The Bermuda-Azores High fills (expands) in summer to cover the middle of the North Atlantic Ocean (including Bermuda), bringing predominantly moderate southwest breezes to Bermuda in those months. It contracts and weakens in winter, allowing stormy weather fronts from North America to whip over Bermuda between December and April.

Unlike the islands of the Caribbean further south, which are influenced primarily by the steady northeast trade winds, Bermuda is constantly swiped by weather systems from the west, coming off the North American coast. The warm waters of the Gulf Stream mitigate the severity of those easterly moving systems. By the time they reach Bermuda they are much more temperate, and milder, than they were over the North American continent.

The proximity of the Gulf Stream is unquestionably the single most important phenomenon to influence the nature of Bermuda's marine environment. The Gulf Stream allows Bermuda to enjoy sub-tropical conditions, with coral reef fauna and fish species ordinarily found much further south. Bermuda is, indeed, a 'coralline oasis' in mid-Atlantic, the most northerly coral habitat on Earth, because of the Gulf Stream.

As a result of the Gulf Stream's influences, including eddies circulating eastwards out from the main northward flow, Bermuda's waters are mild considering its geographical position at 32° North latitude. Sea temperatures around Bermuda range from an average of 17–18°C (low to mid-60s F) in February, to 28°C (mid-80s F) in August.

Studies by marine scientists at The Bermuda Biological Station have shown that mean surface temperatures in waters around Bermuda extend as deep as 450 metres.

A variety of sub-tropical oceanic and inshore fish species are found around Bermuda because of its relatively warm waters. Their food chain ranges from the fauna of microscopic organisms drifting in the currents around the islands, and other prey fish, to the marine grasses, seaweeds, corals, and crustaceans of the island's sheltered, shallow inshore waters.

The change in seasons (from relatively placid summer to often stormy winter conditions), the mild surface water temperatures, the availability of sub-tropical and North Atlantic fish species, a deep sea pelagic and coastal demersal fishing environment, and the erratic nature of weather conditions at any time of the year (including occasional hurricanes from July to as late as November and very occasionally December) all influence the types of fishing practised in Bermuda.

Wind

When the Bermuda-Azores High is well established in the summer, the predominant wind direction around Bermuda is from the south to southwest. Although the strength of summer winds may sometimes be quite strong (above force 5), generally they tend to be light to moderate breezes (force 2–4).

Winter winds around Bermuda tend to blow more from the north, northwest, and northeast quadrants. Winds above force 5 are quite common. Gales (minimum force 8) and even storm conditions occur regularly from November to April. The duration of stormy conditions varies from a few hours as a cold front moves through, to a few days or more if a low pressure cell remains stationary near Bermuda.

The weather around Bermuda can change rapidly. Deteriorating conditions can be dangerous for small craft on the open ocean. Fishermen are vigilant and take note of local weather forecasts at any time of the year, but more particularly in winter months.

Commercial fishermen in Bermuda fish throughout the year, although less in winter when many take time off to service their boats and equipment. Recreational offshore fishing is mainly a warm weather activity. At any time of the year, however, when the sun is warm, breezes are light, and the sea sparkles, fishermen will be out.

In spring and summer the predominant southwest breezes give a moderate sea and swell in offshore waters to the south and southwest out to the banks, even when the strength of the wind is relatively light (10–15 knots).

The north and northeast fishing grounds, in the lee of the island, are much calmer with a southerly or southwesterly breeze, even if the wind is quite strong. In winter, however, strong northerly winds can roughen up the north coast waters to a very agitated state, leaving calm conditions to the southwest, in the lee of the island, to a distance of four or five miles offshore.

Generally, fish, and fishermen, like at least a little sea action. Wave height up to three or four feet is ideal. Waves and swell help turn over the water masses. They bring a constant upwelling of nutrients and create better feeding conditions for the fish. Lines trolled over a wavy sea skip better than in calm conditions, imitating the flight of flying fish, a favourite prey of tuna, wahoo, and other gamefish, over open water.

An exception appears to be an easterly wind of whatever strength. 'Fish bite least when the wind is in the east' is an old saw from many parts of the world, including Bermuda. Why this should be so is not known. Nor has it been tested by hard evidence with scientific rigour. It is simply so.

Bermuda Tides and Currents

Fishermen in Bermuda often use the term tide when they really mean current or tidal stream. It is common to hear a fisherman say, for example, that a tide is running in a particular direction, especially as it acts on his fishing gear.

Tides are regular vertical (upward and downward) movements of water masses governed by moon phases. *Tidal streams* are horizontal movements of water that occur in response to tide-raising forces. Mixed up with tidal streams are *currents*, which are horizontal movements of water due to causes other than tidal forces. Some currents are more or less regular. Some are entirely random and erratic. Ocean currents may be generated or influenced by winds, undersea topography, variations in sea temperature or salinity, and the rotation of the earth, among other things.

Tides may generate currents (tidal streams), but most currents exist independently of tidal action. Open ocean currents, like the winds, may be regular, sporadic, erratic, localized, trans-oceanic, seasonal, deep, mid-water, or on the surface.

Along continental coasts tidal ranges (the height between successive low and high tides) can be extreme: over 12 metres in parts of the United Kingdom, northern Australia, and Nova Scotia, for example. In the Mediterranean, by contrast, there is no tide at all, and so no tidal streams – but plenty of currents (including whirlpools)!

In mid-ocean environments tidal ranges are small because of the much greater depths of water than around coastlines. Since Bermuda is well out in the Atlantic, its tides are modest, but enough to be a consideration in fishing. The tidal range in Bermuda's inshore waters averages just 1 metre, from a minimum of 0.5 metre (*neap tides* at half moon) to as much as 1.4 metres (*spring tides* at new and full moon). Harrington Sound has the smallest tidal range of any inshore body of water: just 20 cm on average.

Inshore Tidal Streams

The average velocity of the tidal stream around Bermuda's inshore waters is quite low. Within the Great Sound system the tidal flow averages 0.5 knot; in Castle Harbour, 0.2 knot; and within St George's Harbour, just 0.1 knot. In most places this amounts to a hardly perceptible flow.

For Harrington Sound, however, the tidal stream averages almost 4 knots: the large mass of tidal water flooding into and ebbing from the Sound has to pass through very small channels (most dramatically under Flatts' Bridge which is only 20 feet wide).

Only about 50% of the tidal exchange of water of Harrington Sound goes under Flatts' Bridge and through Flatts' inlet. The other 50% apparently goes through subterranean passages in the rocks around the Sound.

Tidal streams are also quite strong around Bermuda under other bridges where the mass of water passes between constricted narrow channels. The rate of flow under Watford, Somerset, and Boaz Island bridges, for example, is 1.4–2.0 knots, depending on the state of the tide.

Tides in Bermuda are predominantly semi-diurnal, that is, there are two high tides and two low tides in every 24 hours. (There is a successive low and high tide every 6.2 hours.)

Tidal action around Bermuda is not particularly strong, consistent with its mid-ocean location. Tides do, however, generate currents (tidal streams) around Bermuda outside the inshore waters. These, in turn, combine, and almost certainly overlap with open ocean currents in the Bermuda area.

What is *not* clear is the extent to which local tidal streams interact with open ocean currents. It seems probable, however, that tidal action has a greater influence on local currents around the Bermuda Platform and the offshore banks than oceanic currents, because local tidal streams are, in general, stronger.

A 1977 report by the Bermuda Biological Station noted, 'The only significant and noticeable currents of the [Bermuda] Platform are induced by daily tidal oscillations.' It added, 'The ocean currents in the Bermuda region . . . are generally weak and variable throughout the year, with an average speed of less than 0.5 knots . . . The Bermuda area is a region of weak convergence (of ocean currents).'

Any ocean currents influencing the Bermuda area are generally from the southwest and west-southwest. Occasional eddies from the Gulf Stream, however, particularly in winter, may approach Bermuda from the east and southeast.

The Bermuda Yachting Guide (1994) has noted that, 'It is generally accepted that there is a circular current revolving around the islands in a clockwise direction, with a speed of about half a knot. This is an offshoot of the Gulf Stream. Along the north and south shores of the island there is little current, but at the east and west ends there is a north/south tidal current which can run up to 2 knots. This current runs south when ebbing (going out) and north when flooding (coming in). *Tide-rips can often be seen around the edges of the off-lying banks.*'

It is nevertheless virtually impossible to predict the behaviour of currents *outside the inshore waters of the Bermuda area* with any degree of accuracy with regard to their direction, velocity, or regularity.

Fishermen may experience sudden strong currents (virtual rip-tides) in very localized areas, dragging anchored fishing floats under water by the force of their flow but with no apparent effect as close as a few hundred metres away. Such currents may disappear equally quickly.

The general picture is of a weak ocean current running clockwise around the Bermuda Platform, with a coastal tidal stream flowing south when it ebbs, north when it floods, and slack for brief periods at low and high tide when the tides turn.

The combination of a south flowing ocean current along the steeply shelving South Shore, together with an ebbing (south flowing) tide, probably produces the strongest *regular* current around Bermuda.

Rip-tides may occur randomly, or where local tidal and oceanic water masses clash, flowing in different directions or at different velocities, especially over a steeply shelving topography such as the edge of the Bermuda Platform or around the banks.

The surface turbulence of rip-tides may be caused by the opposing interaction of a tidal stream and an ocean current, or by abrupt changes in the undersea topography, or both. All three phenomena (tidal streams, ocean currents, abrupt undersea topographical changes) exist around Bermuda and are factors governing the nature of currents in the Bermuda area.

Despite the unpredictability and uncertain behaviour of currents converging around the Bermuda Platform and the banks, the strongest influence on their behaviour is likely to be the strength of interacting tidal movements. The precipitous undersea topography of the Bermuda Platform and banks intensifies this effect.

New and full moons exert the strongest tidal influence, when the tidal range (and movement of water mass) is greatest. In between the new and full moon (and vice versa), tidal range (and movement of water mass) is least.

In general the best time for fishing around Bermuda is at, or to one or the other side of, the full moon. At those times the vertical movement of water masses and flow of nutrients is greatest. It is also a common spawning period for fish, when they aggregate in larger than usual numbers and in a heightened state of excitement.

Why reef fish aggregate to spawn around the full (and new) moon has been of interest to marine biologists for many years. One plausible explanation has been offered by R. E. Johannes in his seminal study of reef fishing communities in the Palau district of Micronesia, in the Pacific *(Words of the Lagoon)*.

Johannes explained the phenomenon by noting that spawning groupers and other demersal species moved to the edge of the lagoon reefs at the full and new moon, the times of the month when tides were strongest (spring tides).

The fish spawned on the ebbing (outgoing) tide, which flushed their eggs off the reef to hatch as planktonic larvae in the deep sea. The larvae were thereby kept away from the many predators on the reef that fed on zooplankton such as fish eggs and larval fishes.

After a few weeks or even months living in the deep sea, the small fish returned to take up their more natural residence over the reef, better equipped by then to defend themselves against reef predators.

Palauans had observed over many generations that fish aggregated around the full and new moon. They also recognized 'runs' of demersal fish that were ordinarily sedentary. The 'runs' were along fixed paths of migration from the inner to the outer edge of the reef where the fish spawned. At those times of the lunar cycle Palauans were able to catch many more fish than at other times.

The lunar rhythm of this behaviour of groupers and other demersal species, with the periodicity of their movement linked to moon cycles, has been likewise observed in other reef lagoon environments, including Bermuda.

Fish do not ordinarily like fast tidal streams or currents, except along the edges of the stream where nutrients are released from the main flow to the adjacent water mass. It may be that the fish need more energy to withstand the current. Or that they use currents to move around their habitat more easily, which may distract them from feeding.

Whatever the reason, fishing is usually not good in the midst of a strong current, tidal or otherwise. Since these currents are largely unpredictable around Bermuda, it is mainly a case of the fisherman being aware of the strength of any current in the immediate vicinity and making a judgement accordingly about where it is best to fish.

Kids fishing off the dock at Flatts.

The Fishing Grounds Around Bermuda

In the waters about Bermuda, fish are to be found in all places from half-dried tide-pools down to a depth of two miles.

William Beebe and John Tee-Van,
Field Book of the Shore Fishes of Bermuda and the West Indies

Fisherman: I marvel how the fishes live in the sea.

Master: Why, as men do a-land; the great ones eat up the little ones.

William Shakespeare, *Pericles*, Act ll, Scene 1

Like fish, like men: the greater swallow the smaller.

Talmud: Aboda Zara, 4a

Fortune favours the fisherman who casts a line into any water, though his rewards will likely be greater when he casts where he has been most regularly rewarded by experience.

Bermuda's fishing grounds are areas where fishermen have found fish in the greatest concentrations over hundreds of years. Other waters around the islands, while hardly marine deserts, are relatively sparsely populated by comparison with the traditional fishing grounds.

The first and most accessible fishing ground is the *shoreline* of Bermuda itself. Anywhere along the shore is a potential fishing spot to catch small fish such as bream, grunts, snappers, or squirrelfish, year-round. Other species such as yellowtail, mackerel, small amberfish and other jacks appear more or less numerously depending on the season, phase of the moon, state of the tide, or time of day.

From a small boat a fisherman might get a similar catch around inshore waters, by handline or light spinning tackle.

There is some seasonal movement of shore fish during the year. Pete Perinchief, in his pamphlet 'Bermuda: Island of Great Fishing', noted that offshore fishing between December and April was hampered by the 'uncomfortable' weather likely to prevail during those winter months. He added, 'Nor can we offer shore fishing as an attractive substitute, for, during our winter, the shore fish move out to deeper water.'

A line thrown off a dock or from the rocks at any time of the year is nevertheless always worth a go: the triumvirate of grunts, bream, and snapper may be more lethargic when the water is cooler, but they will be there.

The most popular fishing locations along the coast are public docks (for example, at Mangrove Bay, Evans Bay, Flatts' Inlet, or Penno's Wharf in St George's), next to main bridges (popular West End spots are Watford and Boaz Island bridges), and off the rocks almost anywhere.

Fish congregate particularly where commercial fishermen clean their catch and throw the guts and carcass overboard.

Bonefish cruise *shallow flats* such as at Somerset Long Bay, Whale Bay in Southampton, Shelly Bay in Hamilton parish, around the Causeway towards the airport, and (only accessible by boat) at Castle Point in St George's, among other places.

Pompano (palometa) are taken mainly by surf fishing along the *South Shore beaches* but also, though less commonly, around bays and inlets.

Away from inshore waters, fishermen go out in boats to grounds scattered around the reef, along the edge of the reef Platform as it shelves into deep water, and offshore over the banks, or in the deep waters surrounding the Bermuda Platform.

Demersal (bottom) fish congregate around the reefs and over the banks. Oceanic pelagic species *(floating fish)* patrol along the edge of the Platform where it shelves into deep water, over the banks, and in surrounding deep water.

The Reef Platform

Most reef fishing for bottom fish such as hinds, other groupers, porgies, and triggerfish, and some small floating fish (yellowtail, jacks, chub) is done around the outer edges of the reef plateau. The tidal and ocean surge of water is greatest along the edge of the reef, in 10–20 fathoms of water. Fish populations of this shallow perimeter feed on the upwellings of nutrients from the open ocean that complement their floral and faunal diet from the reef itself.

Fishing over the reefs is most concentrated at the extreme southwest and northeast corners of the Bermuda Platform, areas where hind and other groupers congregate in the summer to spawn. The so-called *northeast hind ground* is located at the extreme northeast edge of the Platform, just to the south of Kitchen Shoals. The *southwest hind ground* is along the southwest edge, due west of southwest breaker.

The three seasonally protected areas (The South Western Area, The Eastern Area, and The North Eastern Area) included within their territories rich commercial fishing grounds before they were closed to fishing between 1 May and 31 August. Spawning groupers in large concentrations were easily caught, often in large numbers, by commercial fishermen.

Nowadays, during the closed season, no handline fishing from boats is permitted in those areas (which extend out to the 100 fathoms contour). Trolling for pelagics is permitted within the restricted areas, but only beyond the 30 fathoms contour. Line fishing from shore within the restricted areas is permitted year-round.

East End fishermen used to fish *Grouper Ground*, a few miles south-southeast of Cooper's Island, off St David's. This small area, in 10–25 fathoms of water, had the great advantage of being close to land. Proximity to the land meant that, in the days before depth-sounders and other electronic gear, fishermen could pinpoint their fishing locations by the use of landmarks. It also meant they could get back to the dock quickly to sell their catch.

In *Bermudian Handline Fishing in the Sailing Sloop Era: A Fisherman's Account*, Captain Geary Pitcher relates how East Enders used to fish Grouper Ground in the spawning season: 'They'd only go south to the Grouper Ground [in] season: the last week in May, or the first week in June. Mostly June 5 to 11, they used to call it "snapping time". The fish would turn crazy. They used to be fish there thick as the hair on your head. By the thousands. And you used to catch a lot of fish . . .'

The Grouper Ground is quite easy to get to 'cause it is just a mile outside the breakers. It was in sight of the land and a very narrow spot. You didn't have to go no more than another quarter mile before you got to the edge of the deep.'

Grouper Ground is not fished intensively these days, because most grouper and rockfish species are now either fully protected year-round, or fishing for them is restricted by a daily bag limit.

Other specific locations nearby on the edge of the Platform, in similar depths of water (out to about 30 fathoms), were well known commercial fishing grounds in those days and fished intensively for grouper, rockfish, and snapper.

Offshore

The *edge of the deep* borders the undersea rim of the Bermuda Platform where it shelves off steeply into deep water. Boats mainly troll for pelagic species along this edge in 20–30 fathoms. The southwest, west and northwest, and north and northeast are preferred areas, but anywhere along the edge may produce good fishing.

The edge off North Rock has for many years been particularly popular with fishermen from the East End. However, fishing within a radius of one kilometre around the rock itself has been prohibited since the Fisheries (Protected Areas) Order of 1990.

The edge of the deep provides an alternative fishing opportunity for boats that do not make the longer run out to the banks (for example, on a short half-day trip), or an additional fishing opportunity for boats going to or returning from the banks.

(a) A 1200 lb blue marlin, hoisted aloft by crane; (b) Marlin among admiring crowds and accompanied by angler. (Photos courtesy of Andrew Card.)

Seven to eight miles southwest of Bermuda a promontory of the Bermuda Platform bulges out slightly before shelving into deep water. This area is known as *Sally Tucker's*, or *The Point*, the closest point of the edge of the Bermuda Platform to Challenger Bank. Boats that make the run to the banks, especially those from the West End, often first take a few turns around Sally Tucker's before heading out to Challenger or Argus.

The deep water separating the Bermuda Platform and the closest edge of the first bank, Challenger, is a four mile stretch of water known as *The Churn*. Marlin and other speedy pelagics may sometimes be hooked in this area by boats trolling at fast speed headed towards Challenger.

The greatest concentrations of fish in the Bermuda area are around *Challenger* and *Argus* banks. The middle of Challenger (the 'crown' of the bank, its highest (shallowest) point) is 14 miles due southwest (240° magnetic) from Pompano Beach, the end of the channel along the Somerset and Southampton shore (Hogfish Cut), marked by a tripod, where boats turn to head offshore. The closest edge of Argus is another three miles on from the southwest edge of Challenger.

Challenger Bank was named after HMS *Challenger*, which visited Bermuda during its research expedition around the world in 1872–1874. Another name for Challenger was *New Ledge* which has fallen into disuse now but which may have predated the name Challenger.

Argus Bank is named after another oceanographic expedition vessel, HMS *Argus*, which surveyed and charted the seabed of Argus Bank and elsewhere around Bermuda in 1879, shortly after the HMS *Challenger* visit. (In 1896 Professor Alexander Agazziz, a renowned 19th century zoologist, charted a 580 fathoms deep undersea canyon nearby, Argus Deep.)

Commercial fishermen have been going to the banks for generations, as G. Brown Goode records in his 1876 *Catalogue of the Fishes of the Bermudas*: 'Most of the line-fishing is done among the outer reefs or on the outer banks, twenty miles distant.' It is only since the 1950s that the banks have become Bermuda's most popular offshore sportfishing ground.

Upwellings of water masses and currents around Argus and Challenger feed plankton and other nutrients to a myriad population of migratory pelagic gamefish, shoals of small bait fish, as well as permanently resident bottom fish species. The food chain around the banks, from microscopic plankton to 'grander' blue marlins, is the richest and most complex of any fishing ground in the immediate Bermuda area.

Argus Bank benefits additionally from an underwater Fish Attraction Device (FAD). A tower, originally named Texas Tower, or Argus Tower, was constructed by the US military in 1961 as part of a network of hydrophone listening devices used by the US Naval Underwater Systems Center. Its upper structure rose to about 60 feet above sea level. The tower was demolished in 1975, but the undersea remnant of the structure rises to within 50 feet of the surface and is marked on the charts as an underwater obstruction. In attracting fish, however, the relic is anything but an obstruction.

Early Surveys of Challenger and Argus Banks

Extract from: Miscellaneous Papers, Vol. 38 (AB6), United Kingdom Hydrographic Office

Remarks re: His M's Sloop *Columbine*
John Townshend Esqre – Commander

South West and Outer Banks off Bermuda

Surveyed in July 1829 by HM's Sloop Columbine the ship lay at Anchor on each of the banks, and boats were sent sounding to the edges of the banks, their distances measured, and the banks strictly sounded, the East Edge of the inner bank [Challenger] is very steep, and a rock at the extreme edge with 20 fathoms on it the shoalest water on the Bank, the West end of the Bank shoaling gradually to 50 and 55 fathoms, and generally the bottom is coral Rock with small stones. Here we found the current setting to the S.W. 1 mile per hour.

The Outer Bank [Argus] is very steep on the West Edge and shortens gradually to the S.E., the bottom here is foul, coral rocks. Here we found the current setting to the Westward and W.N.W. at the rate of one mile per hour.

From: Narrative of the Cruise of *HMS Challenger* 1873–76

About 4 miles southwest of the southwest extremity of the 100 fathom edge of the Bermuda Bank [the Bermuda Platform] the Challenger sounded and anchored on the 'inner bank' of the 'Columbine', in 30 fathoms, with Gibb's Hill Lighthouse, N. 54° 14′ E. (true), distant 13 miles. The boats were employed one day in obtaining soundings on this bank, but owing to rough weather rendering the men sick, and to the barometer falling, the officers

were unable to define its limits or to look for the 'outer shoal' [Argus Bank], out of sight of land, on which the 'Columbine' anchored in 1820 [*sic*], and on which soundings were also taken by the 'Larne' in 1836. From the depths obtained, the inner or Challenger Bank appears to be of some extent, certainly not less than 10 miles in circumference, the shallowest water found being 24 fathoms, and it is quite possible that it joins the outer or 'Columbine' Bank, or that at any rate the depths between the two do not much exceed 100 fathoms. [In fact, they exceed 500 fathoms.]

In the depression, $3\frac{1}{2}$ miles wide, between the Challenger Bank and the southwest extremity of the Bermuda Bank, the soundings, in all probability, do not exceed 1000 fathoms, as a cast of 1075 fathoms was obtained just east of the northwest part of the depression and another of 1250 fathoms just west of it.

From: *North Atlantic Memoir,* by A.G. Findlay (1879)
Bermudas or Somers Islands

The South-western Banks – There is a rocky fishing bank, now named *Challenger Bank*, lying from S.S.W. to S.W. from Gibb's Hill (or S.W. part of Bermudas), from 4 to 5 leagues distant [1 league = approx. 3 nautical miles, or 4.8 km], and having 22 to 40 fathoms. These banks were surveyed in 1829 by the officers of H.M. sloop *Columbine*, according to whom the northern extremity of the *Inner Bank* [Challenger] lies in 32° 6′ N. and 64° 53′ W.; the S.W. in 32° N. and 65° W. The least water found is 22 fathoms, corally and rocky bottom. On the edges are 40 fathoms. To the S.W. of this bank is another, called the *Outer Bank* [Argus], the N.E. end of which is in lat. 31° 59$\frac{1}{2}$′, long. 65° 2$\frac{1}{2}$′; the S.W. end in in 31° 57′, and 65° 5′. The least water found on this bank was from 33 to 47 fathoms, rocks and coral. From this Outer Bank the land is distant 32 miles, and consequently not visible.

Challenger Bank, S.W. of Bermudas

This bank was named by H.M.S. Challenger, in April, 1873, and Sir Wyville Thomson, after speaking of the soundings at about 2,000 fathoms between the bank and Bermudas Island, says: 'In the evening we sounded in 32 fathoms, about 13 miles to the S.W. of Bermudas; this is a bank well known to fishermen, and is said to have been discovered from the large number of fish swimming near the surface. We anchored on the bank, and the fishing lines were soon out, but we were very unfortunate, for only one or two "snappers" were taken. . .The bank, which seems to be about 5 miles across, consists mainly of large rounded pebbles of the substance of the Bermudas' Serpuline [fossilized marine worm] reef. There is an abundant growth all over the pebbles of the pretty little branching corals *Madracis asperula* and *M. hellena*, and other invertibrates [*sic*] were abundant . . . As the weather did not look by any means promising, we weighed anchor, and proceeded on our course to the N.W.'

Fishes from Around Bermuda

A gallery of original watercolour paintings
by Kat Cruickshank

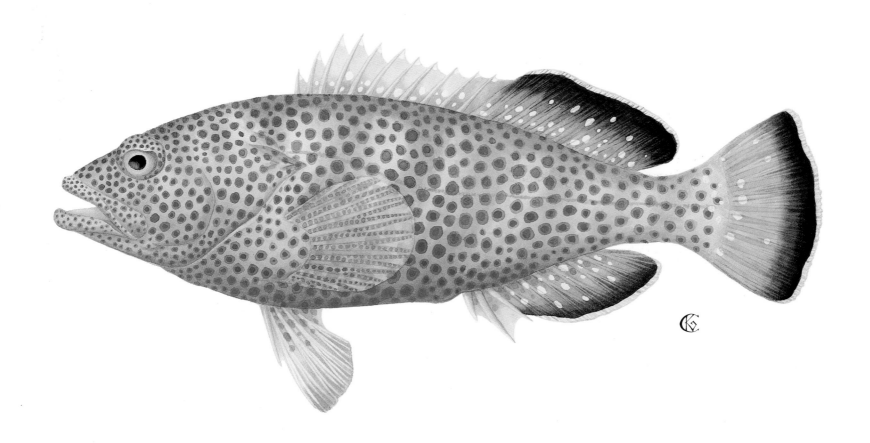

Red Hind

Epinephelus guttatus

Plate i

Nassau Grouper

Epinephelus striatus

Plate ii

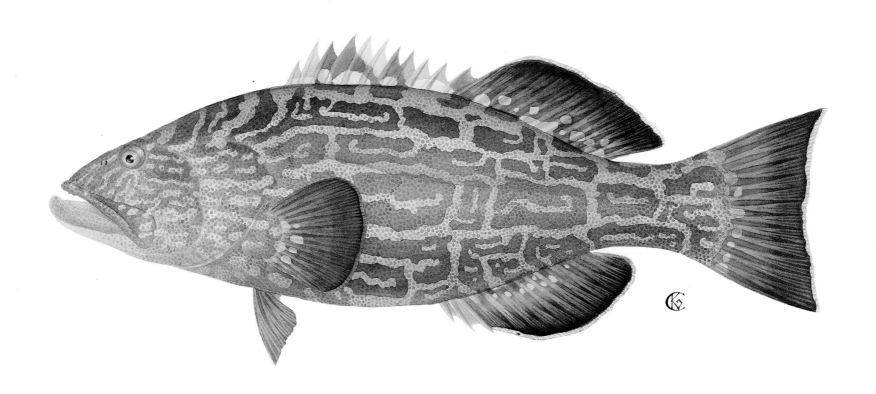

Black Grouper

Mycteroperca bonaci

Plate iii

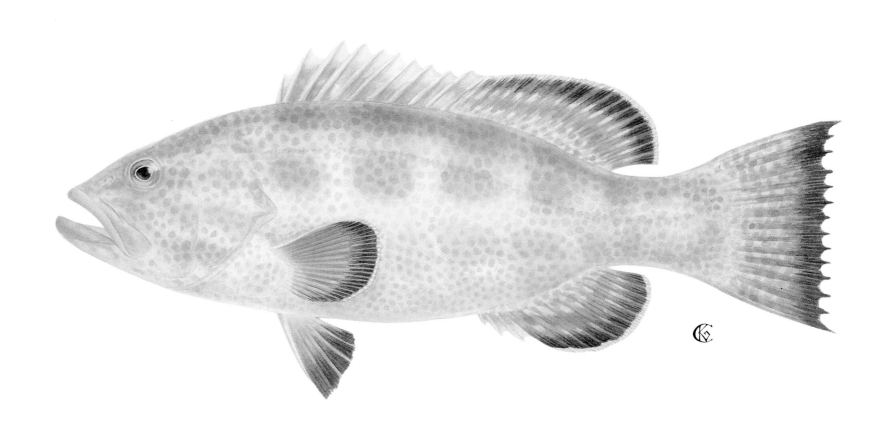

Monkey Rockfish (Yellowmouth Grouper)

Mycteroperca interstitialis

Plate iv

Tiger Grouper

Mycteroperca tigris

Plate v

Coney

Cephalopholis fulva

Plate vi

Hogfish

Lachnolaima maximus

Plate vii

Bluebone (Jolthead) Porgy

Calamus bajonado

Plate viii

Bermuda Chub

Kyphosus sectatrix

Plate ix

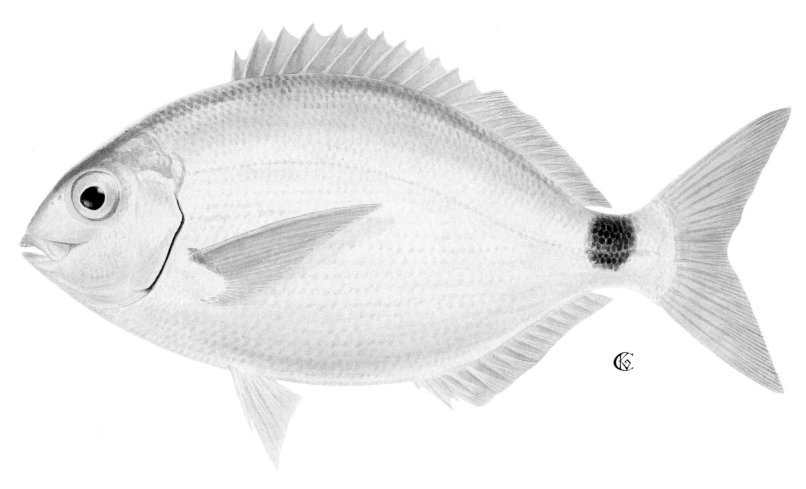

Bream

Diplodus bermudensis

Plate x

Whitewater (Lane) Snapper

Lutjanus synagris

Plate xi

Silk Snapper

Lutjanus vivanus

Plate xii

Yellowtail Snapper

Ocyurus chrysurus

Plate xiii

Bluestriped Grunt

Haemulon sciurus

Plate xiv

Gwelly

Pseudocaranx dentex

Plate xv

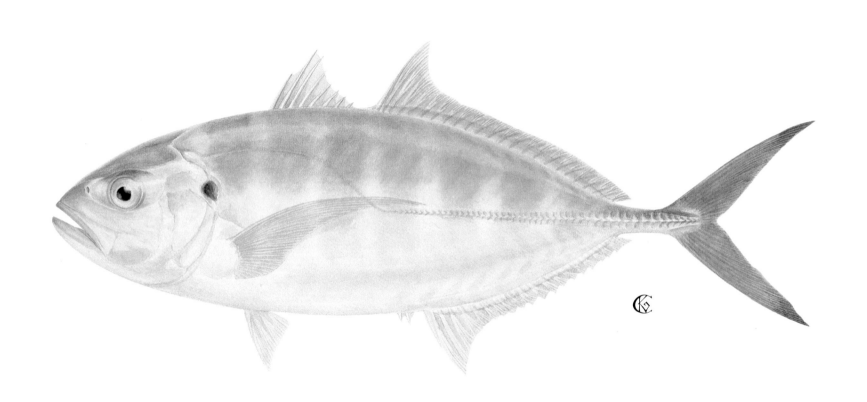

Blue Runner

Caranx crysos

Plate xvi

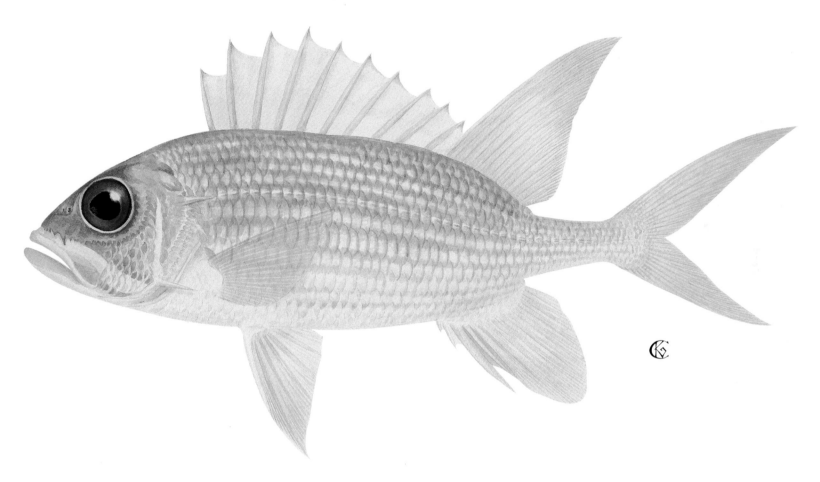

Squirrelfish

Holocentrus ascensionis

Plate xvii

Bonefish

Albula vulpes

Plate xviii

Galapagos Shark

Carcharhinus galapagensis

Plate xix

Great Barracuda

Sphyraena barracuda

Plate xx

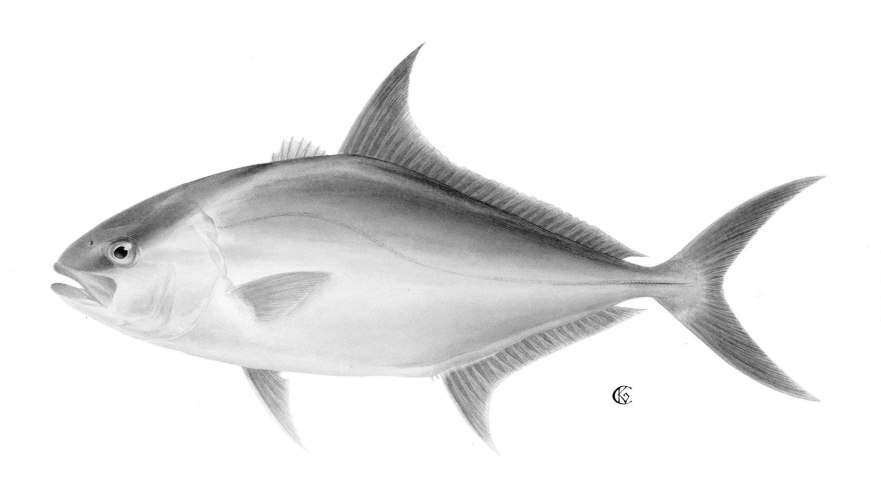

Almaco Jack

Seriola rivoliana

Plate xxi

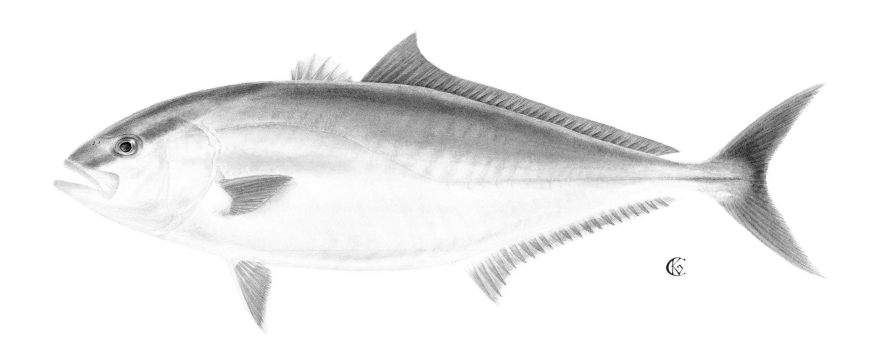

Greater Amberjack

Seriola dumerili

Plate xxii

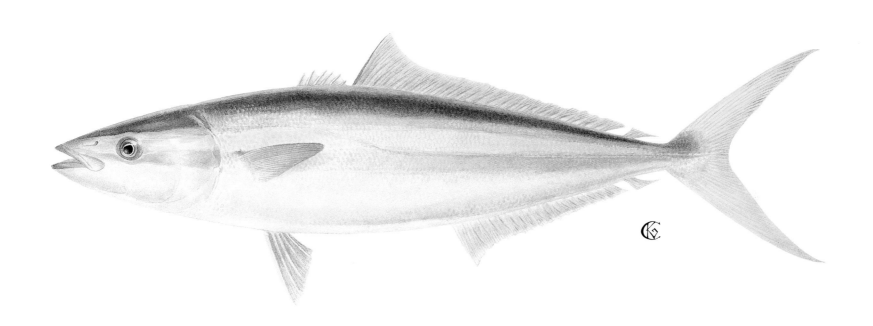

Rainbow Runner

Elagatis bipinnulata

Plate xxiii

Common Dolphin

Coryphaena hippurus

Plate xxiv

Little Tunny

Euthynnus alletteratus

Plate xxv

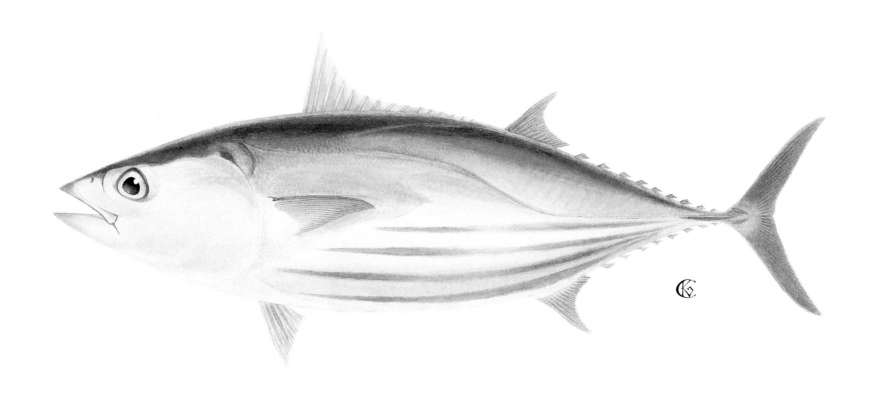

Skipjack Tuna

Katsuwonus pelamis

Plate xxvi

Blackfin Tuna

Thunnus atlanticus

Plate xxvii

Yellowfin (Allison) Tuna

Thunnus albacares

Plate xxviii

Wahoo

Acanthocybium solandri

Plate xxix

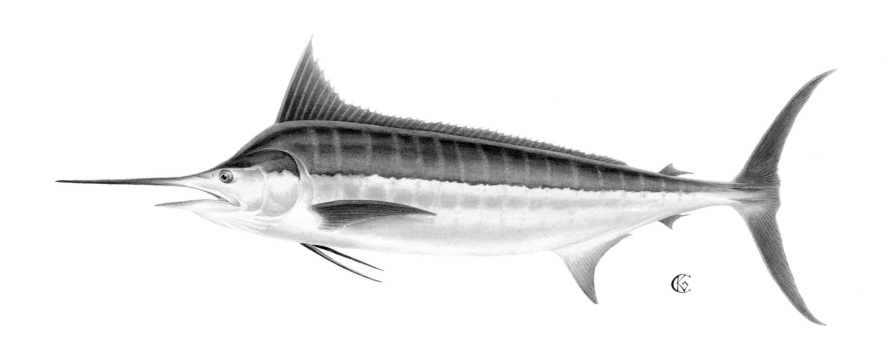

Atlantic Blue Marlin

Makaira nigricans

Plate xxx

Fish Species Around Bermuda

And fish is there so abundant, that if a man steppe into the water, they will come round about him: so that men were faine to get out for fear of byting. These fishes are very fat and sweete, and of that proportion and bignesse that three of them will conviently lade two men: those we called Rockfish. Besides there are such store of mullets that with a seine [net] might be taken at one draught one thousand at the least, and infinite store of Pilchards, with divers [diverse] kinds of great fishes, the names of them UNKNOWN to me: of tray fishes very great ones, and so great store, as that there hath been taken in one night with making lights, EVEN sufficient to feed the whole company a day.

A Discovery of the Barmodas, now called the Sommer Islands 1609–1610, Silvanus Jourdan's Narrative, 1610

There is great store and variety of fish, and so good, as these parts of the World affords not the like; which being for the most part unknown to us, each man gave them names as they best liked: as one kind they called Rock-fish, another Groopers, others Porgy-fish, Hogg-fish, Angel-fish, Cavallyes, Yellow-tails, Spanish Mackerel, Mulletts, Breame, Cony-fish, Morrayes, Sting-rayes, Flying-fish, &c.

'The Description of the Summer Islands, once called the Bermudas', Mappa aestivarum insularam alias Bermudas dictarum, etc.
John Speed, 1626

This rogues' gallery of fish species is a compilation of the main catch fish around Bermuda. The fish that fishermen from the age of 2 to 102 throw their lines out to catch. It excludes most of the multicoloured reef fish, the decorative wrasses, angelfish and parrotfish that nibble and glide around Bermuda's shoreline, surging in the surf, illuminating the depths, bejewelling the coral heads of the reef flats.

Bermuda is distinguished by its variety of fish species and types of fishing. Shore fishing turns up snappers, grunts, bream, squirrelfish, chub, and hogfish, among others, using similar bait and tackle. Away from the shore, groupers, jacks, larger snappers, and porgies, among other species, populate the reef habitat. Premium deep water gamefish in the deeper waters offshore from Bermuda include blue and white marlin, wahoo, half a dozen tuna species, amberjack, amberfish, dolphin (*dorado*, or *dolphin fish*), rainbow runner, barracuda, and sharks.

Gamefishing offers the greatest opportunity for specialization in the use of tackle, bait, and method. Bermudian fishermen have refined trolling methods, in particular over the past 30 years, to target specific gamefish such as blue marlin. At the same time they have adopted more sophisticated tackle and methods to catch other gamefish more successfully.

Most fishing expeditions in Bermuda nevertheless bring in a mixed catch, from the few hours of casual shore fishing to the all day game-fishing excursion offshore. Bonefishing, which requires such specific techniques as to preclude virtually any chance of landing other species incidentally, is the conspicuous exception.

Beebe and Tee-Van, in their *Field Book of the Shore Fishes of Bermuda and the West Indies*, first published in 1933, identified 602 species of fish in Bermuda waters: 267 'deep sea and oceanic surface fish' (*pelagics*, or, to use the old fashioned Bermudian term, *floating fish*), and 335 shore fish.

Twenty-eight of the 335 species of shore fish were indigenous to Bermuda waters. Most of the rest were common to Bermuda, Florida, and the West Indies.

It is generally supposed that the reef fish around Bermuda arrived as spawn hitching a ride up from the Caribbean in the course of the Gulf Stream. Eddies that skimmed by Bermuda would have thrown the spawn out of the main stream. That spawn would finally attach to the Bermuda reef platform where they would grow to take their place as permanent members of the resident reef fish population.

Inshore Waters

Littoral and reef fish populate the coast and shallow reef waters of Bermuda. Primarily bottom dwellers (*demersals*), these fish congregate around coral heads and, inshore, over weedy, sandy, or muddy broken bottom areas.

Demersal species are sedentary, territorial fish. They stay in one place most of their lives, feeding on a range of rather static food from, or just above, the seabed: small crustaceans (crabs, shrimp), molluscs (mussels, oysters), worms, or other smaller fish.

Bottom fish rarely stray far from their home territories, as long as there is food to support them. Beebe and Tee-Van nevertheless noted that they moved into deeper water with the onset of cooler winter conditions. 'The most marked migration of [shore] fishes about Bermuda is a general outward shift into deep water of many species at the approach of cold weather.'

In reef communities around other islands of the world, certain species seem to migrate around the reef at different times of the year, their movements coinciding with lunar cycles and spawning times. Fishermen have observed their movements over generations and have attuned their fishing practices accordingly, to catch the most fish where they are most numerous and most disposed to feed.

Research in Bermuda has shown that reef species which are usually sedentary and territorial do travel to other parts of the reef at specific times of the year, in aggregations of fish, to spawn. Many of the groupers were particularly vulnerable at these times, before they were

protected, because they were easy to catch. Now that there are restrictions on catching these species, with, in some cases, full year-round protection, the relevance of their migratory habits is not as significant to fishermen as it is to marine biologists.

Fish Names

Fishermen in the Western Pacific island archipelago of Palau catch 'tkuu' (or 'manguro'), 'desui', 'keskas' (or 'mersad'), and 'katsuo'. On the other side of the world in Bermuda, fishermen catch yellowfin tuna, rainbow runners, wahoo, and oceanic bonito (skipjack tuna). No doubt the Hawaiians, Seychellois, Sri Lankans, and Pitcairn islanders have their own names – even nicknames – for these fish.

But in all cases they are the same species, each individually identified by their scientific Latin labels: *Thunnus albacares* (tkuu; yellowfin tuna), *Elagatis bipinnulata* (desui; rainbow runner), *Acanthocybium solandri* (keskas; wahoo), and *Katsuwonus pelamis* (katsuo; oceanic bonito (skipjack tuna).

Whatever fish are called, in whatever language, wherever in the world, each species has one single, uniformly accepted Latin name. No matter how often the waiter has to explain that it's 'dolphin', 'dolphin-fish', 'dorado', or 'mahi-mahi', rather than a fillet of 'flipper', on the menu, there is one, and only one *Coryphaena hippurus* in the Indian, Pacific, Atlantic or any other ocean (although unlikely to be so designated when offered as grilled, sautéed, or broiled with lemon butter and a sprig of parsley).

Each scientific name for a species, fish or fowl, flora or fauna, has two parts: the first (always capitalized) is the genus, like a surname; the second (almost always in lower case) refers to the species, like a first name.

Grouper and rockfish species, for example, are members of either the *Epinephelus* or *Mycteroperca* genera (plural of genus).

A group of closely related genera constitutes a family (for example, the Serranidae family, comprising all groupers and rockfish).

Bermudians use some common fish names almost indiscriminately for different species (especially among the groupers), according to prevailing vernacular, the knowledge of the person using the names, and changes in species identification over the years.

To add to the confusion, common usage has changed over time. Names from 50 years ago may be different today.

'Bonito' (or sometimes 'bonita') is an example of a name used in Bermuda at different times for various different species. Nowadays bonito in Bermuda may include, colloquially or otherwise: almaco jack (horse-eye bonito, amberfish) (*Seriola rivoliana*); oceanic bonito (skipjack tuna) (*Euthynnus pelamis*); or, occasionally among amateur anglers, little tuna/tunny (*Euthynnus alleteratus*).

For all that, *true* bonito (*Sarda sarda*), which school in great numbers around the Western Atlantic, shun Bermuda and are not generally encountered in local waters.

Groupers

The Serranidae family comprises sea basses and groupers. Groupers are actually large basses belonging to two genera, *Epinephelus* and *Mycteroperca*. In Bermuda the *Mycteroperca* are mainly known as rockfish while the *Epinephelus* are primarily groupers and include hinds. Rockfish is the colloquial name for a variety of species, all of which are technically groupers. The term rockfish is used here to reflect its colloquial usage in Bermuda. Scientists, however, would prefer that the term grouper be used exclusively to include all *Mycteroperca* and *Epinephelus* species. The term rockfish more properly refers to a Pacific Ocean species of the Scorpaenidae family.

(Groupers are so named because of their tendency to group together, forming especially large aggregations during spawning periods.)

The description on the back of the early Bermuda map by John Speed indicates that groupers and rockfish have been known in local waters since the earliest days of Bermuda's colonization. Over the centuries they have become a staple fish for Bermudian tables. Generations of local fishermen have fished groupers in large numbers around Bermuda's shallow reef waters and out to a depth of about 30 fathoms off the edge, as well as on the outlying banks.

Two youngsters, Teko Ingham (14 years old) and Shannon Philpott (13 years old), with the 100 lb rockfish they caught with their friend Anthony ('AJ') Hayward (not pictured), off the rocks near Granaway Heights, on the Little Sound, in Southampton, 4 January 2000. The boys had been baiting the site ever since they first spotted the fish two months before. They struggled for half an hour to catch the rockfish, hauled it 20 feet up the cliff face, and finally called on neighbour Richard Quinn to help them cart the fish home in a wheelbarrow. (Photo courtesy of Flybridge Tackle.)

The best known grouper fishing grounds are near where the first settlers were shipwrecked off Bermuda, at the East End. Grouper Ground lies about a mile and a half to the southeast of St David's Island. Other important grouper fishing areas off the East End are nearby, around Kitchen Shoals and Northeast Breakers. All areas to the east and southeast of St David's are easily accessible, because the edge of the deep is just a few miles from land. These areas are no longer fished specifically for grouper since most species are fully or partly protected. The outlying banks have also been fertile grouper fishing grounds.

It is almost inconceivable these days to imagine the number of groupers caught in earlier years, even well into this century, by small boat fishermen. E.A. McCallan notes in his 1948 narrative *Life On Old St David's*: 'A good grouper season stocked the ponds of the Island [St David's] with, perhaps, 5,000 fish.'

Although this abundance had dwindled even by the time of McCallan's account, when most of St David's 'forty-odd' fish ponds had fallen into disuse, it was not so many years beforehand that ponds held hundreds of fish at any one time. McCallan records that 'one [fish pond] at the Villa had a capacity of five hundred, but fifty to a hundred and fifty was the capacity of most'.

There used to be around the coast of Bermuda hundreds of concrete or stone fish ponds. Families with waterside homes built ponds to keep fish fresh. By the 1940s most had been abandoned. Ice boxes, refrigerators, and freezers in Bermudian homes made fish ponds redundant. (The large pond at Waterlot Inn in Southampton, which kept four or five green turtles as well as live fish, was used until the late 1960s to keep lobsters fresh. New owners subsequently filled in the pond.)

In his monograph *Bermudian Handline Fishing in the Sailing Sloop Era: A Fisherman's Account* (1975), Raoul Andersen quotes Captain Geary Pitcher, Sr: 'There were about 15 fishermen at the time [early 20th century], and every one had a pond. Some would hold 1,000, some would hold 4-500 lbs.' Most of the fish in those St David's ponds were groupers and snappers.

*Fireman Michael ('Minch') Rawlins and the pillion passenger 102 lb rockfish he caught off the shoreline on 15 December 1992. ('Minch' stands for **M**ichael **I**s **N**ot **C**oming **H**ome . . . because he's out fishing!)* (Photo courtesy of Flybridge Tackle.)

The amiable nature and willingness of groupers to take a bait, combined with their territorial habits (making it easy to 'bait up' and fish sites where they abounded), contributed as much to their decimation as any other factor. The effort needed by fishermen to catch them was not particularly arduous, especially in the pre-1990 era of fish pot fishing. So they were taken in large numbers, and most easily during spawning periods when they congregated in large groups.

Commercial fishermen have caught far fewer groupers since the 1970s, in part because of the prohibitions against taking them as endangered species. In 1975 all groupers (including rockfish and hinds) accounted for almost half the total catch of fish taken by commercial fishermen in Bermuda. By 1986 that was down to just over 15%, and by 1995, just over 10%. (The catch of pelagics and other 'miscellaneous' fish increased in inverse proportion.)

A characteristic common to all groupers is that they change colour, like chameleons, according to their environment. In general, the colour of groupers darkens with the depth of water of their habitat. Red coloration predominates in deeper habitats. Lighter browns and yellows distinguish fish from shallower water. Beebe and Tee-Van have confirmed the phenomenon: 'Some of the Bermuda fish, such as the Hind, have shallow and deep water colour forms, those from deeper water being redder.'

Because groupers change colour, it is sometimes difficult to identify different species. (Even marine biologists do not agree on all the classifications, which have changed periodically.) The main identifiers to notice, apart from colour, are body markings (stripes, bars, blotches, and spots), peripheral colorations (along the borders of fins), and the size of the fish.

Some groupers are among the largest of all fish species. Jewfish (*Epinephelus itajara*), rarely found in Bermuda waters, exceed a weight of well over 500 lb. The black rockfish (*Mycteroperca bonaci*), which grows up to 200 lb, is the largest grouper species commonly found around Bermuda.

Groupers eat a range of small bottom dwelling and reef organisms, including small fish, shrimp, and other crustaceans. It remains to be ascertained whether this basic food source for groupers has been seriously disturbed by pollution from the growing number of small and large craft around Bermuda's waters, as well as by demographic pressures from the increase in the island's population and tourist visitors, all of which might have contributed to the depopulation of the grouper community.

Most groupers now have protected status in Bermuda waters, some year-round, some seasonally, and some by a bag limit restriction. The following profiles are therefore mainly for descriptive purposes, but also in recognition of a family of fishes that have played a leading role in Bermuda's fishery in the past and still constitute a valuable marine resource for Bermuda.

The colloquial names for grouper species in Bermuda can be confusing, and even contradictory. This is partly because it is difficult to distinguish some species from others, given their predilection for changing colour. It is partly also because groupers are nowhere near as common as they used to be. Familiarity with the different species has diminished. So, by casual delinquency, names have become attributed somewhat indiscriminately.

Wolfgang Sterrer, in his reference work *Bermuda's Marine Life*, encapsulates the problem (with a footnote nod to Jennifer Gray-Conklin):

> Much as in fry, sardines and anchovies, local names don't mean a thing to the uninitiated. The Red Grouper, for instance, is known in Bermuda as Deer Hamlet, not to be confused with the Red Rockfish which is also called Princess Rockfish or Yellowfin Grouper; the latter, however, is not the same as the Yellowmouth Grouper a.k.a. Monkey Rockfish. The Gag Grouper, or Fine-Scale Rockfish, is definitely not identical with the Gag Rockfish, which is just another name for the Tiger Grouper. On the other hand the Runner Rockfish, which Bermudians may call a Black Rockfish, is actually a Black Grouper. Not even the Nassau Grouper is only the Nassau Grouper: in Bermuda it is referred to as Hamlet.

You pays your money and you takes your choice . . .

Nassau Grouper (*Epinephelus striatus*), a.k.a. Hamlet

Incredibly, in the days when Nassau groupers were still abundant around Bermuda, fishermen sometimes forked this beautiful fish into the ground as fertilizer when they caught more than they could sell on the local market or stock in fish ponds.

As early as the 1950s the survival of the Nassau grouper in Bermuda waters was under threat. By the 1980s the potential peril had become a discernible reality: between 1975 and 1981 commercial landings of Nassau grouper declined by 95%.

Since then (1981) 'the species has not shown any evidence of a subsequent recovery' and has become, apparently, a commercially extinct species. This has ostensibly been because 'spawning aggregation sites on the Bermuda platform and on the offshore banks were intensively fished with fish pots during this period and it appears that the spawning stock biomass was reduced below a critical but unknown level so that the population has apparently been unable to recover' (Luckhurst, 1996).

In other words, commercial fishermen have taken so many Nassau groupers out of the waters around Bermuda over the years that there are not enough of them left to reproduce and increase in numbers. Whether they can be regenerated like the cahow remains to be seen.

What is left of the Nassau grouper population around Bermuda waters is fully protected: the fish may not be taken at any time of the year. It is no longer, therefore, a fish for either recreational or commercial fishermen, at least until, and *if*, the species revives.

Hamlet, as Nassau groupers are most commonly called in Bermuda, are strikingly attractive, variously coloured fish. In shallower reef areas the fish is light grey-green to ochre-yellow. A dark stripe runs longitudinally from the snout, through the eye, and along the back to about the start of the dorsal fin. Up to six dark bars stripe its body vertically from the back to the belly. Towards the tail of the fish, three of these bars may sometimes form a 'W' shape.

As with other groupers, hamlet are able to modify their colour according to their surroundings. The general coloration of the fish darkens with the depth of water to a more reddish brown. The bars along the body often disappear altogether. A constant square black spot will always be visible, however, on the upper part of the caudal peduncle, whether in shallow inshore waters or offshore in greater depths. This mark identifies the hamlet from all other grouper species which it might in other respects closely resemble. Hamlet reach a maximum size of about 60 lb.

Red Grouper (*Epinephelus morio*), a.k.a. Deer Hamlet

This grouper is often mistaken for the Nassau grouper: its markings are similar and coloration may appear similar if the fish is from deeper water. Although primarily found in shallow waters around the outer reef, it may relocate to deeper water in its spawning period of April–June. The red grouper is typically light brown or reddish in colour, but it lacks the Nassau grouper's distinctive black mark on the caudal peduncle. Maximum size is about 30 lb.

Like the Nassau grouper, this fish is protected year-round as an endangered species.

Mutton Hamlet (*Epinephelus* (previously *Alphestes*) *afer*)

Another endangered grouper, the mutton hamlet, cannot be taken in Bermuda waters at any time, under the Protected Species Order. This is a rather small grouper, growing to just about a foot long. It inhabits mainly weedy bottoms and areas around coral reefs. It is identified by a skin covered spine on its cheek, which no other grouper has.

Red Hind (*Epinephelus guttatus*)

Until the 1960s and 1970s, the red hind was considered a rather unseemly, low value, almost 'trash' fish in Bermuda. Compared with the more esteemed flesh of tuna, dolphin, and wahoo, which were being taken in larger quantities as gamefishing became more popular, the red hind was of marginally acceptable quality. Despite being somewhat sniffed at, it nevertheless provided the bulk of grouper fish for the commercial fishery and had been a staple catch for generations.

By the 1960s, and into the 1970s, fishermen began catching the red hind in increasing, and sometimes vast, numbers. Boatloads of hundreds of fish caught in a single day were not unusual. Recreational fishermen caught hind easily. Charter boats complemented their gamefishing business by bottom fishing for hinds. There was also a growing demand for fresh fish to feed the increasing number of tourist visitors to Bermuda. The hind was enjoying its heyday. Perils, however, loomed.

By the early 1970s fishermen were beginning to notice smaller catches of hind, and smaller fish. As it was being fished heavily, there was growing concern for the hind population. Fishermen persuaded fisheries officials that it was time to give the hind protection from overfishing. Seasonally protected areas for the hind were introduced from 1974.

The 1975 catch of red hind by commercial fishermen was 175,000 lb. (No official figures exist from before 1975 to record fish landings, so there is no accurate way to compare the catch with earlier years.) Ten years later, in 1985, after seasonal protection had been introduced, landings of red hind were down to just 70,000 lb, a decline of about 60%. In the years since the 1990 fish pot ban, landings of red hind by commercial fishermen have averaged 18,000–20,000 lb/year.

The hind is still probably the most common of all the grouper varieties in Bermuda waters. It seems to hold its own against overfishing, assisted in no small part by the Species Protection Order, established specifically to protect spawning aggregations of red hind, and by the 1990 fish pot ban, which has redirected fishing for hind to line fishing, requiring much greater fishing effort by fishermen and consequent lower catches.

Hind, like other groupers, habitually aggregate at specific sites to spawn in the summer months. The protection of those sites, and the fish pot ban, have been the two most important factors allowing the population around Bermuda at least to stabilize above a critical level and, possibly, to recover from the depleted numbers caused by heavy fishing in previous years.

The red hind varies in colour between a very bright red, to pink, to a brownish red. Lighter colour vertical bands run down its body. The fish is speckled all over with reddish brown spots. The dorsal, anal, and caudal fins have dark edges.

Another hind species, the **rock hind** *(Epinephelus adscensionis)*, has similar markings to the red hind, but with, additionally, four or five large black spots on its back which distinguish it from its cousin. The rock hind is quite rare in Bermuda waters.

It used to be thought that the maximum size for red hinds was about 10 lb and 2 ft in length. Any fish over 8 lb was considered exceptional. In June 1990, however, a local fisherman caught a red hind off Bermuda weighing 18 lb and measuring $2\frac{1}{2}$ ft long. The Department

of Agriculture's Fisheries Division examined the fish and verified its size. The specimen confirmed anecdotal evidence of previously reported catches of large hind up to 12 lb.

Black Grouper *(Mycteroperca bonaci)*, a.k.a. Black Rockfish, Runner Rockfish, Rockfish

As Louis S. Mowbray notes in his *Guide to the Reef, Shore and Game Fish of Bermuda*, 'This is the common rockfish of Bermuda.' The fish often exceeds 50 lb and may grow up to 200 lb. Although the fish is usually found around and just beyond the reefs of Bermuda, the following stories record unusual shoreline catches. Most large groupers caught from the shore in Bermuda are black rockfish.

In October 1979 two beach attendants at the (then) Holiday Inn in St George's caught a 93 lb fish that they noticed browsing among the rocks just off the beach. The manner as much as the location of their catch attracted the attention of the news media. Not having a fishing line handy, the two men stunned the fish with a rake and fork, attached a rope to the struggling fish, and brought it ashore. They finished it off with a well directed blow of the fork to the fish's head.

(A follow-up to this story in *The Royal Gazette* was a letter to the editor a few days later, criticizing the cruelty of the manner in which the rockfish was dispatched.)

In September 1978 *The Royal Gazette* reported that Ross Talbot, a member of Bermuda's foremost singing group The Talbot Brothers, caught a rockfish estimated to weigh 75 lb. The newsworthy feature of this catch was that Mr Talbot caught the fish from shore, off a rocky promontory near John Smith's Bay (not far from the Talbots' home). Mr Talbot had been baiting the area 'every day for a long time' before catching the fish.

Yellowfin Rockfish *(Mycteroperca venenosa)*, a.k.a. Red Rockfish, Prince Rockfish, Princess Rockfish, Yellowfin Grouper, Black Grouper

One of its common names, black grouper, derives from the yellowfin's similarity in body shape and markings to the common black rockfish (*M. bonaci*). It differs by the mainly red coloration of its body and yellow tinges around the base of its pectoral fins. Like the black rockfish, it has mottled dark patches along its body. Both fish have a rather elongated body shape. Maximum size for the yellowfin is around 35 lb.

The **princess rockfish** is a slightly different variety of this species, with light brown, rather than red, body colour. As its lighter colour might suggest, it is a shallower water cousin of the yellowfin.

The yellowfin now has year-round protection and may not be taken at all in Bermuda waters.

Tiger Grouper (*Mycteroperca tigris*), a.k.a. Gag, Tiger Rockfish

Another protected grouper species in Bermuda, the gag cannot be taken at any time of the year. It inhabits waters of up to 30 fathoms around the outer reefs. The fish is usually dark brown, with distinguishing 'tiger stripes' running vertically along its body from the back to the lateral line. It also has several slightly elongated finlets on the dorsal, anal, and caudal fins.

The common name 'gag' is said to derive from the fact that it disgorges its stomach when brought to the surface, *'gagging'* its mouth (although this phenomenon is also common to other groupers taken from deep water). Maximum size is around 25 lb.

Finescale Rockfish (*Mycteroperca microlepis*), a.k.a. Gag Rockfish/Grouper

The distinctive feature of the finescale (gag) rockfish is the set of stripes radiating out from the eye to the base of the pectoral fins and start of the dorsal fin. Irregularly dispersed brownish blotches mark its somewhat elongated body. Maximum size is about three feet.

Yellowmouth Grouper (*Mycteroperca interstitialis*), a.k.a. Monkey Rockfish, Salmon Rockfish, Flag Rockfish

A semi-protected grouper (year-round bag limit of one fish per day per boat), the yellowmouth gets its name, not surprisingly, from the yellowish colour of its mouth. All its fins also have a yellow tinged edge. It is more commonly known in Bermuda, however, as the monkey rockfish.

Misty Grouper (*Epinephelus mysticinus*), a.k.a. John Paw(s)

Beebe and Tee-Van described the misty grouper found in Bermuda as John Paw or speckled hind (the latter because of its densely speckled white spots). At the time (1930s) it was classified as *Epinephelus*

A generation ago the misty grouper was a common grouper around Bermuda's waters, both over the reef platform and the offshore banks. These days the species is a rarity. This 92 lb specimen is accompanied by its captors Richard Allen (left) and Craig ('Cakes') Soares (right), July 1994. (Photo courtesy of Flybridge Tackle.)

drummond-hayi (Goode and Bean). *Epinephelus mystacinus*, the true misty grouper, was identified by Beebe and Tee-Van as the black grouper. The speckled hind, the only grouper with white spot markings, is now separately classified as *Epinephelus drummond-hayi*. The true black grouper is *Mycteroperca bonaci*.

The misty grouper used to be common in deep water around Bermuda. It is now a rarity. A beautiful fish of yellowish ochre to umber brown coloration, it is marked by dark bands running vertically from its back to below the lateral line. The head is marked by darker bands running diagonally across the face to the gill coverings.

John Paws typically weigh in the region of 25–30 lb but may grow to a maximum of around 100 lb. Over 50 lb, their flesh is rather mushy and unpalatable. The fish is primarily a deep water dweller, found in depths of 300 feet or more.

Coney (*Cephalopholis / Epinephelus fulva*), a.k.a. Butter-fish

Very similar to the hind in shape and spotted body markings, the coney is differentiated by its smaller spots. Unlike the hind, it displays two more distinct dark spots behind the soft dorsal fin just before the caudal peduncle. There are also two distinct spots on the lower jaw. These spots are apparent in all colour phases. Coney are somewhat smaller than hinds, with a maximum weight of about 2 lb and maximum length of about one foot.

Coney exhibit changing colour phases, from brownish red to, less commonly, bright yellow, and even a bi-colour phase of dark black and light yellowish sides and belly. In its solid colour phase it is typically dark red in deeper waters beyond the reef platform, and a lighter brown colour in shallower waters inside the reef boundary. In its yellow phase it is known as the **yellow coney**, but it is the same species.

There are no restrictions on catching coney in Bermuda. As a result, it is one of the few grouper species to have been caught in greater numbers by commercial fishermen in recent years. Landings of coney by commercial fishermen increased from 10,000–20,000 lb/year in the 1970s, to an average of about 50,000 lb/year from 1985 onwards, compensating for the diminished availability of other grouper species to the local commercial fishery.

Barber (*Paranthias furcifer*), a.k.a. Creole Fish

The barber appears still to be abundant in Bermuda waters. Its small size (usually less than 2 lb) probably made it less desirable than other groupers as a commercial catch before restrictions were established, allowing the local population to thrive.

The name *barber* is thought to derive from the razor sharp spines along the upper edge of its opercal (gill) cover. The alternative name *creole fish* may derive from its flame red and bright yellow colour displays.

Barbers are typically dark red along the dorsal surface, fading along the sides and belly to a light pink or pinkish white. Three or four white or light grey spots along the base of the dorsal fin identify the species. Barber also have a deeply forked tail and small mouth, unlike other grouper species which have a rounded tail and large mouth.

Another distinctive feature of barber is their habitat. They are mid-water feeders of the open ocean that travel in small schools, unlike most groupers which keep to the bottom in one place for most of the year. They feed on small organisms (krill, small shrimps, plankton), typically rising and falling in the water column, as a school, in cone formation. Barbers inhabit the waters beyond the outer reef and over the banks, in depths of at least 80–100 ft.

Small hooks and firm bait are needed to catch barber as they tend to pick at baits with their small mouth. Fishermen often use small size multiple hooks to catch the fish in large numbers.

Wreckfish (*Polyprion americanus*)

Wreckfish are similar in external appearance to groupers but with a few differences that classify them in their own family, Polyprionidae, rather than among the Serranidae family of groupers and sea basses. The fish are bottom dwellers found in waters from 25 to 500 fathoms. Their preferred habitat is similar to that of groupers, namely, rocky outcrops and holes or undersea caves. The steep drop-off of the Bermuda Platform is typical wreckfish territory.

Only one species of wreckfish, *Polyprion americanus*, is thought to inhabit the deep waters off the Bermuda reef platform, caught by fishermen mainly looking for deep water snappers. Coloration is greyish brown, with lighter mottling around its body. The largest specimens locally have been in the region of 100 lb. (Outside Bermuda the wreckfish is also known as the **stone bass**.)

The average total catch of wreckfish by commercial fishermen in Bermuda is now just a few hundred pounds a year, compared with several thousand pounds a year in the early to mid-1980s. (Wreckfish may have been even more abundant in earlier years, but records from before 1982 do not identify them specifically.) That suggests either that the local population of wreckfish has been severely depleted by overfishing, or that fishermen are no longer fishing the same depths they used to.

Either way, the role of the wreckfish on the stage of commercial fishing in Bermuda has diminished greatly.

Hogfish (*Lachnolaimus maximus*)

Once one of the most common fish taken by the commercial fishery in Bermuda, hogfish are widely distributed around the shallow reef waters of the Bermuda Platform, as well as in harbours and bays of inshore waters. The fish, a member of the wrasse (Labridae) family, is so called because of its hog-like snout which it distends when foraging along the bottom for its favourite foods (mussels, clams, scallops, crabs, sea urchins, and virtually any other available shellfish or crustacean).

The legal minimum size for catching hogfish in Bermuda is 14 inches fork length, to protect the juveniles of the species.

The hogfish is clearly identifiable by the first three elongated spines of its dorsal fin which extend like trailers, and by its elongated tail fin lobes. The dorsal and anal fins near the caudal peduncle are also rather elongated.

Hogfish, like groupers and other reef fish, change colour according to their environment. When excited, the fish may change colour abruptly. Generally, however, the adult fish is reddish brown (lighter pink in juveniles), mottled with irregular off-white patches along its body and fins. Whatever changes of coloration or body markings, the head remains a constant reddish brown. There is also always a dark spot at the rear base of the dorsal fin.

Hogfish can reach up to 25 lb, which would be a very large looking fish indeed given its deep compressed body shape. Large hogfish in other parts of its range in the Western Atlantic have reportedly become very scarce because of over-zealous predation by spearfishing. The average size in Bermuda waters is 8–10 lb.

Hogfish have traditionally been considered a fine eating fish. They used to be a staple of the local commercial fishery when reef and pot fishing predominated. Now they appear for sale in far fewer numbers than previously.

Another wrasse family member found in Bermuda is the **Spanish hogfish** (*Bodianus rufus*), which has a more slender body shape than the common hogfish. It also lacks the three extended dorsal spines. Its tail fin lobes are slightly elongated, but nowhere near so much as on its common cousin.

The Spanish hogfish has vivid coloration and colour changes. Its most brilliant colour phase is bright blue or purple along the dorsal surface, and bright yellow along the sides and belly. The fish roams the reef and inshore waters in depths of up to about 100 ft. It grows to a maximum size locally of about a foot, hardly ever exceeding a few pounds in weight.

Blueboned Porgy (*Calamus bajonado*), a.k.a. Goat-head Porgy, Jolthead Porgy

For generations of Bermuda's commercial fishermen, the blueboned porgy has provided a source of fish (and income) in the early months of the year when they spawn but when other fish may not be caught so easily. They also appear to be quite abundant still throughout the year. There are no restrictions on taking them.

Sea urchins are by far the favourite food of blueboned porgy which forage for the spiny little echinoderm around the sandy and grassy shallows of the Bermuda Platform. The sea urchins are thought to give the bones of the fish a bluish tinge, and its common name. The body of the fish is most commonly silvery grey.

Its alternative name, **goat-head porgy**, derives from the large head and snout profile resembling the shape of a goat's head. It gets another

Captain Michael Baxter (Ellen B) *and guest angler with freshly caught blueboned porgy.* (Photo courtesy of Captain Mike Baxter.)

name, **jolthead porgy** (not used in Bermuda), from the way it jolts or shakes loose molluscs from rocks, for food. All porgies have a distinctive humped head area and deep, compressed body.

A bone near the anus of the porgy contains a powerful solvent to dissolve the spines of urchin. This bone should be removed before cooking the porgy. It would otherwise give the flesh a strong taste if left in place. The fish also often has urchin spines embedded in its thick reddish lips.

In the early 1980s long spined sea urchins (*Diadema antilla arum*) around Bermuda contracted a lethal affliction from a marine fungus that eddied up from Gulf Stream waters. Affected urchins lost their spines and died in large numbers. The size and quality of porgies taken by commercial fishermen diminished, while their usually firm, translucent, white flesh became dense, opaque, and unsavoury.

Even under normal conditions the blueboned porgy yields only around 20% of its ungutted weight as fillets. What the porgy lacks in abundant fillet flesh, however, it more than makes up for as a prime base for fish stock and chowder. The bones and large head are particularly well suited for making chowder stock.

Blueboned porgy average 8–10 lb in Bermuda waters. Their natural habitat is the weedy and sandy broken bottoms of the coast and reef platform, in depths of 30 feet to as deep as 100 feet, wherever sea urchins and other succulent molluscs and crustaceans might be rooted out.

The **sheep's-head porgy** (*Calamus calamus*) is very similar to the blueboned porgy in shape, habitat, and preferred prey, but its maximum size is just about 3 lb. Named, like its cousin, for another farmyard animal, the sheep's-head has a smaller mouth, which makes it difficult to catch. As a quick change artist, the sheep's-head is adept at rapidly modifying its colour and markings, from blotched to striped, and vice versa.

Common Triggerfish (*Balistes capriscus*), a.k.a. Turbot, Grey Triggerfish

The triggerfish is known as 'turbot' in Bermuda and the West Indies in general. A number of flat fish in the Atlantic and Pacific Oceans are known as turbot, like the cold water Greenland halibut and the arrowtooth flounder from more temperate areas of the Pacific. Their common characteristic is a flat compressed body, but real turbot have the distinctive feature of two eyes on the same side of the body. In most other respects, too, these flounder type fish are very different from the triggerfish, a member of the Balistidae family.

Triggerfish have a peculiar ocular ability: they are able to rotate their eyes independently, enabling them to see in two different directions simultaneously. The eyes of triggerfish are located quite far back on the head so that they can prey on sea urchin, their favourite meal, without the urchin's spines injuring their eyes. The fish bite off the urchin's spines and, rotating the urchin on to its side or back, proceed to eat its underbelly. The triggerfish also has hard, plate-like scales to afford its body protection from the spines of its prey.

Common grey triggerfish have populated most of the Bermuda Platform, particularly around the grassy broken bottoms of inshore waters and coastal shallows.

The tail of the trigger is similar to the hogfish in that its lower and upper lobes are slightly elongated. The 'trigger' of the triggerfish is its second dorsal spine. The fish uses its strong dorsal spines as a defence mechanism, locking the first, and largest, spine in the erect position by raising its second spine, the trigger. The only way to move the hard front spines down is to apply pressure to the third set of spines towards the tail, which unlocks the two forward sets.

The common grey triggerfish is darkest along the dorsal surface and lighter along the belly. Maximum size is around 4 lb.

Other triggerfish found in Bermuda include: the **ocean triggerfish** (*Canthidermis sufflamen*), a mid-water inhabitant of deeper waters and, increasingly numerous, over the banks, with a maximum size of around 10 lb; and the less common but much more colourful **queen trigger** (*Balistes vetula*), also known as **old wife**, found mainly around reefs, with distinctive bright blue bands radiating from the snout downwards towards the belly, and bright blue radial stripes on the dorsal, anal, and caudal fins against a yellow surface.

Snappers

Alongside the grunts and bream families, snappers are one of the most common demersal fish around the shallow waters of Bermuda. Anyone who has ever fished off a dock in Bermuda has at least a visual acquaintance with a member of the snapper family (usually, in those circumstances, the grey snapper). Small snappers of up to a few pounds cruise around inshore coastal waters. Larger specimens up to 20–25 lb inhabit the outer reefs and deeper waters.

Like other demersal species around Bermuda, the forward rays of the snapper's dorsal and anal fins are spiky while the back rays are soft. Fishermen handling snappers should first smooth down the forward spiky rays of the dorsal fin in particular, running the hand snugly along from its forehead, or risk being spiked.

Whitewater Snapper (*Lutjanus synagris*), a.k.a. Lane Snapper, Spot Snapper

Predominantly pinkish in colour, the whitewater has up to 10 yellow horizontal stripes along the body, with three or four broad stripes along the head. There is a conspicuous dark spot high on the back of the fish where the soft rays of the dorsal fin begin. The slightly V-shaped tail is distinctly pinkish red.

This snapper is common over weed-strewn sandy or grey 'clay' (white water) bottoms but is also found around coral heads. A 2 lb fish would be a good size specimen. Maximum size is 4–5 lb.

The whitewater feeds at night on small crustaceans, small fish, and worms. As with other nocturnal feeders, it is easier to catch at night while it feeds. The glare of the sun against the clear bottom also makes it more difficult for the whitewater to see a baited hook during daytime. Just before sunset is also a good time to fish for the whitewater.

These fish are adept at throwing a hook with a soft bait, so a combination bait of a tough piece of squid or mussel, together with fry or anchovy, is recommended.

Unlike its cousin the grey snapper, which grabs and runs, the whitewater nibbles at a baited hook. Prime catching time is from April throughout the summer, during its spawning cycle, and as late as November or December. Fishermen are restricted to a bag limit of 30 fish per recreational boat per day, and minimum size limit of 25 cm (about 8 inches) fork length, year-round.

Although the whitewater is sometimes misnamed 'silk snapper' by amateur fishermen in Bermuda, the true silk snapper is quite a different fish, and much rarer nowadays than it was in the past.

Silk Snapper (*Lutjanus vivanus*), a.k.a. Red Snapper

There are several different species of silk (red) snapper, including the **red snapper** itself (*Lutjanus aya*), the **chub-nosed** (or **cubera**) **snapper** (*Lutjanus cyanopterus*), and the **black fin** (*Lutjanus buccanella*) which has a dark spot at the base of the pectoral fin. All are characterized by a dark pink or red body colour, with a yellowish sheen on the tail and fins. The common identifying feature of this species is its bright yellow eye.

Silk (red) snapper inhabit the dark depths off Bermuda, from the edge of the deep at around 200 feet to the real deep over 600 feet. It is the largest snapper found in Bermuda waters, peaking at around 25 lb.

In past years the silk snapper played a more important role in Bermuda's commercial fishery than it does today. There used to be a number of commercial fishermen who actually specialized in catching this one species. Silk snapper was one of the island's more common table fish in the days before mass imports of frozen fresh and prepared packaged fish.

The abolition of fish pots, which accounted for many silk snappers brought to the market, and the relatively labour intensive effort needed to target this fish, has mainly accounted for its relative scarcity now as a commercial fish. Recreational anglers, however, still go fishing specifically for the silk snapper, such is its premium as a fine food fish.

Silk snapper tend to come up from the deeper reaches of their habitat to feed at night in shallower water around and just on the edge of the Bermuda Platform. They eat mainly small crustaceans, squid, and other small bottom prey.

Grey Snapper (*Lutjanus griseus*), a.k.a. The Lawyer, Greydog, Mangrove Snapper

Grey snapper are the most ubiquitous of all the shallow water snappers in Bermuda, lurking around docks, rocks, and coral heads, and under anchored or moored boats. The fish often looks virtually motionless, seeming to tread water, and affecting an impression of supreme aloofness and disdain for the baited hook.

Typically the grey snapper is all grey coloured, with a dark tail and slightly lighter grey belly. It adapts its colouring to its surroundings, appearing lighter grey in shallow sandy areas and darker grey in deeper rockier waters. Maximum size is around 15 lb for specimens in deeper water around the reefs and on top of the banks, diminishing to a few pounds (and often less) around inshore coastal habitats.

The grey snapper is among the most fastidious of Bermuda's small inshore fish. Fishermen should disguise a relatively small hook as much as possible with bait, dropping an unweighted line to drift among loosely scattered chum. Even then the fish appears able to discern with impunity the difference between a free feed and a murderous hook. It often seems to pick off bait that drifts free of a hook, eluding capture by the patience and prudence that have earned it the sobriquet 'The Lawyer'.

One clue to its feeding inclinations (and catchability) is the hue of the dark chevron running from just above the eyes to just forward of its gill cover which darkens when the fish is more excited (when feeding or around spawning time, for example). The chevron mark is lighter coloured when the fish is relaxed and less interested in feeding or procreation.

Whether, at a distance from above, an angler is able to recognize, much less exploit the nature of this lighter or darker chevron is a moot point. At the best of times the grey snapper remains an elusive catch and equal to most inducements offered his way via hook and line.

The peak spawning activity for grey snapper is just before or at the full moon, over a cycle of two to four full moons, from April to August. Since the fish is a nocturnal feeder, anglers have the best chance of catching grey snapper in the nights leading up to the full moon in the warmer months of the year.

Grey snapper feed mainly on smaller fish found within the surrounding environment, including fry and anchovy when the fish 'goes pelagic'. Anglers are best advised to use fresh bait on a well camouflaged hook, although white bread balled up to form a tough nugget of dough, bread crust, or bits of fatty raw bacon are all equally common baits for many young fishermen casting off the local dock in hopes of catching 'The Lawyer' with its briefs adrift.

Schoolmaster Snapper (*Lutjanus apodus*)

The schoolmaster is not as common as the grey snapper around the coast of Bermuda but may be found in similar locations, especially around weedy bottoms. Identification of the schoolmaster is made by the eight or nine whitish stripes running vertically down its olive green to brownish body, from the dorsal to the ventral areas. In larger fish the stripes may be less apparent, but the olive green and brownish colour of the body overall distinguishes it as a schoolmaster.

Around shallow coastal waters the fish typically weighs in at a pound or two but may grow to as much as 10 lb in deeper waters. Squid and crustaceans are a good bait for the schoolmaster, as they are for most snappers.

Yellowtail (*Ocyurus chrysurus*)

The yellowtail is one of the most important snapper species in Bermuda's commercial fishery, for its value as a prized catch much in demand by consumers. It is related to but not strictly part of the snapper family proper. The fish is identified by a dark yellow stripe running from the snout past the eye to the deeply forked yellow tail along the mid-lateral line. Its back varies in colour from an olive green to light blue violet or pinkish colour, and is marked by irregularly sized yellow spots above the lateral line. The lower sides and belly exhibit horizontal reddish and pale pink stripes.

The yellowtail is more elongated and streamlined than bona fide snappers which typically have a rather humped back and flattish belly silhouette. In Bermuda waters the average yellowtail is 1–3 lb. Maximum weight is about 15 lb.

An environmental feature of yellowtail that distinguishes them from their snapper relatives is that they are more like pelagic roamers than territorial demersals, although they may be found virtually anywhere around Bermuda waters, from shallow reef areas to the banks.

When conditions are right (abundant food supply, towards a full moon, with a favourable tide), yellowtail may aggregate in large numbers, especially over reefs and coral heads. Yellowtail feed on shrimp, fish larvae, other crustaceans, and, in a pelagic environment, small bait fish such as anchovy, fry, and pilchards.

The best fishing for yellowtail is in the warmer months around the full moon, using a relatively small hook baited with fresh anchovy or other similar fresh bait. There is no bag limit on catching yellowtail, but there is a minimum size restriction of 25 cm (10 inches) fork length.

As voracious feeders, yellowtail often have a very full stomach when caught. This makes them susceptible to 'belly rot', a condition brought on by the continued digestive process that occurs particularly in well fed fish.

Digestive juices used to break down the fish's food continue to work after death, softening and eventually rotting the stomach wall. If the process is not halted by gutting, cleaning, and icing, the whole fish soon becomes tainted and spoiled by bacteria allowed to flourish in the gut of the dead fish.

It is therefore imperative to gut, rinse, and ice the fish as soon as possible after it is caught. Icing the fish without gutting it will retard bacterial activity and spoilage, but only for a limited time, and only if the fish is not particularly well fed. A well gutted, clean, and iced fish should retain an acceptable degree of freshness for up to a week.

Grunts (*Haemulon*, five or six species)

Grunts are members of the Pomadasyidae family, closely related to snappers (with a 'snapper look' body shape), and named for their grunting noise when caught. The grunt is made by the fish grinding its teeth, amplified by its air bladder. The inside of the mouth of grunts is typically blood red. Several varieties express a sort of 'kissing' behaviour where two fish will oppose each other with open mouths. It is theorized that this practice is of territorial significance, intended to frighten and drive away intruders.

About half a dozen types of grunts inhabit Bermuda waters. The most abundant are **yellow grunt** (*Haemulon flavolineatum*) and the **bluestriped grunt** (*Haemulon sciurus*). For most Bermudians a yellow grunt is the first fish they ever catch. This small fish is found all around the coast of Bermuda, near docks, off the rocks, under bridges, as well as in shallow reef waters.

Yellow grunts are burnished yellow in colour along the back, fading to white along the belly. The bluestriped grunt has fine blue stripes running the length of its body from snout to tail. The grunt has a single dorsal fin, the forward part comprised of a dozen or so spines and the posterior, soft fin rays.

Grunts spawn in large aggregations in the early to mid-summer months, around the full moon phase. Their diet is mainly worms, small molluscs, and crabs, although larger grunts may sometimes eat other smaller fish (like fry). Grunts feed primarily at night.

Most yellow grunts near the shore are small fish, averaging no more than six inches in length and less than half a pound in weight. Larger specimens, however, in deeper water, can reach a weight of up to about 2 lb. Grunts do not struggle much when hooked and are one of the easiest Bermuda fish to catch, using anything from bread or squid to cut up fish as bait.

The **white grunt** (*Haemulon aurolineatum*) is the smallest of the grunts found locally. Its body is grey-white, with a few dark lines running longitudinally, and a black spot by the caudal peduncle. Local anglers often use small white grunts whole as live bait to catch larger grey snappers.

Away from the shore, the **white margate** (*Haemulon album*) is the largest grunt found in Bermuda waters. It may grow to as much as 15–18 lb but more usually averages 5–8 lb. The fish is quite common around broken sandy or weedy bottoms of the reef platform, often in the same neighbourhood as porgies.

The adult margate has a silvery grey background colour, with dark black or grey stripes along the dorsal surface and lateral line. Younger fish have no stripes. The fish was apparently named by early settlers of the Bahamas who came from the southeastern English coastal town of Margate in Kent.

Bermuda Chub (*Kyphosus sectatrix*); Yellow Chub (*Kyphosus incisor*)

Like turbot, chub is a name applied to a number of fish in different parts of the world, some being freshwater species. In Bermuda there are two chubs from the Kyphosidae family: the **Bermuda chub** and the **yellow chub**.

Both fish have a grey coloured background, are medium bodied and oval shaped, with small mouths. Yellow stripes run along the body with two horizontal yellow bands on the snout. The yellow chub has more pronounced yellow stripes than the Bermuda chub whose finer markings may not be as clearly discernible.

In an excited state, when chasing prey, for example, chubs may display a white spotted mottling effect on their body and fins.

Chub are omniverous fish, feeding on plant and algal growth over rocky bottoms, as well as on crustaceans and small fish like fry. Their diet actually depends more on their immediate environment than any particular preferences. They may nibble on seaweed at the surface, or go quite deep to prey on whatever food is available at the time (including the bait you are using to catch something else).

The Bermuda chub reaches a substantial size. Both species are good fighters on light tackle. The local record for Bermuda chub is 16 lb 10 oz on a 12 lb test line. The yellow chub is, on average, slightly smaller. The average size of both fish in Bermuda waters is in the range of 5–7 lb.

Bream (*Diplodus bermudensis*)

If the first fish a Bermudian youngster catches is not a grunt, it is most likely to be a bream. Bream are from the same family as porgies (Sparidae), and elsewhere are called spot porgy, or silver porgy (as well as spottail pinfish).

As abundant as grunts around Bermuda, bream are unmistakable for their oval shape, bright silver colour, dark spot on the caudal peduncle, and a rather messy habit of ejecting copious amounts of faecal fluid when caught and handled. They closely resemble Bermuda chub in shape and colour but are not as large as chub, nor as dark. The chub, moreover, lacks the bream's dark spot at the base of the tail.

Bream often congregate in large groups around the same neighbourhoods as grunts but are considered more of a menace by fishermen. They often take bait intended for other fish and may make it virtually impossible to catch other more desirable fish like snapper. The average size of bream in Bermuda is around half a pound.

As food fish, bream are non-starters. Their one potentially redeeming feature is that they are easy to catch, provide more fight than grunts, and so offer more satisfaction to the less discriminating fisherman who is mainly interested in the thrill of a catch (*any* catch) than the reward of a prize specimen. When other more desirable food fish are not so abundant, bags of mixed fillet sold by commercial fishermen may include bream fillets.

Squirrelfish (*Holocentrus*, several species)

The holocentrids, or squirrelfish family, are so named for their large squirrel-like eyes. The fish is very common around the Bermuda Platform, both along the shore and in reef areas. It is mainly nocturnal in its habits when its dark red colour effectively camouflages its activity. Their preferred habitat is the cover of small holes along rocky shores or under coral reef heads.

Handling the squirrelfish constitutes a prickly hazard. Apart from its bright red colour, the sharp spines of its dorsal fin and equally painful opercular spine on the outside gill cover are its most characteristic feature. Squirrelfish extend these barbs, when handled, as a defence mechanism. The scales of the fish are rough and sharp. While the body is usually bright red, the membranes between the spines of the dorsal fin have a yellowish coloration.

Several types of squirrelfish are found in local waters, the most common being the **longjaw** (*Holocentrus ascensionis*). The fish grows to a maximum of about two feet in length. Most are considerably less than half that around inshore waters but larger over deeper reef areas.

Bonefish (*Albula vulpes*)

Of all the types of inshore fishing around Bermuda, bonefishing is the most specialized. In the 1950s and 1960s bonefishing was more popular than now, although interest is reviving. Stalking bonefish requires more of the patience and concentration of freshwater flyfishing than any other type of fishing in Bermuda.

The bonefish itself, a member of the Albulidae family, is one of the most attractive of saltwater fish. Similar in appearance to bass, it has a slender, elegantly streamlined shape, a single triangular dorsal fin, and homocercal V-shaped tail. The upper body is streaked longitudinally by dark striations. Faint crossbands extend from the dorsal surface to the

Kevin Pelletier, from Simsbury, CT, with a 10–12 lb bonefish he caught and released off the beach at Willowbank in Somerset, 9 October 1990. Mr Pelletier used a spinning rod with 8 lb test line, a plain hook baited with a live crab, and no leader or weights. (Photo courtesy of Flybridge Tackle.)

lateral line. The body of the fish is generally silvery white, with a darker olive green, or bluish back.

The head of the bonefish extends to a conical snout which overhangs the lower jaw to give a rather 'buck-toothed' appearance. The slightly longer upper jaw allows the fish to snuffle around the bottom with its snout, to root out food. The eyes are protected from sand and mud by a cartilaginous membrane. The outer extremities of the fins of the bonefish are black.

'Bonefishing country' is characterized by broad expanses of shallow water flats, with sandy, grassy, or muddy bottoms. There are a number of such locations around Bermuda where mid-tide depths are typically no more than a few feet, and the water is relatively protected and still.

'Bones' often make their first appearance to the angler while feeding, waving their tail fin slowly just above the surface of the water as they skim the bottom for food, a phenomenon known as 'tailing'. Preferred foods include worms, crabs, shrimp, other small shellfish, and small bottom fish.

The simplest way to fish for 'bones' is by wading quietly over the shallow flats, or casting from the shore. In a boat, one person usually poles or sculls quietly while the angler casts. The angler on or in the water stalks fish that are 'tailing' or just visible below the surface. Bonefish are easily spooked. Stealth and patience are indispensable qualities. A background in deer hunting might come in useful, although a naturally placid temperament would serve as well.

Any angler new to bonefishing will, unless forewarned, be startled by the action of a striking fish. Bonefish rip line off a reel on the first run at a faster speed than almost any other gamefish, and certainly of any inshore fish. Initially the fish will strip off at least 100 metres of line as it heads for deeper water. After that it provides as much excitement as any big gamefish offshore.

Bonefish grow to a substantial size in Bermuda. This one was probably close to the Bermuda record (a 14 lb fish taken on 20 lb test line way back in 1950).
(Photo courtesy of Flybridge Tackle.)

Palometa (*Trachinotus goodei*), a.k.a. Pompano

Pompano fishing, like bonefishing, used to be more common in Bermuda when the beaches were more tranquil environments than they are today. Although the fish are still there, it has become more difficult to find a quiet beach where surf casting for pompano does not constitute an annoyance to other swimmers.

A Carangidae (jacks) family member, the pompano is a feisty little surf fish found along sandy bottoms. Against the white translucent background, their silvery colour provides perfect camouflage. Four dark vertical bands usually mark the fish from dorsal area to just below the lateral line of their highly compressed body. The bands may also be absent since pompano are able to regulate their colouring. Without the dark banding, pompano are practically invisible against a white sand bottom.

In Bermuda the average size of pompano is less than a pound or so, although they can reach up to 5 lb. The body is oval shaped, with a snubbed snout, small mouth, and distinctive elongated dorsal and anal fins. The tail is deeply veed with long streamlined lobes. All fins on the fish are black tipped.

Pompano feed mainly on small crustaceans and molluscs. Despite their generally small size, they provide very game qualities as typically pugnacious carangid fighters on light tackle for anglers wading in the surf. Scattered bread for chum and a small spoon lure, or bread for both chum and bait, may attract pompano off any of Bermuda's sandy beaches.

The **Atlantic permit** (*Trachinotus falcatus*), also known as great pompano, is essentially a big pompano. Permit are common around the Gulf of Mexico and Florida but rarely caught in Bermuda waters. Juvenile permit closely resemble pompano. For a long time they were thought to be the same species. The snout of the juvenile permit is snubbed like the pompano. Coloration is similar, as are the elongated dorsal and anal fins.

Any confusion between permit and pompano will be in the permit's juvenile phase. As they mature permit begin to look more like jacks, with a more elongated body, less snubbed snout, and diminished length of the dorsal and anal fins.

Captain Allen DeSilva fighting a good size yellowfin tuna on light spinning tackle.
(Photo courtesy of Captain Allen DeSilva.)

All permits, as both juveniles and adults, lack the pompano's dark vertical bands. As adults, the permit's dorsal and anal fins are much shorter than those of the pompano, although still notable for their extension. Adult permit, moreover, grow to a substantial size (around 60 lb) compared with the flyweight pompano.

There have been occasional catches of permit from Bermuda waters, but these have been incidental rarities. The fish inhabits similar sandy environments to the pompano but with a bias towards tidal inlets and channels from which they move to sandy flats on a rising tide. Not a surf fish, like pompano, they are likely to be found in Bermuda, if at all, around coral marl bottoms near a sandy environment with a distinct tidal influence. This is exactly the type of environment from which a 52 lb specimen was caught by net some years ago, near Shelly Bay, according to Mr Louis Mowbray.

Pelagics/Gamefish

A conspicuous feature of early accounts of fish found in Bermuda waters is the absence of any mention of offshore species now considered gamefish. Recreational fishing to catch tuna, wahoo, and other pelagic species offshore is a recent phenomenon of the second half of the 20th century. The abundant demersal fishery, dating to the earliest days of Bermuda's colonization, obviated the necessity for going offshore.

Tourism and the increased affluence of the local population after the Second World War, in particular, spawned the interest in recreational offshore fishing. The charter fishing business evolved mainly since the 1950s, to cater to the arrival of greater numbers of affluent tourists, especially from North America (although there was some charter fishing as early as the 1930s).

The pelagic gamefish of Bermuda are mainly caught off Challenger and Argus Banks, and along the shelving wall of the Bermuda Platform as it rises up from the deep ('the edge of the deep'). Boats may, less frequently, get fish in very deep water, at high boat speeds, when going to or returning from the banks, but this often depends more on good fortune than dedicated fishing.

Captain Allen DeSilva with an 86 lb, yellowfin tuna he caught on 20 lb test line, with spinning tackle. (Photo courtesy of Captain Allen DeSilva.)

A good day's catch (17 wahoos, dolphin, and several tunas) for commercial fishing captain Monty Ible (centre) and mates Clarkie Showers (left) and Antoine ('Short People') Simmons (right). (Photo courtesy of Flybridge Tackle.)

Most Atlantic saltwater gamefish are found in Bermuda waters, although tunas, wahoo, dolphin (dorado, or dolphin fish), amberjack, blue marlin, and, to a lesser extent, barracuda account for the majority of all catches. Common sub-tropical Atlantic and Caribbean species not ordinarily found around Bermuda include cobia, king mackerel, snook, and tarpon. (Some of these species, it should be noted, e.g. tarpon, king mackerel, have been caught in Bermuda waters but as rare occurrences.)

Her first blue marlin. Nowadays very few blue marlin are boated and brought ashore in Bermuda. Charter captains have become increasingly conscientious about conserving vulnerable fish stocks. (Photo courtesy of Captain Allen DeSilva.)

Records for gamefish around the world are ratified and registered by the International Game Fish Association (IGFA). Many IGFA world records have been set in Bermuda over the years, especially for tunas, amberjack, and wahoo. There are currently around 20 IGFA line class and several all-tackle world records for fish caught in Bermuda waters.

Billfish

The billfish family is comprised of nine major species: sailfish (two species: Atlantic and Pacific); marlin (five species: Atlantic blue, Pacific blue, black, white, and striped); swordfish (single species); and spearfish (two species – longbill and shortbill – but so rare as to be considered, for practical purposes, a single gamefish species).

Atlantic blue marlin and white marlin, and, occasionally, sailfish, are the main billfish caught around Bermuda. (Striped and black marlin, and the Pacific blue, are only found in the Pacific and Indian Oceans, although some black marlin are occasionally caught in deep South Atlantic waters by longliners.)

To all intents and purposes, the only billfish regularly caught in Bermuda waters are blue and white marlin.

Atlantic Blue Marlin (*Makaira nigricans*)

Blue marlin are the largest and most spectacular gamefish regularly fished in Atlantic waters. They average 200–300 lb, frequently exceed 500 lb, and make headlines at over 1000 lb ('granders'). Females grow fastest, and largest, and usually take much longer to boat than the male. (A visitor to Bermuda in July 1987, using 125 lb test line, took just 18 minutes to boat an 810 lb, 13-foot-long blue marlin, according to a report in *The Royal Gazette* of 1 August 1987.)

Any specimen over 300 lb is almost always female. Large female marlin are the largest of all bony fish.

Blue marlin spawn in the summer months in the Western Atlantic, from about 15°–25° N. Peak activity is in July.

The blue marlin is easily recognizable by its long body shape, dark blue back and silvery sides and belly, pointed anal and dorsal fin tips, long dorsal fin rising to a semi-sail at the head, falcate tail, and rounded elongated upper jaw projecting forward as the bill. Blue marlin also exhibit a pattern of light grey vertical bands running down their back and sides.

The bill on blue marlin, as with other billfish, is thought to be used in part as an instrument for stunning, if not killing, its prey. Fish found inside the stomachs of marlin often show slash marks, indicating how the bill was used just prior to ingestion.

Juvenile blue marlin, occasionally taken in Bermuda waters, have a veed rather than falcate shaped tail. The falcate shape only develops with adulthood. The juvenile also exhibits a high dorsal fin throughout its length (like sailfish), whereas the dorsal of the adult is only high at the front. Pelvic fins, too, are disproportionately long in the juvenile.

In Bermuda 'big blue' have been taken in increasing numbers since the late 1970s and 1980s as fishermen have refined their techniques for catching them, and as they have targeted the fish more specifically. Before then they were caught regularly but rather infrequently.

The more widespread use of heavy 130 lb test line from the mid-1980s onward dramatically improved the catch rate for marlin, as well as reducing the average time needed to boat a fish. When 50 lb or 80 lb line was the heaviest in common use (in Bermuda), marlin took longer to catch. That reduced the time available to fish for them in a day trip and, therefore, limited the numbers caught. The heavier drag fished with 130 lb line also improved the hook-up and catch rate.

By the mid- to late 1980s an average of about 100 blue marlin a year were being caught off Bermuda. By the mid-1990s the average was closer to 200 a year. A peak of 231 fish were taken in 1991 (on a reported catch basis).

Up until the mid-1980s, most blue marlin caught around Bermuda were landed ashore. Since that time tag-and-release has been increasingly promoted, in the interest of the conservation of the species. The World Wildlife Fund indicates that Atlantic populations of marlin have fallen by over 50% since 1980 'and are still in decline'.

The large majority (over 80%) of all blue marlin reported caught around Bermuda since the mid-1990s have been tagged and released. The main exceptions have been unusually large trophy specimens in excess of about 800 lb, although smaller fish may also be kept from time to time, for one reason or another (ego playing a prominent role on those occasions). Less principled fishermen who catch marlin may cut the fish up for bait rather than tag and release it, but that practice tends to be of a clandestine nature and, not surprisingly, is largely unacknowledged.

There is no particular reason for landing marlin in Bermuda apart from showing the fish as a trophy. There is virtually no local demand for it as a food fish, unlike in the Caribbean and other parts of the world where it provides an important local food source. Its oily dark flesh is not to Bermuda tastes (unless cured, like smoked salmon), accustomed as local consumers are to the more refined flavours of tuna, wahoo, snapper, and other lighter flesh fish.

Relatively few tagged marlin are re-caught. In the summer of 1992, however, a 260 lb specimen with a tag in its shoulder was caught on the north side of Argus Bank. Captain Allen DeSilva, a leading Bermuda charter boat captain, had tagged and released the fish almost exactly two years before, and estimated its weight then (August 1990) at 180 lb. It was surmised at the time of the second tagging that the fish had almost certainly not spent two years in the same waters but had returned to Bermuda along its migration route.

Tag returns elsewhere indicate that marlin follow trans-Atlantic migration routes, usually from west to east. Bermuda may be a staging post along those routes, especially in the warmer months of the summer spawning season.

All adult blue marlin are big fish and so generally taken on heavy tackle. The IGFA all-tackle world record for the fish is a whisker over 1400 lb. The Bermuda record (the largest fish ever caught by rod and reel in local waters) is just 50 lb under that, at 1352 lb, taken on 130 lb test line. This fish was caught near Challenger Bank by a fisherman on the charter boat *Mako 4* (Captain Allen DeSilva) on 1 August 1995. It was hooked by an artificial lure and boated after a 40 minute fight.

Even more astounding than the big marlin taken on heavy tackle are relatively big marlin taken on relatively light tackle. A fish of 471 lb 8 oz was caught in July 1979 on just 20 lb test line, the Bermuda record for that line class. A catch of that size on line which might ordinarily be used to fish for snapper rather than a gamefish of almost a quarter of a tonne equates to 23 lb of fish per pound of line test.

By comparison, the Bermuda all-tackle record, taken on 130 lb test line, equates to just about 10 lb of fish per pound of line test. For all other Bermuda line class records, the specimens amounted to less than

The Bermuda all-tackle record blue marlin, 1352 lb, caught by US visitor Ken Danielsen Jr (with white cap, to the left of the fish), on board Captain Allen DeSilva's Mako 4, 1 August 1995. The fish was raised in the deep water between Argus and Challenger Banks as Mako 4 was heading home after a day's fishing. Danielsen boated the biggest fish ever caught in Bermuda after just a 40 minute fight. (Photo courtesy of Captain Allen DeSilva.)

15 lb per pound of line test. (In 1996 an angler fishing off the Azores caught a 573 lb blue marlin on 4 lb test line.)

The first 'grander' (marlin over 1000 lb) taken in Bermuda waters was in 1984. Since then half a dozen more have been caught. One charter boat captain (Captain Alan Card) has caught five of all the 'granders' taken off Bermuda (to 1999), more than any other charter captain in the Atlantic region (and possibly more than any other in the world).

Other highly successful marlin catchers among the charter boat operators in Bermuda include Captain Allen DeSilva and his father Captain Henry 'Buddy' De Silva (who started targeting marlin in the early 1970s and who still holds the Bermuda 80 lb line class record of 805 lb), from *De Mako*, and Captain Russell Young Jr, from *Sea Wolfe*. Captain Russell Young Sr, one of the first charter fishing captains in Bermuda in the 1950s and considered one of Bermuda's most successful charter fishermen until his death in 1990, once played a marlin for 36 hours before the angler fighting the fish lost it.

Techniques for catching marlin around Bermuda have evolved significantly over the past 50 years. Ballyhoo (garfish) or small tunas, trolled from outriggers, were originally the preferred baits. In more recent years artificial lures have become the main trolled bait, although ballyhoo and whole fresh tunas or bonito are still used.

Most recently some fishermen have trolled teasers (coloured artificial lures or baits with no hooks) a short distance behind the boat to raise the marlin, throwing out a baited hook only when the fish

Another big blue marlin. This one, brought in by Captain Allen DeSilva's Mako 4, weighed in at 1031 lb, at Dockyard, July 1994. Angler Bill Kaas's first 'grander' after a 30 year wait!. (Photo courtesy of Captain Allen DeSilva.)

White marlin make a regular appearance in Bermuda from the spring months throughout the summer and are caught in rather more numbers than their blue cousin. 'Whities' most often strike the smaller lures and baits used to catch wahoo, Allison tuna, and the like, rather than the heavy outrigger lines baited for blues.

Blue marlin are sometimes found with partially digested white marlin in their stomachs, or with a white marlin bill stuck in their throats, suggesting that the law of the jungle dictates the nature of relations between marlin species rather than family ties.

One of the first white marlin caught after the war was reported by *The Royal Gazette* on 5 June 1950. The report is noteworthy for the unusual way the marlin took the bait, but also for the large number of bonito taken that day. Charles Christianson, the boat captain, was one of Bermuda's first charter boat operators.

Captain Alan Card's Sea Maid, *one of the early post-war sportfishing boats in Bermuda from the 1960s. Compare the straight stem, long foredeck, low freeboard, and basic flybridge design with the more specialized, technologically advanced design of modern sportfishing boats.* (Bermuda News Bureau photo courtesy of Captain Keith Winter.)

appears. Teasers made of soft plastic or, in the early days, of wood, have been used for many years around the world to raise billfish, but mainly in conjunction with a hooked bait trolled simultaneously off the outriggers. By raising a fish first with teasers it is possible to assess by eye its potential gameness (or record breaking potential) for different line classes. The angler can then present a hooked bait on a line class commensurate with the apparent size of the fish.

White Marlin (*Tetrapturus albidus*)

Two features immediately distinguish the white marlin from its big blue brother: first, it attains a maximum weight of only about 200 lb; and second, the tip of the dorsal, pectoral, and anal fins is rounded. The light coloured dorsal fin usually displays some dark blue spots on its surface.

Like the blue, the white marlin's back is dark blue and its belly silvery white. Unlike the blue, it lacks the vertical stripes along its back. White marlin also have a visible, sometimes prominent, lateral line which is missing on the blue.

White Marlin Caught From The 'Dolphin'

It promises to be a fine fishing season for Bermuda, for yesterday Charles Christianson, fishing with a party aboard his 'Dolphin', had the pleasure of seeing Mr. Dexter H. Simpson, manager of the Inverurie Hotel, catch a 40-pound white marlin. 'It was a little one', said Charlie, 'and it only took ten minutes to land, but at least we know they're here again and waiting to be caught . . .' The strange part of this particular catch is that the fish took the outrigger bait first, was not hooked, then went for the feather and gar-fish [ballyhoo] streamed from the stern of the boat. Charles Christianson gave the party a good trip for they ran into a school of Bonito, and in half an hour had 74 aboard. They lost one Wahoo during the day.

An even earlier specimen, however, deserves special mention. The oldest Bermuda fishing record pertains to a 128 lb 10 oz white marlin caught on 50 lb test line in May 1948, as noted by the following report in *The Royal Gazette*.

New White Marlin Record Set Locally

Carl Bridges, of 'Sea Bright', Paget East, set a new Bermuda record for White Marlin on Sunday, when fishing from Roy Taylor's motor cruiser 'Wally II', he landed one weighing 128 pounds, 14 ounces. The fish measured eight feet, ten inches in length.

The old record was one of 83 pounds, on February 23 of this year [note how early in the year] by Mr. L. Douglas Murray . . . The world record is 161 pounds.

According to Mr. Louis Mowbray, Jr., Curator of the Government Aquarium, any White Marlin over 110 pounds is an exceptional White Marlin. It will be recalled that at the start of the Bermuda Game Fishing Tournament, Mr. Mowbray predicted that some large Marlin would be caught. He now predicts that larger Blue Marlin will be hooked before the end of the tourney.

The White Marlin was Carl Bridges' first, and he was plenty thrilled with his catch. It took Mr. Bridges fifty minutes to land the giant and called upon all his skill and strength to capture it. 'It came out of the water six or eight times' he told the Sports Editor of The Royal Gazette shortly after landing the fish, 'and leapt from five to eight feet out of the water. He was really dancing.'

Mr. Bridges had the Marlin up to the stern of the 'Wally II' three times before he was able to get him gaffed. Each time he brought the Marlin in close, he found the fish had too much fight left in him and had to let him go again. When he finally gaffed him, it was a toss-up as to who was the more tired, the White Marlin or Carl Bridges.

A Tuna belly was used for bait and the bait skipped from an out-rigger. The Marlin was caught about 11 miles southeast of St. George's [note: in very deep water].

Henry ('Buddy') DeSilva, a pioneer of dedicated marlin fishing in Bermuda, with his catch of sailfish (a billfish rarely caught in Bermuda waters) and (on the deck) wahoo and yellowfin tuna. (Photo courtesy of Captain Allen DeSilva.)

Atlantic sailfish (*Istiophorus platypterus*)

This fish is not at all common in Bermuda. Its natural habitat is further south, in warmer waters around the Gulf of Mexico, and off the east coast of the United States as far north as Cape Hatteras, but especially

The first swordfish ever caught on rod and reel in Bermuda, mid-1970s. To the left of the 132 lb fish, two of Bermuda's best known commercial fishermen, Captain Alan Card (standing) and his brother Captain Andrew Card (kneeling), from Somerset Bridge. (Photo courtesy of Flybridge Tackle.)

abundant off the southeast Florida coast. The largest specimens, however, have been caught off the west coast of Africa (Angola northward).

The migratory nature of the Atlantic sailfish as it follows warm water currents suggests that it may arrive in Bermuda waters as a result of following Gulf Stream eddies flowing northeast off the main flow of the Stream. The fish is another pelagic speedster, having been clocked at almost 70 mph over a short distance.

Spearfish (*Terapturus pflugeri*)

A few spearfish are taken most years in Bermuda waters. Although somewhat similar in appearance to sailfish, the spearfish sail is not as high nor as dramatic, its body is more slender, and it is smaller in size. The Bermuda all-tackle record for a spearfish is 37 lb (IGFA world record: 94 lb 12 oz) compared to 73 lb for sailfish (IGFA world record: 135 lb 5 oz).

Swordfish (*Xiphias gladius*)

Swordfish are caught at depth (typically 150–600 feet) mainly by commercial longline fishing. They feed nocturnally on squid and surface apparently to aid digestion in warmer water. This behaviour would explain why swordfish on the surface, having eaten their fill, rarely take an interest in a surface trolled bait. There is sporadic interest in swordfishing around Bermuda waters, by commercial fishermen, but it is almost exclusively an occasional rather than a full time interest.

Tunas

Although some tuna species have readily identifiable features (yellowfin/Allison, albacore), it is often difficult to distinguish among others, especially juvenile specimens. Counting the number of gill rakers (individual hair-like protuberances along the inside of the gills) provides a useful means of identification, but observation of and familiarity with the external aspect of the fish is still the most reliable guide. (The average number of gill rakers for each type of fish, moreover, falls within a fairly wide range of minimum and maximum numbers, leaving considerable scope for mistaken identity.)

Tunas are members of the larger Scombridae family of fishes which includes mackerels. Some of the smaller tunas so closely resemble true mackerels that they are colloquially, but mistakenly, called 'mackerel' in

Bermudians are known for their friendly character. This bigeye tuna, a rare visitor to Bermuda waters, nevertheless had the misfortune to cross the path of a less than friendly local shark with a particular sweet tooth for bigeye tuna tail.
(Photo courtesy of Captain Allen DeSilva.)

Bermuda. (The main difference between tunas and mackerel is that the tunas, with a few exceptions, do not have large cutting teeth as mackerel do.)

A distinguishing feature of Scombridae (tunas and wahoo) is the row of finlets found along the top and bottom of the fish, starting immediately after the secondary dorsal and anal fins and continuing towards the tail.

Tunas are one of the few pelagic fish that are warm-blooded. Their internal temperature may be as much as 10°F higher than the surrounding sea temperature, mainly because of the high metabolic rate they generate to sustain their dynamic migratory lifestyle.

The amount of blood tuna need to support oxygen levels for this high metabolic and aerobic activity means they should be bled, gutted, and iced as soon as possible after being caught. Icing soon after catching the fish is imperative. The flesh might otherwise be tainted by an accumulation of high histamine levels that can cause illness (scombroid fish poisoning) if consumed. The same conditions apply to dolphin which, like tuna, have a highly active metabolism.

Yellowfin Tuna (*Thunnus albacares*), a.k.a. Allison Tuna

According to Louis L. Mowbray, founder of the Bermuda Aquarium, the yellowfin was named 'Allison's tuna' (*Thunnus allisoni* at the time) 'in honor of James A. Allison, President of the Miami Aquarium and Biological Laboratory'. Mr Mowbray was director of the Miami Aquarium in the early 1920s.

Yellowfin tuna are the most prized of all tuna varieties both around Bermuda and elsewhere, for their size, gameness, and the high quality of their flesh. The fish is a prime quarry of large-scale commercial fisheries and accounts for 35% of the total world tuna catch. Their numbers are declining. According to the World Wildlife Fund, 'Atlantic populations [of yellowfin] are believed to have declined by 30% in the past ten years.'

Apart from bluefin and bigeye, which are rarely caught around Bermuda, the yellowfin is the largest tuna taken regularly in Bermuda waters and the most abundant tuna species found locally in the warmer months.

Yellowfin tuna are unmistakable for their long yellow second dorsal and anal fins which become elongated with age, especially after the fish attains a weight of 25–30 lb. The pectoral fins usually reach beyond the start of the second dorsal fin but not beyond the end of its base. Yellowfin have a dark blue back with a yellow lateral band on the upper sides. The lower sides and belly are silvery grey. Finlets are yellow with a narrow black margin.

Fish of 50–80 lb are quite common in Bermuda waters. The local record is a shade under 200 lb.

The minimum legal weight for taking Allison tuna in Bermuda is 3.2 kg (7 lb). Pound for pound Allison are considered the most game

Andrew Down with the 99 lb 8 oz yellowfin tuna he caught on 8 lb test line. The line over-tested, however, and was therefore not a world record. Still, an exceptional catch on very light tackle. (Photo courtesy of Flybridge Tackle.)

of all gamefish in Bermuda waters (and, in fact, in temperate waters all around the world). Although caught surprisingly close to shore in deep waters off South Africa and Australia (from fishermen on the shore), around Bermuda Allison tuna roam the conventional steeply shelving fishing grounds along the edge of the deep and over the banks.

A good size yellowfin tuna showing its elongated yellow dorsal and anal fins that identify the species. (Photo courtesy of Captain Allen DeSilva.)

Yellowfin tuna coming in to be gaffed. (Photo courtesy of Andrew Card.)

Waters over the banks regularly roiled with the activity of Allison tuna thrashing across the surface in pursuit of their prey.

Over time, and as a result of stocks depleted by industrial fishing, the sight of Allison tuna engaged in a mass feeding frenzy has become more of a rarity in Bermuda waters. They nevertheless remain one of the major components of Bermuda's pelagic fishery, exceeded only by wahoo for the amount of fish landed each year.

Official government statistics seem to show that the abundance of Allison tuna has increased since 1990, according to reported landings by commercial fishermen. It is more likely, however, that commercial fishermen have been engaging in more pelagic fishing since the 1990 fish pot ban, thereby increasing the catch of Allison around Bermuda while not necessarily reflecting a more abundant stock *per se*.

There have nevertheless been spectacular runs of yellowfin in some years, for no apparent reason other than an abundance of prey food. Sporadic warm water eddies from the Gulf Stream might also be responsible for directing more tunas towards Bermuda waters.

In June 1993 *The Royal Gazette* reported that the recent catch of yellowfin tuna was 'the best in 20 to 25 years', amounting to a glut on the market, if only temporarily. So many fish were being caught that storage was a problem. Restaurants and hotels were demanding fresh chilled rather than frozen fish.

Blackfin Tuna (*Thunnus atlanticus*)

The blackfin, like other tuna, is a streamlined, torpedo shaped, high speed predator. The back is blue-black, the sides silvery, and the belly milky white. A golden lateral band runs the length of the fish from eye to tail, luminescent in life but fading out soon after death. Dorsal fins are grey-black, with a silvery tinge on the second set. The dusky coloured finlets just after the second set of dorsal fins, near the tail, have only a light yellow tinge, unlike the bright yellow finlets of other tunas. The brightness of the silver and white coloration of the fish fades to a dull grey after death.

There are more line class world records set in Bermuda for blackfin tuna than any other gamefish, from 6 to 50 lb test. The IGFA all-tackle record was, from 1978 until 1995, a 42 lb specimen caught off

Boats anchored around the banks off Bermuda pioneered the practice of chumming for Allison tuna in the 1950s and 1960s. Bermuda is also one of the few places in the world where these tuna prefer to take a bait trolled from an outrigger more often than from a flat line trolled from the stern.

When the charter fishery in Bermuda first developed in a big way in the 1960s, and into the 1970s, fishermen regularly witnessed schools of hundreds of tuna feeding on squid, flying fish, and other pelagic prey.

Bermuda. One of the world's great gamefish on light tackle, this tuna is considered, pound for pound, equal to the yellowfin tuna for strength, power, and endurance.

The blackfin population around Bermuda seems to remain stable year-round, unlike the yellowfin tuna which is more numerous in the warmer water summer months. Blackfin spawn in the open ocean during the summer. Juveniles grow quickly, to as much as 18–20 lb in two years. Any blackfin over 20 lb is a hefty specimen.

Blackfin will take live bait in a chum, or an artificial lure or strip bait from a trolling line. The largest specimens have been caught with live bait in a chum. There is otherwise no particularly preferred method of taking blackfin tuna. It was common, many years ago, to catch them incidentally on heavy tackle while trolling for billfish.

Little Tuna/Tunny (*Euthynnus alletteratus*), a.k.a. Mackerel, False Albacore

Most commonly known in Bermuda as mackerel, the little tuna has wavy blue-black markings along the back within a well defined border never extending further forward than the middle of the first dorsal fin. Its most conspicuous identifying feature is a scattering of four or five dark spots just below the pectoral fins. The pectoral and ventral fins are short and broad. The two dorsal fins are separated at the base by a small interspace.

In Bermuda juvenile little tuna are known as frigates (or frigate mackerel). The bona fide frigate tuna species (*Auxis thasard*) is actually found further south, in warmer waters, and not around Bermuda at all.

The International Commission for the Conservation of Atlantic Tuna (ICCAT) has re-named this species the **Western Atlantic black skipjack**. In Bermuda, however, the fish continues to be called mackerel, and, because of the predominant colloquial use of that name, it will be identified as such here. (False albacore is another commonly used name for this fish, in Bermuda and elsewhere.)

All tuna species have streamlined bodies with highly developed musculature, built for speed and manoeuvrability. If anything mackerel are even more streamlined, equally robust, and predaceous. They feed voraciously on fry, anchovies, squid, small herrings, shrimp, and a variety of other small pelagic organisms. At certain times of the year young mackerel can be found in schools feeding around the inshore waters of Bermuda all over the Platform.

In turn mackerel are preyed upon by, and provide an important bait for, larger gamefish such as marlin, dolphin, Allison tuna, and especially wahoo, among others. After mackerel spawn in the summer and early autumn, juveniles provide a plentiful food for such gamefish around Bermuda in September through October and November. The abundance of rapidly growing frigates offshore towards the end of summer attracts the second big wahoo run of the year. Wahoo spawn year-round with peak activity in the spring and autumn. Gorging on late summer frigates nourishes the wahoo for autumn spawning as well as for the accumulation of protective fat in the winter.

Like most of the tuna family, the mackerel is a lively gamefish. Maximum weight is around 35 lb. In Bermuda waters they most commonly average 10–12 lb. Four line class world records for this fish are attributed to catches on Challenger Bank (at 8 lb test, 16 lb test, and 20 lb test). The largest was a 32 lb 4 oz specimen caught on 16 lb test line, a women's line class world record and not far off the IGFA all-tackle world record of 35 lb 2 oz.

Albacore (*Thunnus alalunga*)

This is not a commonly caught tuna in Bermuda waters, because it is rarely found at the surface. In the Atlantic, albacore feed in deep water below about 200 feet. They rarely take a lure or bait unless it is deep trolled or long-lined at, or even well below, that depth.

Albacore are long distance migrators. A fish tagged off California was recovered 294 days later near Japan, a distance of 5000 miles (swimming an average 17 miles a day). The albacore migrates *within* water masses rather than *across* them, accounting for the substantial depths which they ordinarily inhabit.

In Bermuda albacore makes its most regular appearance in cans on supermarket shelves. The species has a high proportion of prized white meat (as the 'chicken of the sea'), unlike other locally caught species which typically have a high proportion of dark blood-red meat running the length of the fillet.

James Pearman stands alongside the 55 lb 12 oz albacore tuna he caught on the christening of Captain Allen DeSilva's then new boat Mako 4, 1 May 1988. *Note the long pectoral fin on the albacore that identifies it as* Thunnus alalunga. (Photo courtesy of Captain Allen DeSilva.)

Most of the albacore tuna taken in Bermuda waters is caught by industrial longliners or purse seiners, fishing in deep offshore waters within the 200 mile Exclusive Economic Zone (EEZ) around Bermuda. Albacore prefer cooler water in a temperature range of 60–66°F (16–19°C). Reluctant to cross the lower and upper thermocline of this temperature band, they are industrially fished around Bermuda mainly in the winter months.

The identifying physical characteristic of the albacore is its elongated pectoral fin (*alalunga* means 'long wing' or 'fin') which is typically around one-third the length of the entire body length of the fish and may reach to a point beyond the anal fin. The belly of the fish is silvery, with no stripes or spots such as are found on skipjack tuna and the little tunny. The tail fin has a thin white trailing edge.

The body itself is also less streamlined than other tuna species, being thicker further back before it tapers towards the tail. It shares this shape with the skipjack tuna, although the skipjack has other distinctive markings.

There are only two Bermuda line class records registered for this fish, both specimens caught on 30 June 1996: a 59 lb fish taken on 16 lb test line, and a 53 lb fish taken on 50 lb test.

Skipjack Tuna / Oceanic Bonito (*Euthynnus* or *Katsuwonus pelamis*)

The most conspicuous identifying markings of the skipjack are the series of four to six prominent dark stripes running the length of the fish's body along the silvery sides and belly. Above the lateral line the back is dark blue, mottled with spots at the front just above the pectoral fins. A herringbone pattern marks the posterior area of the back from about the middle of the first dorsal fin.

The species has a similar body shape to albacore in that the greatest depth (or girth) is further back than for other tunas. Its body is deepest at the point where the secondary dorsal fin begins. In other tunas the greatest girth is approximately in line with the base of the forward dorsal fin. After the second dorsal fin, the body slopes rather steeply downwards towards the tail.

Skipjack are usually called **oceanic bonito** in Bermuda, although it is not the true bonito. *Sarda sarda*, the true bonito (also known as 'horse mackerel' and 'little bonito'), has horizontal stripes along both its back and sides just below the lateral line, and is not usually found around Bermuda.

Skipjack are widely distributed throughout the Atlantic, Indian, and Pacific Oceans, tolerating a minimum sea temperature of about 65°F. Spawning usually takes place in warm summer water of around 75°F. They are 'known to be cannibalistic, and will eat their own young'. Their habitat is the epipelagic regions of the ocean, usually delving no deeper than about 200 feet.

Commercial fisherman Andrew Card with fresh filling for his skipjack tuna sandwich lunch. (Photo courtesy of Andrew Card.)

Skipjack is the smallest variety of tuna caught by large-scale commercial fishing. Like albacore, skipjack are sought by longliners and purse seiners for their fine flesh, destined for canning factories and supermarket shelves. The fish accounts for 40% by weight of the world tuna catch.

Around Bermuda the skipjack is not caught in particularly large numbers, although it is by no means uncommon. The maximum size for this fish is probably around 45 lb (the all-tackle world record being just under 42 lb). Any fish caught over 20 lb would be a well regarded specimen. In Bermuda waters the average size is 10–15 lb. Small to medium size fish may be trolled on outriggers as bait to catch marlin, wahoo, and larger tunas.

Keith Winter with his world record 39 lb 4 oz skipjack tuna for 20 lb test line. Keith caught the fish on 12 lb test line, but the line over-tested. The record was therefore ratified for the 20 lb test class, the next highest line class then available (before the introduction of a 16 lb line class). Caught on Challenger Bank, 13 July 1978. Photo taken at Cambridge Beaches, Somerset. (Photo courtesy of Flybridge Tackle.)

Wahoo (Acanthocybium solandri)

The most abundant year-round large gamefish in Bermuda's offshore waters is the wahoo, a species of mackerel within the broader Scombridae family which includes tunas. Wahoo are similar in shape to king mackerel (also called kingfish), which are not generally encountered in Bermuda waters, but are considerably larger (maximum weight possibly as much as 180 lb compared with king mackerel's maximum 100 lb).

The name *wahoo*, according to fishing writer Peter Goadby, originated from Hawaii. Whalers and early missionary visitors to those islands were often based on the island of Oahu ('pronounced and

Freshly boated wahoo positively crackling with the luminescence of its irridescent blue stripes which fade to a dull metallic grey after death. (Photo courtesy of Andrew Card.)

Angler Ken Henneberger and larger-than-average wahoo.
(Photo courtesy of Flybridge Tackle.)

sometimes spelt *wahoo'*) from which they derived the name of the fish commonly eaten there. For economy of style and precision of character, the native Hawaiian name for wahoo, *ono* (good), takes some beating. The scientific Latin species name (*solandri*) commemorates Daniel Solander, the Swedish scientist on board Captain Cook's ship *Endeavour*. The crew of the *Endeavour* were ostensibly the first Westerners to catch and scientifically name this fish.

Wahoo has been by far the most important commercial fish species taken in Bermuda waters since 1975 when official data for fish landings were first formally compiled. The 1998 catch of wahoo by the commercial fishery in Bermuda (238,000 lb) was more than twice the amount of yellowfin tuna (116,000 lb), the next largest catch.

Wahoo have an elongated body up to six feet long. The back is cobalt blue, sides are bluish green, with a silvery underbelly. Dark blue stripes run vertically from the back of the fish to the belly.

When a wahoo is hauled aboard a boat, its blue stripes are incandescent, lit up like an electric shock, but they fade and eventually disappear soon after death.

The tail of the wahoo is lunate and homocercal in shape (top and bottom lobes of equal length). The tail is stiffened by three pairs of scutes, of which the central median pair are most prominent.

Around Bermuda wahoo average 30–40 lb although 50–60 pounders are common. The current Bermuda all-tackle record is 129 lb 4 oz, from February 1976. In June 1987 a 128 lb specimen was taken off St George's.

Conventional wisdom has it that there are usually (though not always) two 'runs' of wahoo a year around Bermuda waters, in spring (April–May) and autumn (September–October). Statistical evidence indicates that the second and third quarters of the year (April–September) account for 60–70% of landings of wahoo throughout the year. The abundance of wahoo in those months might be related to spawning and migration patterns. More probably, however, catches of wahoo are greater in those months because the weather is more conducive to fishing.

Landings of wahoo by regular fishermen working throughout the year have historically been very consistent, suggesting that the general availability of wahoo in Bermuda waters has not changed much, at least in recent years. Since they are not targeted by industrial fishing fleets, as tuna are, wahoo stocks are not so vulnerable to depletion by commercial overfishing.

Schools of wahoo include fish of a wide range of ages and size (unlike schools of tunas, which are comprised mainly of fish of the same age and size). Aggregations of wahoo in schools are relatively small, typically averaging 10 or 12 fish. There are regular instances, however, of large catches of wahoo in a single day. On 11 May 1988 *The Royal Gazette* reported a catch of 50 wahoo by two local fishermen, offloaded at Albuoy's Point in Hamilton.

Years ago I went out fishing with the two Card brothers, from Somerset Bridge, both well known charter fishermen at the time. That particular trip was to catch fish for the commercial market. On Challenger Bank we hit a run of wahoo. Over less than two hours we took 16 fish. A very satisfactory arrangement for the real fishermen as they spent less than a minute hooking each wahoo of from 30–50 lb

Angler Micky Johnson shows a pedigree wahoo. (Photo courtesy of Captain Allen DeSilva.)

while their compliant amateur guest displaced most of his vertebrae reeling them in. And, in the process, earning the Cards $5/lb or so for fresh wahoo for sale.

The wahoo is the cheetah of the sea: when it takes a bait, it runs . . . and runs and runs and runs. Fast. But, like a cheetah, it has limited stamina and endurance for long runs. It can attain a speed of up to 50 mph, for short periods. The angler should be prepared to watch as much as 300 yards of line scream off the reel on the wahoo's first flight, but considerably less thereafter. For that reason wahoo are not considered as lively overall as tuna, but they do provide initial excitement and, especially on lighter tackle, very game qualities.

The adoption of downriggers since the 1970s, used to troll stern lines deeper below the surface, has significantly increased the catch rate for wahoo in Bermuda. Before the advent of downriggers (and other improved fishing methods generally), two or three fish boated in 10 strikes (20–30%) was considered good. Now fishermen would expect to achieve a success rate of 60–70%.

Common Dolphin (*Coryphaena hippurus*), a.k.a Dolphinfish, Dorado, Mahi-Mahi

Sometimes called dolphinfish to distinguish it from the mammalian dolphin (porpoise), this fish is not as abundant in Bermuda waters as it is further south. It is nevertheless regularly caught around Bermuda, if not in great numbers, especially in the warmer summer months of July–September.

In the 10 year period 1987–1997 an average of 5000 kg/yr (11,000 lb/yr) of dolphin was reported caught by commercial fishermen in Bermuda, out of an average annual 160,000 kg/yr (350,000 lb/yr) catch of all pelagic species reported taken in the same period (3% of the total). As much as 60% of the annual dolphin catch in Bermuda is in the three month period July–September.

The Spanish name for dolphin, *dorado* (golden), and the Hawaiian name, *mahi-mahi* (very fast), suggest both its colour and its speed through the water.

Dolphin are not only speed merchants. They also jump as much as 20 feet in the air to pounce on a trolled bait or lure. They attack virtually anything that moves, often speeding in to take a trolled bait just ahead of other bigger fish like marlin.

Bull (male) dolphin have a butt-shaped blunt forehead. The forehead of the cow (female) is more rounded. In both the bull and cow dolphin

A very nice bull (male) dolphin of around 30 lb, on board Captain Allen DeSilva's Mako 4. *(Photo courtesy of Captain Allen DeSilva.)*

the black dorsal fin sweeps back from the top of the head, diminishing in height towards the tail which is elongated and close-forked. The bull male attains a larger size (up to about 100 lb) than the female.

The body of the dolphin tapers from its blunt or ovaloid head, through an elongate, laterally compressed, almost flat body. Alive, the dolphin has a bright green back, with silver belly. The trailing edges along its fins and tail lobes are golden yellow. Lines of dark blue spots are arrayed horizontally along the back, with more sparse distribution below the lateral line along the belly.

Dolphin are exceedingly flappy fish when landed, thwacking their tail and body rapidly for some time after they are caught. They lose their brilliant coloration soon after death, turning a uniform grey-blue.

In the Western Atlantic the range of the dolphin is from as far north as Nova Scotia to as far south as southern Brazil. They are, however, essentially warm water fish, tolerating a minimum water temperature of approximately 68°F (20°C). Their appearance well north of the tropics is attributable mainly to eddies of the Gulf Stream or other warm water currents.

Dolphin typically congregate around seaweed or any other floating debris where smaller bait fish or crustaceans may be seeking shelter from larger fish in the hostile open ocean. The Sargasso Sea surrounds Bermuda, and dolphin are often caught near drifts of sargassum weed in the local area.

Most large schools of dolphin are comprised of smaller fish (under 15–20 lb). Larger adults tend to roam singly or in pairs.

Researchers have proposed that there are two distinct stocks of dolphin in the Western Atlantic. The hypothesis is based on evidence of different seasonal peak landing times in the Caribbean (winter) and further north (spring–summer). There might also be genetic differentiation between the southern and northern groups.

The separation point, it is suggested, is around the Virgin Islands, the northernmost of the chain of eastern Caribbean islands. The northern group is purported to migrate in a circular clockwise flow up the southeast coast of the United States, arriving in Bermuda waters in July–August as they head back south towards the northern Antilles.

(The southern group is thought to exhibit a similar clockwise migration route, travelling from the northeast coast of South America and southern Antilles north to as far as the Virgin Islands before heading back south to repeat the migration loop.)

The dolphin is a high energy converter among fish: it processes a large proportion of what it eats into body mass. Dolphin therefore mature very rapidly, growing by as much as 5 lb a month. A dolphin might reach 50 lb within a year. Maximum age for a dolphin is thought to be around four years, but the vast majority die by the age of two years.

Like other pelagics, dolphin produce a large number of eggs (1–1.5 million) at spawning times. This ensures that at least some individuals grow to maturity in a hostile open ocean environment where juveniles of most species are food for other fish.

Young angler with a very fine dolphin of 20–25 lb. (Photo courtesy of Flybridge Tackle.)

The IGFA all-tackle record for dolphin is 87 lb. The Bermuda record is 63 lb, taken on 30 lb test. Dolphin caught around Bermuda tend to be relatively large, averaging 10–15 lb. In warmer parts of the world where they are more abundant as juveniles, catches may average just 5–10 lb. The larger weight of Bermuda fish might be because they migrate northwards in the Western Atlantic which brings them into the Bermuda area at a more mature stage of their life.

Dolphin provide not only a very game fishing experience but an exceedingly fine dish for the table. Local dolphin does not, however, make a regular appearance at local supermarkets because: (i) it is not so plentiful; (ii) imported fish is cheaper; and (iii) fishermen are understandably niggardly with their catch, preferring to eat the fish themselves.

Barracuda (*Sphyraena barracuda*)

The notorious reputation of this fish precedes it. There is, however, nowhere near as much evidence to warrant its ferocity as its notoriety implies. Barracuda are actually a much greater danger, when dead, as the cause of ciguatera fish poisoning when their flesh is eaten by humans, than they are alive as predators of human flesh in the water.

A hefty size barracuda held up by its captor, commercial fisherman Andrew Card. Note the dull grey and blue coloration, good set of teeth, projecting lower jaw, and robust girth. And as for the barracuda . . .
(Photo courtesy of Andrew Card.)

Ciguatera poisoning is caused by eating the flesh not only of barracuda, where the toxin may be particularly prevalent in larger specimens, but also of some jacks, snappers, and even groupers, among other species which sometimes carry the toxin. Ciguatera can be present in fish randomly: fish of the same species might be toxic in one area but completely free of toxin at another location nearby.

In the West Indies barracuda is a common food fish and therefore responsible for occasional ciguatera cases in that area. Until recently in Bermuda barracuda was only rarely consumed by humans. It is still virtually never sold as whole fish in Bermuda but sometimes makes an appearance in bags of mixed fillet sold by commercial fishermen. (It may be more common in mixed fillet bags than otherwise indicated. Fishermen fill such bags with 'Bermuda fish', often without specifying the types of fish included.)

Of the 18 species of barracuda that are found worldwide, the **great barracuda** (*Sphyraena barracuda*) predominates in Bermuda waters. It most resembles a pike in appearance, with a streamlined elongated body and a very discernible longer lower jaw than upper jaw. Arrayed along both jaws are sets of needle-like teeth used to spike and hold prey.

The fish is marked by a number of irregular dark spots along the sides of the body, starting nearer the tail than the head. All fins of the barracuda, including the tail, are rather stunted in size, especially compared with the long body form.

The colour of offshore barracuda is usually gunmetal grey, with a dark blue dorsal surface. The fish becomes lighter coloured in shallower waters nearer the reef.

The great barracuda can reach a weight of almost 100 lb. The all-tackle world record is 85 lb. The local Bermuda all-tackle record is a 64 lb fish caught on 30 lb test line around the outer reef in 1974. (That mounted fish can now be viewed over the entrance to the aquarium hall at the Bermuda Aquarium at Flatts.)

Around Bermuda barracuda roam the outer reefs, the edge of the deep, and over the banks. They are found well offshore mainly in the warmer summer months. Barracuda often keep their distance from a chum, racing in only to snatch a hooked fish and leaving the angler to land a grossly deformed and diminished version of the fish originally hooked.

The only fish the great barracuda is likely to be confused with is the **Sennet** (*Sphyraena picudilla*). This small barracuda species is similar in shape to its great cousin but much smaller, only about 3 lb at most. Young great barracuda may look like sennet, but sennet lack the great barracuda's black spots on the body. Sennet also have several light brown or yellow stripes running the length of their body, which the great barracuda does not have.

Sharks

In one sense sharks need no introduction. They are common in all the oceans of the world. More has been written about sharks than about any other fish. Sharks have been idolized and fetishized, publicized and lionized, but mostly, and above all, they have been villified and reviled.

More information, anecdote, film footage, and media coverage of sharks may readily be found elsewhere in abundance, for which reason they will be dealt with here rather summarily.

For identification purposes, however, it is important to include in this section profiles of sharks most commonly found in the Bermuda area, because some species are notoriously difficult to distinguish from others.

About 250 species of sharks have been identified worldwide. In the Western Atlantic there are an estimated 30 species. Around Bermuda half a dozen species are either habitually resident or regular visitors, although it is likely that others among the 30 or so species in the Western Atlantic may visit the Bermuda area from time to time.

There are established recreational fisheries for sharks in many areas of the world, particularly where there is a lack of variety of other gamefish. For Bermuda fishermen most sharks are a nuisance. Few are game fighters. Their intimidating presence drives away other fish. They often rip into a hooked fish, leaving only the mutilated remains of an otherwise potentially fine catch.

When hooked themselves, most sharks typically run out a length of line at first but subsequently offer hardly more than a token struggle, bullish resistance, and leaden deadweight to the angler's efforts to land the fish. Exceptions include mako, hammerheads, blue sharks, tiger sharks, and the great white, all of which are fished around the world as game fighters and potential record breakers.

Mako (*Isurus oxyrinchus*)

Although not particularly common around Bermuda, makos are occasionally hooked by recreational fishermen trolling offshore for more usual gamefish like wahoo, marlin, and tuna. The mako ranks among the most gymnastic of any gamefish. It often leaps 15 or 20 feet in the air when hooked, twisting and pirouetting to attempt to throw the hook, and diving back into the water, porpoise-like, head first.

Makos are solitary deep water ocean wanderers, not usually seen in large groups or schools. The fish is dark blue to blue black in colour, with a conical pointed snout and almost homocercal tail. The teeth of the mako are often described as among the most awe-inspiring dentition

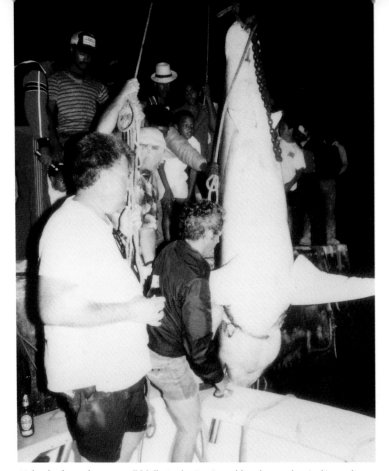

Mako shark weighing in at 720 lb. Angler Lee Estes, blue shorts, white(-ish) tee-shirt, beer in hand, weighing about half that. (Photo courtesy of Andrew Card.)

of the entire shark family (which, considering the competition, is saying something): long, sharply edged, unserrated, curved like scimitars, and flattened on their forward surface. The teeth remain erect most of the time, unlike in other sharks where the teeth are drawn back in the jaw until the mouth opens.

A distinctive feature of the mako is its well defined, wide, tapered keels at the join of the tail (caudal peduncle). These caudal keels add support to the powerful propulsion of the mako's tail, especially when it jumps clear of the water for which it requires a minimum 'escape velocity' of about 20 mph. Most sharks describe a sinuous, fluid body motion through the water. The motion of a mako is more rigid, with a propelling action dominated by its powerful tail.

Makos, along with white sharks and porbeagles, are unique in the shark brotherhood for being warm blooded: their blood temperature is up to 14°F (8°C) warmer than the water in which they live. Like tunas, they need the high internal temperature to maintain a high metabolic rate for their dynamic acceleration and muscle power.

In common, too, with the whites and porbeagles (as well as threshers, tiger sharks, and blue sharks), makos have distinctive dark black eyes. Most other shark species have lighter grey or yellowish eyes, with a cat's eye slit pupil.

The eyes of the mako are further differentiated by the lack of a white nictitating membrane (third eyelid) that covers the eye when the shark is excited or in attack mode. The dark eyed great white also lacks the nictitating membrane. Other dark eyed species such as tigers and blues have this membrane, as do all carcharinids with cat's eye pupils.

However, should you find yourself close enough to a live shark to observe the absence or presence of this membrane, especially in working order, your survival to report the phenomenon may be seriously prejudiced. To be on winking terms with another human is usually a sign of cordial intimacy. To be on nictitating terms with a live tiger shark at close quarters is, at best, inadvisable, and, at worst, fatal. To be on non-nictitating terms with a mako is best conducted from the rod and reel end of a long line of piano wire.

Makos reach up to 1000 lb in weight. The Bermuda record is a fish of 827 lb, taken on 130 lb test line. Maximum length for a mako is about 15 feet. Mako flesh, being firm and similar to swordfish in consistency, is one of the highest eating quality among shark species.

Other sharks commonly or regularly found in Bermuda waters include: **dusky** (or **cub**) **shark** (*Carcharhinus galapagensis*), known elsewhere, more correctly, as Galapagos shark which is grey in colour, with a rounded short head, and attaining a maximum size of about 12 feet, the most common shark around Bermuda and the main local source of shark fillet for steaks (from older individuals) and shark hash (best taken from young pups); **blue shark** (*Prionace glauca*), exclusively an open ocean shark, characterized by very long pectoral fins, elongated upper lobe of the tail, long and pointed head, and dark blue back; **hammerhead** (*Sphyrna zygaema*), easily identifiable by the hammer-like shape of the head with eyes on either extremity of the 'hammer', elongated upper lobe of the tail, and with a maximum size of 15 feet (not common in Bermuda); **tiger shark** (*Galeocerdo cuvier*), grey coloured, marked by vertical lighter grey tigerish stripes and spots along the body, elongated upper lobe of the tail, almost square blunt-snouted head, and exceeding 1000 lb in weight and over 20 feet in length, it comes into shallower water closer to shore during spawning summer months.

Most sharks have five gill slits. The exception is the aptly named **six-gilled shark** (*Hexanchus griseus*), a member of the Hexanchidae (cow sharks) family. A rarely seen shark species, because it lives mainly in deep water of 1500–6000 feet. Nevertheless there have been several catches recorded off Bermuda.

In late summer 1989, staff from the Bermuda Aquarium accompanied well known diver and fisherman Teddy Tucker on an expedition aboard his boat *Miss Wendy* to find deep sea specimens in the Bermuda area, for investigation and exhibition by the Bermuda Aquarium and the New York Aquarium. Among the organisms retrieved from longlines set at 230 fathoms (mid-water) and on the bottom at 650–1100 fathoms, was an 8-foot-long six-gilled shark.

In January 1982 *The Royal Gazette* reported that a St David's fisherman brought up a six-gilled shark about 12 feet long and weighing 'more than 1000 pounds'. The shark was taken on a deep line about five miles southeast of Cooper's Island where the depth of water is 650–850 fathoms.

The six-gilled shark is thought to grow up to 16 feet. It spends most of its life in the darkness of the depths but may come closer to the surface, or approach shallower water, to feed at night. Otherwise not much is known of its behaviour. The shark has a round, bluntly pointed head and dark brown to dark grey coloration. Its most conspicuous feature is its one small dorsal fin near the tail. The eyes are large and translucent yellow.

Right: *A nice size amberfish (almaco jack) coming over the transom.*
(*Bermuda News Bureau photo courtesy of Captain Keith Winter.*)

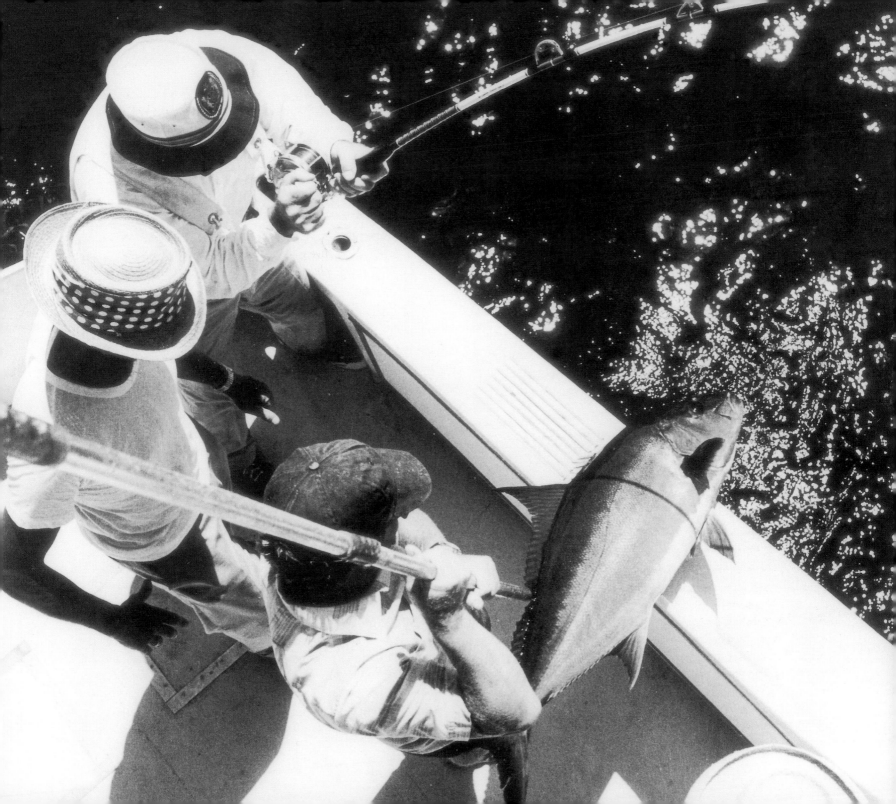

Angler Teddy Gibbons and amberfish on board the Coral Sea, *a well known sportfishing boat from the 1960s. (Bermuda News Bureau photo courtesy of Captain Keith Winter.)*

Jacks

The range of Carangidae (jacks) family members extends from world class gamefish such as amberfish, amberjacks, and rainbow runners, to small schooling species such as the robins and a half dozen variously named jacks in Bermuda waters. Even the smaller species not commonly caught by hook and line display great tenacity when hooked, shaking their head, runnning, and generally resisting capture with every sinew of their pugnacious temperament.

All jacks are predatory, voraciously hungry fish. With a few exceptions they feed during the day, swallowing their prey whole. Bony scutes (bony plate scales) along the lateral line of the posterior part of the fish, running to the caudal peduncle, are the common identifying feature of the Carangidae. The scutes act as stabilizers, like ailerons, to help the fish maintain stability when it travels at high speed.

Jacks also have, notably, two separate sets of dorsal fins: a smaller primary set, and a longer secondary set running to the tail. The falcate shape of the pectoral fin is also common to most true jacks.

Amberjack (*Seriola dumerili*), a.k.a. Amberfish, Greater Amberjack
Horse-eye Amberfish (*Seriola rivoliana*), a.k.a. Almaco Jack, Bonito, Horse-eye Bonito

These *Seriola* cousins are sometimes indiscriminately called amberfish in Bermuda, but the **amberjack** (*S. dumerili*) is considerably larger than the **horse-eye amberfish** (*S. rivoliana*). The greater amberjack often exceeds 100 lb, the amberfish, most often called bonito or almaco jack in Bermuda, not more than 60–70 lb.

The **lesser amberjack** (*Seriola fasciata* (previously *falcata*)), known colloquially in past years as bastard amberfish, madregal bonito, and, sometimes, Bermuda bonito, is smaller still, with a maximum weight of about 10 lb. Less commonly seen in Bermuda than its greater amberjack cousin, the lesser amberjack inhabits deep water in excess of 200 feet. *Seriola fasciata* has relatively large eyes, because it needs better vision in the dark depths. The body above the lateral line has a pinkish tinge, diminishing in intensity below the lateral line towards the belly.

Both the lesser and greater amberjack, and the amberfish, have a characteristic light amber coloured stripe running from the eye to the tail, hence their shared name. They also typically show a dark chevron ('nuchal crest') running from the mouth through the eye, backward to a point just in front of the dorsal fin.

Amberjack and amberfish have well defined caudal scutes, a line of bony protuberances running towards the tail along the lateral line, which help with stability when the fish swims at high speed. Caudal scutes are common to the Carangidae family in general.

Apart from size, the main visible differences between the greater amberjack and the amberfish are the relatively slender body shape of the former compared with the deep body of the latter, and the darker colour of the amberfish, compared with the more silvery amberjack. Around inshore waters small almaco jack of a few pounds in weight are

Two world records in one day! On the right, Joey Dawson with the 153 lb amberjack he caught off Bermuda on 24 June 1981. A new all-tackle world record. On the left, his father, Joe Dawson Sr, with the 155 lb amberjack he caught on 80 lb test line 20 minutes later. (Photo courtesy of Flybridge Tackle.)

often silvery white, flashing through schools of fry or other bait fish like streaks of lightning.

The dorsal and anal fins of amberfish are long and falcate (sickle or scythe) shaped. The same fins on the amberjack are much shorter, more streamlined, and never falcate. Both fish have two distinct sets of dorsal fins, the first spinier and shorter than the main fin which runs from the middle of the back tapering down to the tail.

Amberjack and amberfish lack well developed cutting teeth. They swallow their prey whole with a violent shaking action. Anglers may recognize the ambers by this characteristic tugging and shaking as the fish tries to dislodge the hook. Both the amberjack and amberfish are powerful, stubborn fighters.

Both, too, are not particularly fussy eaters and devour bait food hungrily. Ocean robin, squid, flying fish, little tunny (mackerel), as well as rays and other pelagic prey constitute their main diet. For the

A 131 lb amberjack taken on 50 lb test line, with a good day's catch of other assorted groupers and jacks. To the left: John Barnes, now Director of the Department of Agriculture and Fisheries. To the right: Eugene ('Gene') Barnes, a long-time commercial fisherman from St David's. Photo taken on Barnes's boat Blue Chip III.
(Photo courtesy of Flybridge Tackle.)

angler this means that a variety of live baits and lures might succeed equally well in attracting a fish to the hook.

Amberjack range from the surface, as gamefish, to as deep as 500–600 feet, at which depth only commercial fishermen catch them. Bonito are usually visible around the coast of Bermuda as they feed, rushing through schools of fry or pilchards. The lesser amberfish is found in deep waters off the reef platform.

The IGFA all-tackle world record for amberjack (*S. dumerili*) is a 155 lb 10 oz specimen taken off Bermuda in 1981. The Bermuda record is shared between the IGFA world record fish and another, 2 oz bigger, taken in 1992. Both were caught on 80 lb test line.

On 25 June 1993 *The Royal Gazette* reported the catch of a large amberjack by handline off St David's:

IT'S A WHOPPA! Brothers Mr. Floyd Pitcher and Mr. Gilbert Pitcher and their friend Mr. Simon Wilkinson could not believe it when they caught this five foot, eight inch long, 124 pound Amberjack off St. David's. Mr. Gilbert Pitcher said: 'We caught a goat fish and threw it back in, then half an hour later we felt a tug and knew we had a big one. It took three of us about half an hour to pull it in. Fishermen rarely see them this size so for one to be hand caught is quite something.'

Commercial fishermen often net large numbers of small amberfish around the shore of Bermuda or over the reef area, especially in early and late summer. These 'bonito' are often included in bags of mixed fillet, though their densely flaky flesh is fine eating on its own.

Rainbow Runner (*Elagatis bipinnulata*)

Another member of the Carangidae family, the rainbow runner is one of the most attractive pelagics roaming the offshore waters of Bermuda. The fish has an elongated body similar to the amberjack, and a brilliant yellow deeply veed tail. The back is dark green to blue and the underbelly is silvery white.

The runner's most conspicuous features are two narrow light blue stripes running horizontally along the body from eye to tail, with a wider yellow band running between them. Small finlets near the tail, just after the second dorsal and anal fins, also identify the species.

The average size for Bermuda waters is around 8 lb, but maximum size is thought to be around 40 lb. Any fish over 10 lb in Bermuda waters is a good specimen. The local record is just over 25 lb.

Rainbow runners are common over the banks and near the edge of the deep but never in shallow waters. They typically appear in small aggregations of half a dozen fish.

Rainbow runners are considered rather timid fish, more inclined to range around the perimeters of a chum than to dart back and forth through it. When hooked, however, they dash around trying to shake the hook, earning their badge as a game fish on light tackle in particular. Although commonly taken in a chum, runners will occasionally hit a trolled line.

Rainbow runners often hang around schools of ocean robin, in proximity to them but not integrating wholly with them. Larger adult runners feed on the smaller robins. Juveniles too small to feed on robins find safety in numbers among such groupings. Both are a favourite snack for larger pelagics like tuna, wahoo, and billfish. The smaller runners feed on fry or anchovies

Spoilage (autolytic breakdown) in rainbow runners commences immediately after death. The fish must be promptly bled, gutted, and iced if the flesh is to remain fresh either for bait or for human consumption.

Ocean Robin (*Decapterus macarellus*), a.k.a Mackerel Scad
Round Robin (*Decapterus punctatus*), a.k.a. Round Scad

There are at least three varieties of robin found in Bermuda waters, the most common being the ocean robin and the round robin. The **ocean robin** (*D. macarellus*) is essentially a larger version of the **round robin** (*D. punctatus*), attaining a maximum weight of about $1\frac{1}{2}$ lb and a length of up to 18 inches.

Round robin reach a weight of less than half a pound. Maximum length is about 10 inches. They display from one to as many as a dozen dark spots along their distinctive curved lateral line. An ochre yellow stripe runs the length of their body along the lateral line.

Robins bear the hallmark of most jacks in the form of the conspicuous bony scutes along the lateral line towards the caudal peduncle. Their backs are dark blue, their sides silvery, and their belly white. The body is elongated and rounded in cross-section, with firm, muscular flesh.

Ocean robins are speedy pelagics, often found in large schools over the banks and elsewhere offshore in water of 100–150 feet. Round robin frequently cruise inshore waters and bays feeding on fry or other small schooling fish, especially in the summer months. Robins spawn year-round but are most active in the spring and early summer months.

Although ocean robin is a good eating fish, both robins are used primarily as bait rather than for food in Bermuda, either cut (as strip bait) or as live bait for wahoo, tuna, and other large gamefish. Their natural predators are the large gamefish but also demersal species such as groupers.

Steelhead Jack (*Caranx hippos*), a.k.a. Horse-eye Jack, Jack Crevalle (or Crevalle Jack), Common Jack

The steelhead is one of the largest jacks in the Western Atlantic, attaining a maximum weight of around 100 lb and a length of 4 feet. It is recognizable by its rather blunt, butt shaped head, as well as by other common features of the Carangidae (bony scutes and falcate pectoral fin).

Sometimes called the crevalle jack (not to be confused with the trevally which is a *Caranx* of the Pacific and Indian Oceans), it is deep bodied, with a dark slate blue-grey to olive-green back, silvery sides, and white belly. The falcate pectoral fins are particularly long in this species. The large forked tail is dark in the adult but yellowish in juveniles. A conspicuous dark spot marks the upper edge of its opercal (outer gill) cover near the base of its pectoral fin.

Steelhead inhabit the shallow reef waters of Bermuda to the edge of the deep and around the banks. They prey on small schooling fish such as pilchards and anchovies, as well as on flying fish and small squid. While most jacks are daytime feeders, the steelhead appears to prefer feeding at night.

This species is considered one of the strongest fighters of all jacks. On a line the steelhead behaves like most jacks, shaking its head to try to throw the hook, lying broadside in the water, and rising and falling through the water column in its dauntless struggle for freedom.

The fish is found around inshore waters, around bridges or docks, especially at night when feeding, as well as in deeper waters of the Bermuda Platform. It appears in patrolling groups of a few individuals to schools of a few hundred when feeding.

In October 1992 a fisherman landed a large steelhead from the shore. *The Royal Gazette* of 14 October 1992 reported:

> Mr Ephraim Bean knows exactly what he'll be having for dinner for months to come. He'll be feasting on prime fillets of steelhead jack after hauling a stunning 100 pound specimen from the water with just a hand line. Mr Bean, 72, pulled in the four foot monster just minutes after spotting it swimming off the North Shore...He had just netted some squid off the public dock near Terceira's auto garage when he spotted the jack. Baiting his line with one of the squid, he hooked the fish in about three minutes. About seven minutes later he was being congratulated by astonished fishermen who identified the catch.

Horse-eye Jack (*Caranx latus*)

The horse-eye may be confused with the steelhead (above) but is distinguishable by its larger eye, yellower tail, black dorsal fins, and, in juveniles, six distinctive bands across its back. Not as large as the steelhead, the horse-eye jack grows to a maximum length of about $2\frac{1}{2}$ ft and weight of about 30 lb. The Bermuda record for this fish is 23 lb 6 oz on 12 lb test line.

Bar Jack (*Caranx ruber*), a.k.a. Never-bite, Skip Jack, Black Jack

The colloquially named 'never-bite' has earned this moniker for its reluctance to take a baited line (although they will, more usually, take a trolled lure). Around the reef flats of Bermuda they sometimes congregate in schools of hundreds and even thousands of fish. Most are taken by net fishing.

Reaching a maximum size of 10 lb, the bar jack has typical Carangidae features. Its distinctive marking is the dark purple or black bar running along its sky blue back, alongside the dorsal fin and down along the lower lobe of its tail. The luminous blue of the back is almost universally described as 'neon' bright. It appears particularly brilliant on fish in shallow water on bright sunny days.

Large adults of this species may appear very dark and even black, which is why they are sometimes called black jack.

Black Jack (*Caranx lugubris*)

The true black jack is unlike the bar jack in that, apart from its black coloration, it has a distinctive sloping forehead. This species also grows considerably larger than the bar jack, up to a maximum 30 lb. The black jack inhabits the deeper waters of the Bermuda area.

Blue Runner (*Caranx fusus*), a.k.a. Whale Jack, Hard-tailed Jack

This silvery olive-green coloured jack is the most common jack in Bermuda waters. Mainly caught by net fishermen, it also takes a trolled bait or artificial lure. The blue runner attains a maximum weight of 10 lb, but the average size for Bermuda is 1–2 lb.

Cottonmouth Jack (*Uraspis secunda*)

The cottonmouth gets its name from the creamy white colour of the inside of its mouth. Not particularly well known in Bermuda, this jack is found in rather deep water around the outer reefs, along the edge of the deep, and over the banks. It feeds mainly on small pelagic fish and squid. The fish is game to catch, behaving in a typically obstinate jack-like fashion and often emitting loud grunts when caught.

The cottonmouth is pearly dark grey in colour, reflecting its dark deep water environment. The average size for Bermuda waters is 2–3 lb and 12–14 inches in length, with a maximum possible size of about 8 lb. Unlike other small jacks which have dark, somewhat oily flesh, the edibility of the cottonmouth's flaky white flesh is equal in quality to better known table fish such as dolphin and bonito.

Gwelly (*Pseudocaranx dentex*)

In its juvenile stage the gwelly appears similar to the blue runner and to the yellow jack (*Caranx bartholomaei*). At that age it is a pelagic predator, feeding on small anchovies and fry. As it matures it develops an elongated snout and thick lips as an adaptation of its predilection for feeding on worms, snails, and crustaceans along sandy or broken seabeds. It spends most of the time feeding on the seabed but may occasionally rise closer to the surface if there happens to be abundant prey to feed on there.

Gwelly are mainly taken while fishing sandy or weedy bottom areas of the reef, although they used to be fished mainly by pot fishermen. The fish grows quite large, up to 20 lb, and is considered game to catch despite its apparently lethargic feeding habits. Perhaps its inherent jack nature kicks in when hooked.

The gwelly is a true jack, exhibiting the Carangidae features of bony scutes, falcate pectoral fins, and black spot on the gill cover. Its colouring is yellow-green along the back, silvery along the belly, and with a distinct yellow line along the lateral line.

The gwelly is one of the higher quality jacks in terms of edibility though probably not quite as good eating as the cottonmouth, because it has a larger strip of dark oily meat. Since the gwelly is a rather bloody fish, it should be gutted and iced immediately, to avoid tainting the firm and flaky white flesh.

Gwelly used to be common all around the shoreline and bays of Bermuda, but its numbers have diminished greatly. Commercial fishermen now catch them only occasionally. Consumers rarely see gwelly for sale as whole fish. The flesh is mainly included in bags of mixed fillet.

Recreational and Sport Fishing in Bermuda

6

To the best of my moderate ability to form an opinion, the finest sport is fishing with a rod, line, and hook . . . If you would be skillful in angling, you must first learn to make your tackle, which is, to wit: your rod and your line of divers colours. After that you must know how to fish, in what depth of water, and at what time of day. Also, you must know the different kinds of fish, and the weather suitable in which to catch them . . . It is necessary to know what implements are needed for that art which is called the art of angling. Particularly you must have a knowledge of what bait is needed for different fishes in every month of the year.

A Treatise On Fishing With A Hook, by Dame Juliana Berners; printed in the *Book Of Saint Albans*, by Wynken de Worde (1496); rendered into modern English by William Van Wyck (1933)

Small angler, big fish. Ben Storey Lyles (12 years old at the time, August 1993), with a yellowfin tuna of around 100 lb. (Photo courtesy of Andrew Card.)

When I was not much bigger than a fresh spawned porgy, my horizon was the other side of Mangrove Bay in Somerset. Even then it had extended from my infant's view of the water's edge along the beach. Later on, large gwelly sized, I imagined, looking out to sea from the top of the hill at Cambridge Beaches, that I could see New York City clouding up out of the horizon. When I was 10 (full size bonito) and our home was by Jew's Bay, my horizon across the Sound was Dockyard and Spanish Point.

We moved, our views changed, but the water defined my horizon.

The fishing horizon for children growing up in Bermuda is about 10 feet off the local dock – 'messin' around' with a fishing line and a piece of bread, catching breams, grunts, crabs, whatever happens to be there. The hooks are usually tiny, the line either thread light or hawser strength, and the bait anything from bread crust or dough to baloney to leftover hamburger to raw bits of bacon. At that age, bait is whatever is available from the kitchen to squidge on to a hook.

For children in Bermuda, fishing is a pastime; for adolescents, a diversion; for adults, a recreation. With a well-powered boat, expensive rods and reels, and the desire to catch big fish beyond the reefs, beyond the childhood horizons of white grunts and breams, it becomes gamefishing.

Many Bermudians never get further than fishing off the shore, twirling a line like a lasoo and throwing it out 20 or 30 feet. This is basic Bermuda fishing: a fisherman holding a line trailing off into the water, a hook and bait at the other end, and, somewhere among the weeds, a hungry yellow grunt.

A few dollars buys a spool of light monofilament line, a dozen small hooks, a handful of lead weights, and a bag of bait. Bait could be crabs caught by the shore, a few pieces of bread from home, or a frozen box of squid from the supermarket. A quiet piece of shoreline, a secluded dock, a small boat are required. Throw your line out. Wait for your first nibble, your first bite, your first fish.

The docks and rocks around Bermuda are littered with clumps of monofilament and rusty little hooks left by fishermen hauling in handlines that get tangled by wind, the rocks, prickly pear bushes, dead fish lying around, their mate's left foot, lunch bags, impatience.

Spinning rods not only minimize tangles, they are highly versatile. They get the line out further than casting a handline. Offshore they can be used to drop a line 50 feet, or 250 feet to the bottom for snappers, porgies, and hinds. They can be used for trolling, surf-casting for pompano, or stalking bonefish. They can be hung out over the side of a boat to drift a line in a chum over the reefs, around the banks, or half a mile from shore.

A 50 lb Allison tuna played on a lightweight line spooling off a heavy duty spinning reel gives an angler the opportunity for an extreme test of gamefishing skill. A six ounce bream on the end of a line from a lightweight spinning rod in the hands of a 10 year old off the rocks along North Shore can be equally rewarding.

Bottom Fishing

A fisherman in a boat becomes more than just a fisherman, he becomes a boatman, needing boat handling skills. Wind and weather change the nature of the water. The sea, waves, and swell roll around the edge of the reef. The fish are different, bigger, more varied. Fishing from a small boat offshore expands the fisherman's horizons.

Years ago Bermudian fishermen sailed or rowed miles out over the reefs to fish, out even to the edge of the reefs, to North Rock, or to the breakers, up to 20 miles there and back in a single day. Rowboats for fishing nowadays in Bermuda are used mainly for net fishing, to catch bait or jacks or bonito around the coast.

Bottom fishing from a boat can be satisfactory anywhere around the reefs, from a few hundred metres offshore, to the northern edge of the platform where Bermuda resolves to a knotty strand of rope along the horizon.

Fishermen who have guided their boats and fished around Bermuda for decades know the reef landscape as well as landlubbers know the road from St George's to Hamilton. They know the depth of the water by their colours, from turquoise to aquamarine to milky azure blue. They know where tides can rip a line flat out behind an anchored boat. They know the channels between the reefs, the ledges, the flats, the wrecks, the hollows, where their boat can clear the reefs with six inches of water under the keel at low tide, where it's grassy, muddy, or rocky, and where the big snappers come out at dusk to feed.

The undersea terrain of the reef platform around Bermuda varies from grey sludgy ooze that dries stiff as clay, to marshy grassland, interspersed by coral heads and boilers along the edge.

Whitewater snapper cruise the clear bottom, in 'white (clear) water', in depths of 40 to 100 feet. Porgies, large grunts, bream, and triggerfish feeding on sea urchins keep the whitewater company. Grey snapper lurk around grassy bottoms.

Coney, porgies, chub, bonito, hinds, yellowtail, and jacks will take a line dropped to sit a few feet off the bottom around the reef flats and coral heads bordering the edge of the platform before it slopes off into

Early Gamefishing Offshore

Offshore gamefishing is a 20th century phenomenon. The first gamefish ever taken anywhere in the world on rod and reel, a bluefin tuna, was caught in June 1898. The first marlin caught on rod and reel (a striped marlin, 125 lb) was in 1903. The first gamefish over 1000 lb taken on rod and reel, a black marlin, was caught as recently as 1952.

Gamefishing in Bermuda in the early years, in the 1930s, was as much a social occasion as a sport. The daily newspaper, *The Royal Gazette and Colonist Daily* (now *The Royal Gazette*), devoted regular columns to news of goings-on at the hotels, including lists of new arrivals, dinner parties, tea receptions, gala affairs, and names of honoured guests at such events. It also included brief reports of sporting activities and the occasional fishing expedition by guests.

The Royal Gazette and Colonist Daily advertised gamefishing tackle for sale as early as 1932. Master's Hardware Co. (now just Master's, on Front and Reed Streets) announced in a series of advertisements that 'Trolling season is now', and that it had for sale 'Spoons, Swivels, Troll Lines and all Fishing Requirements'. The ads appeared in the summer, suggesting that, other reports to the contrary, there was at least some understanding of seasonal fishing for offshore gamefish around Bermuda by the early 1930s.

With the Depression still as tight as a noose around the neck of the common man, gamefishing in those years was the sport of the resident gentry in Bermuda, and of affluent North American visitors. Its development as a more popular sport was delayed by the Second World War.

The first 'organized' game fishing in Bermuda originated from the Castle Harbour, one of Bermuda's landmark hotels, opened in December 1931.

Donald Stillman, editor of the 'Rod and Gun' column of the *New York Herald Tribune*, reflected the novelty of gamefishing offshore from Bermuda in the early years. Stillman wrote a series of three articles published over three days in the *Herald Tribune* in February 1935 (below). Two of the articles, from the 20 and 21 February 1935, describe brief fishing trips out of Castle Harbour. In the third, from the 23 February, he speculates on the gamefishing potential of Bermuda.

Peter Pearman shows off the 22 lb red snapper he caught on a bucktail jig ('a single hook moulded into a lead head and dressed with bucktail hair'). Jigs are not commonly used for fishing the deep water around Bermuda, but innovation and novelty in fishing often breed success. (Photo courtesy of Captain Allen DeSilva.)

water thousands of feet deep. Some (chub, yellowtail, jacks, bonito, coney) will snatch a bait from a line drifted in a chum behind a boat.

In deep crevices off the edge of the platform, down past 200 feet and as far as 800 feet or more, silk (red) snapper have been left in relative peace over recent years. Commercial fishermen have fished them less in the past few decades, because they require so much effort that no longer pays adequately. Half a dozen deep water snapper species growing to 25–30 lb, including the silk snapper, are found in the depths bordering the Bermuda Platform.

Fishing for silk snapper, often at night, is an adventure, with the muted lights of Bermuda in the distance, Gibb's Hill Lighthouse's pulsing beam, alone, in a small boat mantled by the stars and cradled by the open sea.

Stillman alludes generally to the virtual absence of information about gamefishing seasons in Bermuda, the variety of gamefish in Bermuda waters, the minimal availability of gamefishing tackle, boats, and guides, but that, 'with development, Bermuda will rank among the famous angling resorts'.

Stillman cited the local knowledge of gamefishing imparted to him by Louis L. Mowbray, founder of the Bermuda Aquarium and an avid sportfisherman, but, surprisingly, says he found no one with experience of bonefishing in Bermuda. Louis L. Mowbray's son, Louis S. Mowbray, aged 36 in 1935, in fact did have a particular interest and expertise in bonefishing in Bermuda around that time. Mowbray wrote regularly to American friends to describe his bonefishing exploits.

20 February 1935
Day 1

The history of rod and reel angling in Bermuda waters is yet to be written. When Louis L. Mowbray, Curator of the Government Aquarium in Bermuda, expressed his belief last December that tuna could be taken trolling with rod and reel in the waters surrounding the island, he had no evidence to support his contention. A few weeks later, however, Mowbray's son, Louis L., Jr. [*sic*], trolled off the south shore of the island and in two hours fishing landed two tuna weighing about thirty and forty pounds apiece. *These are the first tuna ever reported taken on rod and reel in Bermuda* [author's italics]. So far as sport fishing is concerned, the waters still are practically virgin.

It can be imagined, therefore, with what eagerness we availed ourselves of the opportunity of fishing those waters during the recent second annual skeet and trap shooting tournament at the Castle Harbor.

Fishing boats and fishing tackle are not very plentiful in Bermuda. We had the tackle, and F.G. Rounthwaite, general manager of The Bermuda Development Company, Ltd., kindly offered us the use of his own small cabin-cruiser, so, with six-ounce and a nine-ounce tips, feather lures and ballyhoo for bait, we put to sea.

The reef at the entrance of Castle Harbor reaches out a distance of a half-mile or more and at the edge of the reef the water deepens rapidly. Once clear of the inlet, we put over our feather baits, and with anticipatory thrills sat back to await what might happen. We knew that enormous wahoo, dolphin, occasional marlin, and tuna weighing up to 400 pounds [bigeye? bluefin?], visit Bermuda waters at some seasons of the year, but we did not know what were the best seasons, or where the fish might be located or if they would hit a trolled bait or lure if we did succeed in locating them. Our boatman, though skilled, knew less about angling than we, so we determined to experiment with different lengths of line and different speeds until we got a strike.

We did not have long to wait. Suddenly my companion's rod ducked and her line began to sing as something at the far end started off on a swift, powerful rush. The fish did not leap but fought savagely, bending the nine-ounce tip as it lunged for the bottom. In about twenty minutes it was played to boat and lifted in. Our boatman pronounced it a 'horse-eye bonita', but it appeared to be some variety of amberfish, closely resembling the Florida 'amberjack'. We had no scales but estimated it to weigh about twenty-five pounds.

Amberfish [amberjack, in fact] weighing up to thirty pounds or so are common in Bermuda waters, while specimens weighing up to 100 pounds are considered not rare. The record fish of this species is said to have weighed 130 pounds dressed. It would appear that this fish runs larger in Bermuda waters than in Florida.

A little later my companion hooked and landed another amberfish, slightly smaller than the first. Then she caught a small tuna . . . Mowbray is of the opinion that tuna spawn in

Bermuda waters. Perhaps so, for I cannot recall ever having seen as small a tuna taken anywhere in our home waters. The fish probably weighed only two or three pounds, but the catch made my companion the second angler to take this species on rod and reel at Bermuda, so far as the records go . . . a strike which somehow or other felt familiar. So also did the rushing, thumping tactics of the hooked fish. When I landed it, it proved to be a fifteen-pound specimen of what the boatman called a 'horse mackerel', but the five black spots on its 'corselet' [belly just under the pectoral fin] showed it to be the little tunny or 'albacore', as it is known to the [New] Jersey boatmen.

This ended our first day's fishing. We had been out about two hours, at no time more than about a mile from the 'inlet' [Castle Harbour], and had taken five fish of four different species, all on feather baits.

21 February 1935
Day 2

Our second day of fishing out from the Castle Harbour added two more species to our four recorded on our first day. The wind had stiffened a bit and an outgoing tide was pouring the blue waters of the harbour through the narrow inlet into the equally blue waters of the outside reefs.

Not even on the Florida outer reefs are the water colorings equal to the Bermuda 'blue', which varies through numerous shadings from the turquoise of the bays and coral reefs to the darker hues of the deep waters. The boat seems suspended in a crystal-blue liquid of exquisite beauty, the colorings less a reflection of the bottom tints than of the liquid itself. Certainly the charm of the Bermuda 'blue' adds much to the joy of a day afloat.

We sailed between the huge coral rocks that guard the entrance to the harbor, past the natural bridge and the ruined fortifications erected years ago to protect the little town of St. George against foreign invasion.

The swift-flowing receding tide suggested the possibility that gamefish might be working on food swept out of the bay, so we put our lures overboard at once. The guess proved to be correct. 'Strike!' and 'Strike!' – a double-header. One fish tore loose from the hook immediately. The other, after ten or fifteen minutes of vigorous battling, was landed. It was a little tunny, a species which in the north seldom is taken except well out to sea, but here was hooked within just a few hundred yards of the inlet.

Apparently a school of these fish was feeding just outside the inlet, for we went back and picked up a couple more. They ran about fourteen to sixteen pounds in weight and fought hard.

Being more interested in variety than quantity, we moved on down the reef to get out of the school and hoping for other species. We next picked up a small amberfish – about fifteen pounds in weight – then my companion got a smashing strike, a long run, and the fish began to circle the boat. We speculated on what it might be, but the fish did not jump and while we decided it battled differently than anything we yet had taken, our experience was too limited even to hazard a guess.

My companion played this fish for fifteen or twenty minutes. Then she led it boatward. We had been told that while barracuda were plentiful on the reefs in summer they were not present in winter, but a barracuda it turned out to be, and a good-sized one at that.

Passing back through the inlet on the way in, something prompted us to put in a few moments trolling inside the coral rocks. I don't know what we expected to catch. I knew big rockfish, a variety of grouper, inhabited the deep holes in the coral, but I did not know if they would hit an artificial lure, so I put on a ballyhoo bait.

These waters are full of surprises. I got a strike and hooked a fish, which fought valiantly against the six-ounce tip. When landed, examination disclosed it to be a frigate mackerel, a species closely resembling the little tunny, an offshore fish in Northern waters, here taken inside the bay and almost in front of the Castle Harbour Hotel. [The fish called 'frigate' mackerel in Bermuda is actually the juvenile little tunny. The true frigate mackerel is a different species.]

Again we had been out about two hours. We caught six fish of four different species, all within a half-mile of the inlet. Five of the fish were caught on feather baits.

23 February 1935
Day 3

Although with the limited time at our disposal we were able to do nothing more than scratch the surface of the angling possibilities here, the little we did and the information imparted by Louis L. Mowbray, curator of the government aquarium, and picked up from commercial fishermen, convince me that, with development Bermuda will rank among the famous angling resorts.

Outstanding among the game fishes of the island is the bonefish. If you asked a Bermudian fisherman about bonefish, he probably would say he did not know the fish. Here this magnificent battler masquerades under the undignified and belittling name of 'grubber'. But it is the same species as the Florida bonefish and is present in numbers in many of the bays. According to reports it reaches weights of twelve to fourteen pounds. I was unable to contact anyone who has successfully angled for this fish, but as the conditions are entirely different from those in Florida, I presume a different method of angling would be necessary. The bonefish here is

caught in water four or five feet or more in depth.

The commercial fishermen annually catch a number of small tuna weighing up to forty or sixty pounds and Mowbray has a record of a tuna estimated to weigh about 400 pounds which became stranded in a mullet net, so the species is present but at what season most plentiful I do not know.

The formation and location of the island suggests the possibilities of marlin, but concerning this species little seems known. Mowbray has records of two marlin, one of which was harpooned, the other became stranded on the reefs. The first mentioned was ten feet one inch in length, the other seven feet nine inches. It may be presumed that these isolated cases were not merely accidental, but that the species does visit Bermuda waters at some seasons.

One of the greatest of game fishes which seems to be present much of the year is the wahoo, or, as it is known here, the 'ocean barracuda'. It is said to reach a length of six feet and a weight of 100 pounds. The record fish taken on a hand line weighed eighty pounds. I agree with Mowbray that the development of wahoo fishing alone would be well worth while.

Dolphin are plentiful in the offshore waters and, according to report, run to lengths of five feet or more.

In addition to the tuna, the mackerel-like fish include the true albacore, the frigate mackerel, the little tunny and the bonito.

Barracuda are said to be in Bermuda waters throughout the summer months, but our catch of a sizable fish of this species during February would seem to indicate that at least a limited number remain on the reefs through the winter.

The most important of the strictly reef fish is the amberfish, which, in Bermuda waters grows to a great size. Specimens of 90 to 100 pounds are said to be not uncommon, while the record weighed 130 pounds dressed. This fish is, I believe, identical with the Florida amberjack. There are several closely related species which do not attain such heavy weights.

Crevalle, the largest of the true jacks found in Bermuda, have been recorded up to twenty pounds. Other reef fish of lesser importance are the groupers, rockfish, yellowtail snappers, margatefish, porgies, hogfish, etc. Rockfish up to 100 pounds have been caught by commercial fishermen . . .

The angler planning for game fish in Bermuda waters must be prepared to pioneer. Boats are difficult to obtain and arrangements should be made in advance if possible. The angler should take his own tackle including leader wire, lures, hooks, etc. He probably will find that his boatman does not know how to cut a strip bait. Possibly he may never have seen a game fish taken on a trolled bait or lure. The angler will be largely on his own, but can depend upon his boatman's knowledge of the water and weather conditions.

Bermuda is, after all, a very small island in a very big ocean. The nearest land is 500 or 600 miles away, so proper precaution should be taken before venturing offshore. In this connection, the Castle Harbour Rod and Gun Club has decided that all boats fishing out from the club shall fish in pairs with positive instructions to keep each other in sight throughout the day. Under such an arrangement there is no reason why anglers should not enjoy the sport of pioneering Bermuda game fish angling with the same degree of safety that it is practiced in Long Island or Florida waters.

The image of a brace of small boats cruising in tandem along the edge of the deep off Castle Harbour, trolling for gamefish in waters that had hardly been fished in that way before, offers a compelling vision of simplicity for Bermuda sportfishing in the years when the tourist trade to the island was a winter relief for East Coast Americans, Easter lillies

were shipped to New York markets, and horse and buggy was the usual mode of island transport.

Stillman was at Castle Harbour in 1935 during the hotel's second annual skeet and trap shooting competition. While he was visiting, a group of individuals organized the Castle Harbour Rod and Gun Club, 'at a luncheon given at the Mid-Ocean Club'. F. G. Rounthwaite, mentioned in the first of Stillman's dispatches, was elected president. Three vice-presidents were elected: Eltinge F. Warner, publisher of *Field and Stream* magazine; Orson D. Munn, publisher of the *Scientific American*; and Stillman himself. Roy Parton, from New York, was named secretary and treasurer.

The report of the club's formation, in *The Royal Gazette and Colonist Daily* of 19 February 1935, noted that, 'Mr. Louis Mowbray attended the luncheon and is an invaluable member of the club particularly due to his expert knowledge of fishing conditions in this region'.

The report added, 'Mr. and Mrs. Stillman, both expert with rod and reel, tried their luck during their stay, bringing in a catch of barracuda, two varieties of amber fish [*sic*], tunny, tuna and frigate mackerel all of which were caught with rod and reel.

'On another expedition Mr. Mowbray and Mr. Orson D. Munn, who has fished the entire length of the Atlantic sea coast, and whose pet diversion was surf fishing, went out in one boat and Mr. and Mrs. Stillman in another. The northerners were enthusiastic about the possibilities for those interested in game fish.'

The Castle Harbour offered a range of activities for its guests, including, in a 1934 advertisement, 'golf, trap shooting, swimming pool, and deep sea fishing'.

From Castle Harbour Notes in *The Royal Gazette and Colonist Daily* of 17 February 1934: 'Yesterday Capt. W.W. Swan took a fishing party out on the "Tautog" which included Mr. and Mrs. Herbert T. Herr, Miss Betty Herr and Dr. and Mrs. G.V. Foster.

'Another fishing group going on Captain Pearman's "Beaut" included Mr. and Mrs. E.B. Brindle, and Mr. and Mrs. James L. Rodgers. Both parties were successful in making a good catch.

'Judge Irving Lehman and Mrs. Lehman of The Castle Harbour enjoyed a drive to various places of interest in Hamilton yesterday.'

Some local residents also kept boats for recreational fishing around this time. When two yachts, *Curlew* and *Spanish Rose*, went missing in the 1932 Montauk Point to Bermuda Ocean Yacht Race (now the Newport to Bermuda race), it was reported in the press that Harold and William Frith's fishing boat *Tucan* assisted in the search for the vessels.

Rod and reel fishing continued to be a noteworthy event in the mid-1930s. Fish species were then accorded the dignity of capitalization in the press, as if they were honoured guests to Bermuda waters much like the hotel guests listed in the social columns. One of the earliest news reports of a gamefishing catch in Bermuda, from *The Royal Gazette* of 21 February 1936, noted the following:

Great Fishing Haul Off South-west Yesterday
Darrell Brothers Return with 24 Tunas

Fishing with rods off the South-west reefs for about four hours yesterday afternoon, Messrs. Reggie and Victor Darrell returned to Hamilton with a great haul of fish, including twenty-two Tuna, 2 Mackerels and two Allison Tunas. The largest Tuna weighed 50 lbs. while both the Allison Tunas scaled 45 lbs. – Not a bad afternoon's sport.

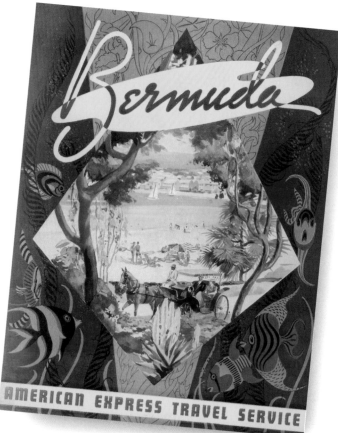

By the 1930s Bermuda was being touted as a paradise tourist resort. This 1938 travel brochure highlights the aesthetic attractions of its coral reef fish and glass-bottom boat excursions. The quality of its sportfishing and offshore gamefishing potential would not be fully realized until after the Second World War.

In the years before the Second World War Bermuda was a true colony of the British Empire. In the summer of 1932 India pith helmets ('Light, Cool and Comfortable') were advertised for sale at 12/6 (twelve shillings and sixpence), for men's sizes ($6\frac{7}{8}$ to $7\frac{1}{2}$) and 10/- for boy's sizes ($6\frac{1}{2}$ to $6\frac{3}{4}$).

Morris A. Gibbons (forerunner of Gibbons Company), the clothing and haberdashery store, offered 'Smart Tropical Helmets, Latest Shape', for 18/6.

The Front Street department store H.A.&E. Smith (founded 1889), still going strong today, was selling 'New Summer Dresses' for 25/- and 30/-.

The shoe store T.J. Pearman & Sons announced the arrival of 'Men's Black and White and Brown and White Sport Shoes with Cuban Heels – Just the thing for smart summer wear', at 25/- a pair.

A now defunct clothing store, Cox & Wilson, sold 'Men's Irish Linen Suits' at the 'Special Price' of 40/- per suit.

The first airport in Bermuda, Darrell's Island Marine Airport, in the Great Sound, opened on 12 June 1937. By 1938, just a year before the outbreak of the Second World War, the air fare to to the United States on Pan American Airways (PAA) was $70 single and $120 round trip. Flights from Bermuda took off on Wednesday, Thursday, Friday, and Sunday.

PAA's Sikorsky flying boat *The Bermuda Clipper* (known to Bermudians as *The Betsy*) flew to Bermuda from Baltimore via Port Washington on Long Island. The Imperial Airways (subsequently BOAC, now British Airways) flying boat *RMA Cavalier* flew from Port Washington to Bermuda.

Most seaborne visitors to Bermuda arrived on the two cruise liners for which Bermudians have the most affectionate memories, the *Monarch of Bermuda* (later the *Ocean Monarch*) and the *Queen of Bermuda*. The train (opened October 1931, closed down May 1948), bicycle, horse and buggy, and foot power were the main means of travel around the island in the 1930s. The automobile was not introduced to Bermuda until 1946.

Gamefishing After the War

Fishing offshore from Bermuda, in boats with a captain and mate, came of age after the Second World War. A few 'guides' offered their services for hire before then, but gamefishing as we know it in Bermuda today evolved from the late 1940s and 1950s, when mass tourism began to take off.

In those early days guides such as Milton Pitman in Somerset, Roy Taylor and Charles Christianson from St George's, and the Darrell brothers from Warwick began to take visitors out fishing as an offshoot of their boating activities. General Glancey, from 'Willowbank' in Somerset, and Ed Olander from the US Navy Base (NOB) were well known gamefishermen in the late 1940s. Russell Young, who was to become one of the most high profile charter captains in Bermuda until his death in 1990, was introduced into the business by Milton Pitman.

Roy Taylor's *Wally II*, Charles Christianson's *Troubador*, Bert Darrell's *Porpoise* and *Pompano*, Milton Pitman's *Marlin* (bought from General Glancey), and Russell Young's *Sea Wolfe* were among the best known of the early charter boats in Bermuda from around 1950.

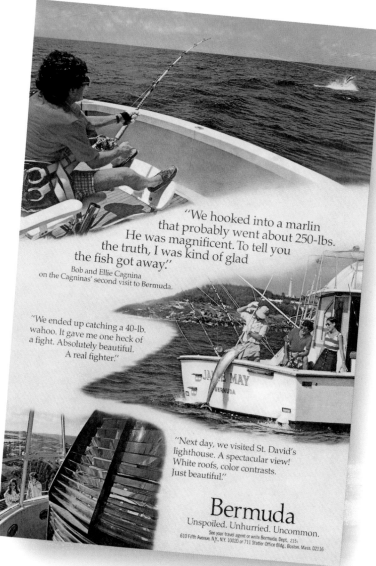

Dedicated marlin fishing in Bermuda took off in the 1970s as charter fishermen began to offer a wider variety of gamefishing opportunities for the tourist trade in particular. This 1976 Department of Tourism advertisement exploited, and promoted, Bermuda's growing reputation as a high quality gamefishing centre within a few hours flying time from its main tourist markets along the east coast of North America.

Troubadour *(left)*, Coral Sea *(centre)*, *and* Sea Wolfe *(right)*, *three well known gamefishing charter boats in Bermuda at a 1971 tournament weigh-in.*
(Photo courtesy of Captain Keith Winter.)

Louis L. Mowbray

Apart from establishing a local aquarium of worldwide renown and gaining a commensurate international reputation as an aquarium expert, Louis L. Mowbray was the first individual of standing in Bermuda to recognize the potential for offshore gamefishing in local waters.

Louis Leon Arthur Mowbray (Louis L. Mowbray) was born in St George's in 1878. He was the son of William Arthur Mowbray, originally from New Orleans and arrived in Bermuda in 1870, and Mary Ann Brown from St George's. Mowbray suffered from numerous childhood ailments. He was prescribed 'plenty of fresh air' for their relief.

Consequently he 'spent his early days running around barefooted and wearing fewer clothes than children of those days were accustomed'. Among his pursuits was 'collecting every specimen of fish and shell that he could find', so that he 'amassed a very large collection of Bermuda fauna' well before his 18th birthday.

Married in 1907 to Hilda Higginbothom (who died in October 1951), also from St George's, their first child was a son, Louis Septaine Mowbray (Louis S. Mowbray), born in January 1909, died in March 1976. A second son, Territ (Terry), was born in 1911.

In 1895 Louis L. Mowbray went to Rochester, New York, to study photography with Kodak. Returning to Bermuda he bought a studio and started a photography business, introducing, apparently, 'the first pictorial postcards in Bermuda'.

Adjacent to his photo studio, Mowbray maintained a room for his growing collection of Bermuda fauna which 'attracted the attention of many visitors', including scientists who took away duplicates of many specimens 'new to science'. The same scientists, in return, sent Mowbray the four volume set of *Fishes of Middle and North America*, which he studied assiduously 'until the four volumes had been gone over many times from cover to cover'. Another cherished gift was Nicholson's *Natural History*. These books would become the literary touchstones of Mowbray's devotion to the natural sciences throughout the remainder of his 75 year life.

Mowbray was eventually invited to become an associate of the Bermuda Biological Station, working on a broad range of subjects related primarily to marine biology.

In 1905 Mowbray participated in the first small motor boat crossing of the Atlantic west to east on a voyage to deliver the motor torpedo boat *Gregory* from Perth Amboy, New Jersey to Sevastopol in Russia. During his seven months abroad, 'he visited and studied at the Biological Station in Sevastopol, the Berlin and Hamburg Aquariums, and at the New York Aquarium on the return trip'.

Shortly after his return to Bermuda, Mowbray was employed by Dr Tarlton Bean who was visiting Bermuda to accumulate a collection for the Field Museum of Chicago. Subsequently, and on the strength of recommendations from Dr Bean, Mowbray, together with Goodwin Gosling from Bermuda, started up an aquarium at Agar's Island, the northern island adjacent to Two Rock Passage at the western end of Hamilton Harbour.

In 1910, a year in which he rediscovered the cahow, long thought to be extinct in Bermuda, Mowbray went to Boston to set up and manage the Boston City Aquarium until 1911. From there he moved to become Superintendent of the New York City Aquarium in Battery Park, until 1919.

With the support of John Oliver La Gorce at the National Geographic, and funded by James A. Allison, Mowbray went on to build and assume the post of curator at the Miami Aquarium. James Allison eventually sold the aquarium to property developers. Mowbray returned to his previous position at the New York City Aquarium.

Mowbray named the Allison tuna after his Miami Aquarium mentor, in the belief that it was a separate species from the yellowfin tuna. Although it has since been recognized to be the same species, the yellowfin still bears the alternative moniker of Allison tuna.

After 1925 Mowbray travelled on expeditions to Cuba, Florida, the Bahamas, Central America, and the Gulf of California, to collect specimens. In 1926 he returned to Bermuda to instigate and oversee construction of the aquarium at Flatts. The penguins originally bred at the aquarium (the first penguins ever bred in captivity) were brought from the Galapagos Islands by the American multimillionaire and naturalist Mr Vincent Astor with whom Mowbray travelled on at least three expeditions.

Mowbray remained as curator to the Bermuda Aquarium until bad health (a result of overwork because of staff shortages occasioned by the war) forced him to retire in September 1943. He died on 5 June 1952.

Louis S. Mowbray

Louis S. Mowbray continued his father's lifelong interest in marine life and natural sciences in general, taking over from him as curator of the aquarium from 1943 to 1969.

As well as pioneering gamefishing (and especially bonefishing) in Bermuda, Louis S. Mowbray was also the local representative for the International Game Fish Association (IGFA). While his father had already surmised that Bermuda offered excellent gamefishing possibilities, Louis S. Mowbray subsequently engaged with fishing in Bermuda most actively to develop its recreational and commercial potential.

Mowbray was instrumental in articulating and promoting the qualities of Bermuda's offshore gamefishing opportunities. He identified those pelagic species (especially tuna, wahoo, and amberjack) that were abundant but still hardly touched by sportfishermen in Bermuda before the 1950s.

In his paper 'The Commercial and Game Fishing Industries of Bermuda', presented at the Gulf and Caribbean Fisheries Institute meeting in Florida in 1949, Mowbray noted:

> Game fishing in Bermuda has had many set-backs since its commencement in 1934. The trade was just about getting in its stride in the summer of 1939 when the advent of World War II terminated all sport fishing activity abruptly.
>
> At that time there were about a dozen boats engaged in charter fishing, and a few of the guides were developing into really first-class men in their trade. Immediately upon the declaration of war most of the boats were taken over by one of the Services, and the skippers were drafted into something else. In consequence, many of the craft suffered irreperable damage due to careless handling and neglect and it was not until 1946 that the few good ones left were turned back into the fishing trade.

Mowbray noted that there were 'about eight boats suitable for offshore charter', and that, while none had 'what may be termed luxurious appointments', they were 'adequately equipped for going ahead with the business'. All the boats had 'fishing chairs, and a minimum of three full sets of rods and reels, etc., and most are fitted with outriggers'.

The gallery of gamefish in Bermuda's offshore waters identified by Mowbray is of some interest for the degrees of importance, abundance, and quality he attached to each.

Blue marlin and white marlin are fairly common, though seldom fished for. The only specimen known of an Atlantic black marlin was caught at Bermuda, and was described as a completely new species. It is called *Makaira bermudae*. The fish was 10 ft. 3 ins. long and weighed 305 lbs. The big-eyed tuna and Allison tuna, as well as a few blue-fin are found, the former being here the year round. Albacore, Oceanic bonito, little tunny, wahoo, dolphin, barracuda, three species of amberjack (one reaching 180 lbs.), mackerel, Bermuda chub, bonefish, pompano, yellowtail, skip-jack, blue runner, hard-head jack, and grey snapper cover about all of the important species . . . Tarpon, cobia, and broadbill swordfish have been recorded, but their appearance is so infrequent that they are never listed. Even the American bluefish appears at intervals, a fine one of 15 lbs being taken during 1949 [by a commercial fisherman while trolling in from his pots]. Surprisingly, kingfish and Spanish mackerel are not here.

The chub (or rudder fish as it is sometimes known) is afforded pride of place as 'the most potentially important small game fish of Bermuda waters'. From other writings it seems that Mowbray had almost as much admiration for the chub as he did for bonefish. Today most fishermen consider chub to be a lower caste species, of dubious commercial value, and a general nuisance when fishing for more pukka quality fish.

From around 1947 sportfishing offshore became increasingly popular. Angling tournaments started up, fishing reports appeared in the sports section of the daily newspaper, and Bermuda began to promote itself as a prime fishing location for visiting sportfishermen.

At the beginning of August 1947 the first post-war fishing tournament was held, the Belmont Bermuda Game Fishing Tournament. Prizes in the tournament totalled $5000, a considerable sum of money in those days and equivalent to at least $50,000 today. Louis S. Mowbray noted at the time that 'there are big fish in Bermuda but up to the present time little effort has been made to go after them'. Mowbray cited 'tuna', oceanic bonito, and amberjack, as well as wahoo and blue marlin as the most game species in local waters offshore.

'Record' catches of gamefish in Bermuda had been made before 1950, but several of them were by handline or net (seine) and therefore not eligible for IGFA consideration. The local records for various

The first post-war fishing tournament in Bermuda was held in August 1947, the Belmont Bermuda Game Fishing Tournament. By the 1960s fishing tournaments were an established part of the summer sporting scene. Many international angling clubs competed with local clubs such as Blue Waters, pictured here at the weigh-in of a 1979 tournament. (Photo courtesy of Captain Allen DeSilva.)

gamefish just before the Belmont Bermuda tournament were as shown in the table, according to Louis S. Mowbray (from *The Royal Gazette*, 16 July 1947):

Fish	Date	Weight	Captor	Method
Amberfish	1946	171 lb	Harry Stubbs	Handline
Horse-eye Bonito	n.a.	54 lb	Fred Burrows	Rod
Barracuda	1945	52 lb	J. Pitman	Seine
Bonefish	1939	17 lb	S. Pitcher	Seine
Dolphin	1938	28 lb	Harry Truran	Rod
Bermuda Marlin	1927	320 lb	Trotter Fox	Harpoon
Blue Marlin	1938	121½ lb	J. Mustard	Rod
White Marlin	1936	66 lb	C. Christianson	Rod
Allison Tuna	1938	140 lb	Bernard Smith	Rod
Bluefin Tuna	1945	180 lb	M.H. Porterfield	Rod
Bermuda Tuna	1935	32 lb	L.S. Mowbray	Rod
Wahoo	1936	101 lb	H.J. Tucker, Sr.	Rod
Rockfish	1947	150 lb	Frank Ray	Handline

Several fish taken by means other than rod and reel in Bermuda exceeded the world records for that time. The world record for 'amberfish' (amberjack) at that time was just 106 lb. Harry Stubbs had taken a 171 lb fish, but by handline. A 17 lb bonefish caught by net comfortably exceeded the official world record of 13¾ lb. The nub of the report was to suggest that, once gamefishing was more highly developed in Bermuda, there would be abundant large fish to catch.

'Bermuda Marlin' was considered to be a species of marlin indigenous to Bermuda. From *The Royal Gazette* of 29 July 1947: 'The Marlin, Makaira, has also been taken here, the most unusual one having a length of ten feet one inch which was harpooned by Mr. Trotter Fox of St. David's Island. It had an exceedingly high dorsal fin and a deep body. Mr. Louis L. Mowbray, former Curator of the Government

Aquarium and father of the present Curator [Louis S. Mowbray], named it *Makaira bermudae*.'

In Beebe and Tee-Van's *Field Book of the Shore Fishes of Bermuda and the West Indies* from 1933, *Makaira bermudae* is called 'Bermuda Spearfish'. The name marlin did not appear to be in use at that time. Its distribution was said to be, 'Off shore Bermuda waters; the only known specimen was taken in 1927 [by Fox] on the northern shore of Castle Harbor. . .The species is known only from an abbreviated description and a foreshortened photograph.'

In *The Commercial and Game Fishing Industries of Bermuda*, Louis S. Mowbray identifies *Makaira bermudae* as 'black marlin'. He notes: 'The only specimen known of an Atlantic black marlin was caught at Bermuda, and was described [by Mowbray] as a completely new species. It is called *Makaira bermudae*. The fish was 10 ft. 3 ins. long and weighed 305 lbs.'

In his later (1965) booklet, *A Guide to the Reef, Shore and Game Fish of Bermuda*, Mowbray does not list this species, suggesting that its identity by that time may have been subsumed into the category of Atlantic blue marlin.

In fact, black marlin are exclusive to the Pacific and Indian Oceans. The true black marlin has a rather low dorsal fin and short bill. Atlantic blue marlin have a higher dorsal fin, which tallies with the original description of *Makaira bermudae* ('It had an exceedingly high dorsal fin . . .'), and its bill is longer than the black marlin's. *Makaira bermudae* may, alternatively, have actually been a swordfish, which are regularly taken by harpoon in other places and even today occasionally caught by Bermuda fishermen.

The evolution of the scientific naming of the Atlantic blue marlin includes '*Makaira bermudae* – Mowbray, 1931' but goes on to various subsequent modifications (including '*Orthocraeros bermudae* – Smith, 1956') before *Makaira nigricans* used today.

Other interesting inclusions in Mowbray's list of records are bluefin tuna and 'Bermuda tuna'. The occasional occurrence of bluefin in Bermuda waters has been known for many years. The early gamefishing article cited previously mentions 'tuna weighing up to 400 pounds', which is well within the size range for bluefin and towards the upper limit for bigeye tuna. Both the bluefin and the bigeye are found throughout the Atlantic but are not common in Bermuda waters.

A *Royal Gazette* report from 29 July 1947 reveals the origin of a large bluefin catch in Bermuda. 'The largest of the game fishes, or those most sought by the angler, are the Great Tunnies, *Thunnus*. The largest specimen ever taken in these waters was taken in Mullet Bay, St George's, and weighed between 300 and 400 lbs. It was found stranded in a mullet net by John Bartram.' This was almost certainly a bluefin (*Thunnus thynnus*), but how it came to be tangled in a net used to catch an inshore fish like mullet must be anyone's guess.

The record 'Bermuda tuna' weight of 32 lb suggests that this fish was either a blackfin tuna (*Thunnus atlanticus*) or, more probably, an oversized little tuna (*Euthynnus alletteratus*), known in Bermuda as 'mackerel', 'false albacore', or 'bonito'. Blackfin may exceed 40 lb, but *E. alletteratus* rarely exceed 35 lb. Blackfin, moreover, are universally recognized by that name, while the 'Bermuda tuna' has several common local names that distinguish its ubiquitous Bermudian status.

Louis S. Mowbray not only raised the profile of gamefishing locally, by his writings and, later, by his ZBM (local radio) broadcasts, he also attracted visitors to the island, inviting his North American friends to come down to enjoy the sport. Through his close personal involvement with the aquarium and with international associations from it related to the natural sciences, Mowbray was able to extend the influence of Bermuda as a gamefishing venue far beyond the horizons of the island itself.

Throughout the 1950s and 1960s Louis S. Mowbray continued to promote Bermuda as a gamefishing centre of potential excellence, although it was only then maturing into adolescence. In 1950 he, along with other charter founding members (Ambrose Gosling, Jay Gould, W.W. Anderson, Harry Smith, Louis L. Mowbray, James Pearman, J. Elliott Cutter, *et al.*), regenerated The Bermuda Anglers Club 'which was started in the Colony before the war' (*The Royal Gazette*, 7 May 1950).

Apart from his activities in Bermuda, Mowbray was a member of the British Empire Tuna Fishing Team for eight years. In 1956, at the Wedgeport (Nova Scotia) Tuna Tournament, fishing for giant bluefin tuna, he fought a 614 lb fish for six hours. Despite the loss of handles on the reel (through breakage) for the final hour, Mowbray eventually landed the fish.

In the late 1960s Mowbray became increasingly concerned about the fate of Bermuda's hind population which was by then becoming fished more intensively as the larger groupers were becoming increasingly scarce. In a July 1969 interview he noted, 'Years ago, the hamlet was Bermuda's most sought after fish. Now they are scarce [because of] overfishing by both commercial and amateur fishermen . . . During the hamlet boom the hind was scorned, it was too small a fish to bother with. Now, with the hamlet seldom seen in large quantities, commercial fishermen and amateurs have turned to the smaller hind.'

Although Mowbray was inherently against government intervention in the fisheries, he acknowledged with increasing frequency, and insistence, that it might ultimately be necessary in order to protect certain fish stocks from overfishing.

Commercial fishermen around that time also began to alert the government about the depopulation of the hind which were being taken in great numbers during their spring and summer spawning period. As a direct result of those concerns, legislation (The Fisheries [Prohibited Areas and Prohibited Period] Order of 1971) was subsequently enacted to protect spawning hind populations. The benchmark Fisheries Act 1972 and related Fisheries Regulations 1972 followed soon after.

Mowbray was instrumental in starting the Bermuda Fisheries Research Programme in conjunction with the Biological Station and the Trade Development Board. (Terry Mowbray, his brother, was a prominent member of the Trade Development Board.) He was also responsible for the creation of the Coral Reef Preserves Act of 1966, which provided sanctuarial protection for three areas of Bermuda's reef. He was awarded the OBE in 1960, became a curator of the Waikiki Aquarium in Hawaii on an exchange basis in 1965, and in the 1970s advised the Seychelles government on its fishing programme. Louis S. Mowbray retired as curator of the Bermuda Aquarium at the end of 1968. He died in March 1976.

Bermuda Anglers Club weigh in at the 1973 Bermuda International Light Tackle Tournament: (left) Norbert Monish; (centre) 'Pete' Perinchief; and (right) Jack Warwick.
(Bermuda News Bureau. Photo courtesy of Captain Keith Winter.)

'Pete' Perinchief

Another bonefishing and all-round gamefishing aficionado from the 1950s and 1960s, S. L. 'Pete' Perinchief, from the Department of Tourism, headed up the Bermuda Fishing Information Bureau (now defunct) which had been originated by Mike Fountain as an initiative to promote Bermuda's tourist industry.

Perinchief in some respects took over the baton from Louis S. Mowbray for the promotion of gamefishing in Bermuda from the 1960s through the 1980s, although as a sportsman and tourism specialist rather than as a sportsman cum natural sciences specialist as Mowbray was.

'Bermuda – Island of Great Fishing', a pamphlet written by Perinchief and first printed in the 1960s, describes with unbridled enthusiasm the range of gamefishing options in Bermuda, the types of fish available, and where, how, and when to catch them. Perinchief hoists his tourism-angling pennant with some pride by his opening statement, 'Bermuda has gained an enviable reputation among the outstanding angling centres of the world – and rightly so!'

The transition from the Mowbray to the Perinchief era reflected the transition of fishing in Bermuda from infancy through childhood under Mowbray's tutelage, to adolescence and adulthood with Perinchief's promotional talents.

Both had a passion for sportfishing which, in different ways, meshed with their professional careers: Mowbray as an internationally renowned natural scientist, and Perinchief as a director of Bermuda's tourism industry. Mowbray, and his father, sowed the seeds of possibilities that Bermuda was a bountifully endowed point of convergence of gamefish in the Western Atlantic. Perinchief, and others, cultivated those possibilities into fuller fruition for Bermuda to reap the economic rewards.

Deep sea gamefishing in Bermuda at the end of the 1950s, while attaining a degree of maturity, was still new enough to provide a frisson of adventure for newsworthy figures. *The Royal Gazette Weekly* reported the following on Saturday 8 October 1960:

Governor to Fish

The Governor, Major-General Sir Julian Gascoigne, and his a.d.c., Captain David Gordon-Lennox, will board Mr. Roland Lines' 38-ton motor yacht 'Baroki' at 5 p.m. today for an overnight fishing trip to the Argus Bank. They will return to Hamilton tomorrow.

By the 1960s tourism had become a pillar of Bermuda's economic growth and stability. Sportfishing and tourism were natural bedfellows. The charter fishing industry was well established by the mid-1960s, thriving on the rapid growth in numbers of affluent tourist visitors to Bermuda.

The local population, however, was also thriving, becoming more affluent, and buying larger, more powerful boats that could be used for gamefishing offshore.

From the mid-1960s onwards the offshore waters of Bermuda became an extended recreation ground for fishermen in Bermuda. As the economic horizon expanded, so, too, did the fishing horizon. At least as far as the banks. Periods of recession in the economy have slowed the growth of gamefishing around the island as tourist numbers have fallen, and, more importantly, the spending power of tourists has declined. Local residents, however, have taken to their boats in increasing numbers to swell the ranks of charter boats fishing the banks and around the edge of the Bermuda Platform.

The number of charter fishing boats in Bermuda has now stabilized at around 20 regular operators. The number of small boats owned by residents, however, has continued to rise, with several thousand craft now moored around Bermuda used at some time or other for offshore gamefishing.

A good day's fishing in anyone's books! Yellowfin tuna, blackfin tuna, skipjack tuna, dolphin, and friends. (Photo courtesy of Flybridge Tackle.)

Wahoo, Allison and other species of tuna (primarily blackfin and oceanic bonito), white and blue marlin, amberjack, and dolphin constitute the bulk of the catch for offshore gamefishing anglers in Bermuda, just as Louis S. Mowbray suggested they would 50 years ago.

Industrial fishing for yellowfin tuna since the 1970s and 1980s, however, has depleted their numbers in the Western Atlantic. Around Bermuda their appearance in the spring and summer months occurs in regular runs of fish that diminish and increase sporadically, but their overall abundance is not what it was in the 1960s and 1970s. The fish also appear to be smaller on average than in years gone by, probably as a result of predation of the species globally by factory ships taking tonnes of fish from the sea in a single haul. Allison tuna is nevertheless considered the prize non-billfish target for amateur anglers chumming or trolling around the banks: during a good run, a boat may count a dozen fish landed as an average day's fishing.

If Allison tuna is the premium non-billfish species in Bermuda waters, wahoo constitutes the steady all-round favourite for its largely undiminished numbers. Since wahoo is not targeted by the world's industrial fishing fleets, the stock of fish around Bermuda has remained fairly constant as gamefishing has developed. Anglers (and commercial fishermen) can usually depend on wahoo to tighten their lines and buckle their rods at any time of the year while Allison and other species appear seasonally.

For some years now tag-and-release has been the norm in marlin fishing in Bermuda. This small blue marlin is about to be tagged in its shoulder as the angler brings it close to the boat. (Photo courtesy of Captain Allen DeSilva.)

Blue marlin figure prominently on the hit-list of some gamefishing regulars now. Tackle and methods used to catch marlin have become more sophisticated and hook-ups more frequent. Boats regularly go out 'marlin fishing' with the specific intent of landing a 'big blue', to the exclusion of other gamefish. Nowadays, however, tag and release is the universal practice when marlin are caught, so that few specimens other than potential record breakers ever get landed ashore as trophy fish.

Explosion of Recreational Fishing

As the early pioneers predicted, the gamefishing grounds off Bermuda now attract a steady ebb and flow of recreational fishing boats,

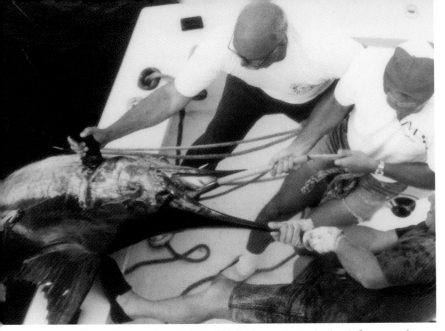

Above: Hauling aboard a 350–380 lb blue marlin, in the days before tag-and-release was common practice. **Right:** *The full size marlin hoisted aloft on the dock, with angler. (Photos courtesy of Andrew Card.)*

especially on summer weekends when Challenger Bank is often corralled by a string of boats hanging anchored off its edge and furrowed by a flotilla of others trolling over its crown.

One of the dangers of this proliferation in numbers of boats is that the offshore waters around Bermuda, and around the banks especially, may become too intensively fished. Since amateur fishermen are not required to keep a log of their catches, there is virtually no hard evidence of overfishing the offshore grounds. Anecdotal evidence (along the line of comments such as, 'The banks are fished out') is inconclusive. There is always the danger, however, that stocks of pelagic fish offshore may be diminished, even by the relatively small fleet of recreational fishing boats cruising Bermuda waters, especially since local boats have virtually open access to the offshore fishing grounds.

Demersal foodfish species (groupers, snappers, and other bottom fish) have always been most at risk from overfishing and other environmental disturbances. Increased numbers of gamefishing amateurs might also constitute a long-term risk to pelagics like tuna and wahoo, especially if there is a resident population of these fish that does not migrate away from local waters.

Commercial fishermen have diversified towards the pelagic species since the 1990 fish pot ban, fishing the same waters as gamefishermen and putting even more pressure on offshore species.

The growth of recreational gamefishing, together with the fish pot ban, has shifted the centre of gravity of Bermuda's fishery away from the platform, further offshore. Just as offshore gamefishing has blossomed, commercial fishermen have been forced to reduce their dependence on the traditional reef fishery to compete for the same offshore pelagics targeted by larger numbers of recreational fishermen.

Species	Jan	Feb	Mar	Apr	May	Jun	Jul	Aug	Sep	Oct	Nov	Dec
Blue Marlin	●	●	●	●	●	●	●	●	●	●	●	●
White Marlin	●	●	●	●	●	●	●	●	●	●	●	●
Sailfish	●	●	●	●	●	●	●	●	●	●	●	●
Spearfish	●	●	●	●	●	●	●	●	●	●	●	●
Yellowfin Tuna	●	●	●	●	●	●	●	●	●	●	●	●
Wahoo	●	●	●	●	●	●	●	●	●	●	●	●
Dolphin	●	●	●	●	●	●	●	●	●	●	●	●

● Excellent ● Good ● Fair ○ Not Available

Although this chart suggests that wahoo are 'not available' around Bermuda in January and February, it would be more accurate to say that wahoo are less abundant in the winter months, rather than absent altogether. Wahoo is one of the few species of gamefish caught year-round by fishermen in Bermuda. (Reproduced by permission of the publishers of Marlin – The International Sportfishing Magazine.)

Sportfishing enthusiasts need no fishing permits and are virtually unregulated except by restrictions on species and closed areas and seasons. Commercial fishermen, who are licensed and highly regulated, argue that the amateurs should be similarly regulated, especially as they fish increasingly around the same common grounds for the same fish.

Bonefishing

In *The Commercial and Game Fishing Industries of Bermuda*, Louis S. Mowbray comments at some length on the excellence of bonefishing in Bermuda, the relatively large size of the fish, their habitat, and the most appropriate bait for catching them.

> Bonefish run very large in these waters, commercial fishermen having seined [netted] them weighing 17 lbs. The average is nearer 9 lbs., though many fish of 11 and 12 lbs. have been taken. Very few local persons fish for them, though quite a number are caught on handlines while fishing for spot [whitewater] snappers in the grassy areas. They have been taken in waters from a few feet to twelve fathoms, though anglers seldom select an off-shore spot for their fishing for bonefish.

Mowbray's personal correspondence reveals his affection for and interest in bonefishing. In a letter to an American friend, J. Eliot Cutter, from late August 1937, he writes: 'Four or five nights ago I went fishing with . . . for bonefish and we got two beauties, one weighing 12 lbs., and the other 11 lbs . . . I certainly wish you had been with us to enjoy the fun but we hope, now that we have located the spot they frequent, to give you some good fishing. The only disadvantage is that we catch them at night. We caught the two mentioned about 10 p.m., just as the moon came up.'

A few months later, in another letter to Cutter: 'I am very glad to know that you are coming down and looking forward to getting you out among the bone fish some evening. The depth at which I am catching them is about 10 to 12 feet, and about 25 yards from the shore.'

After the war, in a letter to a friend at *The Miami Herald*, from November 1948, Mowbray recounted further memorable bonefishing experiences.

> Just a few lines to let you know that things are really beginning to percolate here in Bermuda along the bonefishing front. You may remember that I said we get lots of big ones here at times. Well, fella, they sure are on the take at present.
>
> A couple of weeks ago a local chap fishing with a handline for something for the pan got two fine ones during the early evening. They weighed $10\frac{1}{4}$ and $11\frac{1}{2}$ pounds. In talking this over with another night fisherman he mentioned that he knew a place close by the Aquarium (and only 200 yds from my own house) where he nearly always got one when fishing for porgy and gray snappers, and also that he had caught one some years ago which looked a bit larger than others he had caught, and weighed it. It scaled SIXTEEN POUNDS.
>
> Always a sucker, I decided to try it myself on the evening of 1 Nov. (two nights ago). I was using my official three-six rod with six thread linen line, and worm for bait.

I got two beauties. One weighed in at TWELVE POUNDS NINE OUNCES, AND THE OTHER ELEVEN POUNDS SEVEN OUNCES. Not at all bad for an evening of fun. The former, incidentally, establishes a new World Record for six thread over the former record of 12 lbs 2½ ozs. Mine will not hold good for more than this month, I fear, as there are several fellows fishing for them now and it won't take much serious fishing to beat it.

A report in *The Royal Gazette* from May 1950 confirms the bounty of large bonefish in Bermuda waters around then. The angler was probably using slightly lighter tackle and line than Mowbray's 'three-six rod with six thread linen line', but the fish caught was not much smaller.

Record Bonefish Caught Yesterday
Eleven-Pound Fighter Landed After Hour Scrap

What may be a world's record Bonefish – depending upon what the nylon line used in catching it tests – was caught at Whale Bay yesterday by Frank Bailey, at present staying at Hampton Head [a large private residence in Southampton].

Frank Bailey, fishing with his brother Aubrey, and his friends Jay Gould and Donald Green, caught the fish at seven o'clock yesterday night after playing him for about an hour.

Using worm for bait, Frank fished for about an hour before getting a strike. The fish made four long runs and fought gallantly, taking about 200 yards of line off the reel with each run.

Mr. Bailey was using a short steel rod, a Penn reel, and nylon line. He did not know how much the line tested at, but if it tests at the equivalent of three-thread linen-line, he will have caught a world's record fish. One other strike was made but no further fish were caught.

Bailey comes of a Bonefish-catching family. Last year his brother Aubrey caught a Bonefish in Bermuda weighing 12½ pounds.

Bonefishing has never attracted a crowd among Bermuda's fishermen. Cognoscenti such as Mowbray, Pete Perinchief, and others around the same time, were on their own to seek out bonefish mainly around the shallow flats along the shoreline. Mowbray continues:

The greatest handicap at present for the visiting fisherman is that no one is engaged in the [bonefishing] guide business, and it invariably falls upon one or two of us, who do fish for bones occasionally, to take time off to show them several places, etc.

My fish were caught from the shore and Cutters from the beach while wading. No boats are necessary in most cases, really all one needs is transportation – which may be either by bicycle, bus, or taxi – to any one of several areas. All [areas] are within very easy reach of most of the hotels and guest houses . . .

Later.

Johnny Cutter and Mr. Lee have just brought in the new bonefish to be weighed in officially by me as the local representative of I.G.F.A. [International Game Fishing Association] Here are a few of the specifications for your blue book. Total length 32 inches, girth 16¾ inches, weight TWELVE POUNDS FOUR OUNCES exactly, and caught on three thread linen line. Rod was a Tycoon Regal Bonefish, and reel was the 185 Penn Bonefish. That sure tears all to hell the three thread record of eight pounds three ounces.

Bermuda: Island of Great (bone-)Fishing

Pete Perinchief, another devotee of bonefishing, affords the bonefish pride of place in his pamphlet 'Bermuda: Island of Great Fishing', allotting two and a half pages to a description of local bonefishing conditions and qualities. Other gamefish in the pamphlet, while generously eulogized, are conceded a page of space, at most.

Few fishermen doubt that the bonefish is one of the outstanding small game fish. Early in May, these wary fish commence to move into shore water, and from then until mid-July bait will be the best means for taking them. From mid-July until the end of October, and frequently well into November, prize battlers will tear up the bottom to get at well presented and skillfully manipulated artificial lures. Bait will work equally well during those times, but it cannot be denied that fishing for bonefish with lures is much more enjoyable.

Bonefish are primarily inshore fish, trawling the shallow flats around the island, grubbing for food around sandy bottoms. Less frequently they roam offshore around the outer reefs, especially during the cooler months of the year when many inshore fish move further out. Spinning tackle has been the traditional means of taking bonefish, with a minimum of 200 yards of 6–8 lb test monofilament on the spool. Flyfishing for bonefish now also appears to be gaining adherents.

For the bonefishing angler using bait rather than an artificial lure, Perinchief recommends a 20 lb test leader of about 18 inches, a small swivel, a 3/0–4/0 size Mustad Beak hook (which has the point bent inwards slightly, like a beak), and a half ounce to one ounce weight egg-shaped sinker to hold the line in position on the bottom if there is a strong tide.

When a bonefish takes a bait, the angler waits a short while for the baited hook to settle in the mouth of the fish. He then strikes sharply to set the hook. With a lure, the angler strikes to set the hook as soon as the fish takes it.

In both instances, the fish will explode into a run that will denude any reel carrying less than 150 yards of line. A large fish (over 8–10 lb) may well strip off 200 yards or more in its first flight. The angler is advised to 'ease the drag slightly until the run is under control, then use firm but fine judgement and tighten the drag (Not too much!), and go to work on the fish. Repeat the procedure for all additional runs.'

Bonefishing is as close to skilled angling as inshore fishing in Bermuda gets. Good knowledge of the tackle, patient stalking of the fish, a sure touch with the cast, the confidently jigged retrieval of the line towards the fish, and finesse with the drag lever to play the hooked fish are the hallmarks that distinguish the sterling silver bonefish angler from the more rough hewn stock of other fishermen.

Pompano Fishing in the Surf

Fishing for pompano (palometa) has qualities similar to bonefishing: similar tackle, casting skills, and the excitement of a small but pugnacious gamefish taken on light tackle.

Mowbray notes:

Shore fishing is mainly a summer sport owing to the fact that, with the exception of the bonefish, pompano, and sennet, most species migrate off-shore in the winter months. The pompano referred to is that species which is often known elsewhere as the gafftopsail, palometa, or longfin pompano. It is found in the surf along most of the southern shore of Bermuda, and takes a bait, fly, or other artificial lures quite readily. Its great gameness on light tackle needs no further comment, nor does its palatability as a dish for the table. The average size is about 12 ounces, though specimens as large as $3\frac{1}{2}$ lbs. have been taken on occasion.

When tourism to Bermuda was in its infancy, the beaches around the island were sparsely populated. Surf fishing for pompano, in peaceful solitude, was easy for the light tackle pompano specialist. Not so today when many more visitors to the island, and residents, speckle the beaches, and surf, from May till October.

The places left quiet for pompano fishing are fewer. Like bonefishing, however, surf fishing in Bermuda attracts a rather small band of dedicated followers who will always find an isolated spot to cast, waist deep in the surf, away from the tanning crowds.

A Year in the Life of a Bermuda Gamefishing Captain

Captain Allen's Weekly Fishing Report 1999
by Captain Allen DeSilva ('Mako 4')

11 April

The first week of April saw good weather, lots of humpback whales and moderate fishing. Trolling is producing scattered wahoo action, with fish between 15–70 lbs, while small yellowfin tuna (15–30 lbs) are being caught by chumming. This is the beginning of Bermuda's fishing season, and the fishing will improve with every passing day.

18 April

A bad week for fishing. A small craft warning's been up up all week, with winds at 15–30 knots. For the brave fishermen that did go out a few days, there was some fair wahoo and yellowfin tuna fishing. The good news is that the weather has broken and should be good the next couple of days, allowing the fleet to get out and find the hot spots. Tuna and wahoo fishing is improving every day. It shouldn't be long before the first marlin of the year is spotted.

25 April

The third week of the fishing season produced some good catches. Wahoo catches of up to 14 fish a day were reported, with some nice size fish like the 76 pounder caught by Mr. Felthan on the 'Mako 4'. The yellowfin are still small (15–30 lbs) . . . As I predicted, the first billfish were seen this week, although all white marlins. I'm sure the blues aren't far behind. The weather has improved greatly and water temperature has reached the low 70s.

2 May

The last week of April saw some good wahoo fishing, with catches of 10 or more fish not uncommon. Frank Feltan, fishing with us on Wednesday, caught the largest wahoo for the season so far – a 114 pounder!! The yellowfin tuna are still small and few, but the billfish are starting to make a showing. We released a small spearfish this week, plus pulled the hook on a 70 lb white marlin close to the boat. Also had a shot at a 400 lb blue . . . With the beginning of May will come the first blue marlin of the season, which is usually a big fish. I guess we'll have to wait and see if the blues make me out to be a liar.

9 May

Well, May is here and so are the fish. What a week! As I predicted, the first blue for the year was caught. PLUS the second and the third! A lucky fisherman, in a 22 ft Aquasport, caught and released the first blue, a 400 pounder. Later in the week there was a 500 pounder, and then a 550 pounder caught. The 550 lb blue was caught on our headboat, the 'Eureka', with our able crew Captains David Soares and Big Jeff. (It looks like it's going to be another big blue marlin year for Bermuda, by the size of what we've seen so far.) THE YELLOWFIN ARE HERE!!! Good tuna fishing all week with catches of 10–25 fish a day, with some fish in the 40 lb range. Wahoo are also still biting well. Plus, inshore, the reef fishing and bonefishing has started. The best thing this week is the weather . . . flat calm all week . . . I mean ccccccalm!! Can't wait till next week.

16 May

The second week of May brought about the same amount of action as last week with the school of yellowfin tuna still biting nicely

(10–15 fish per trip). We caught a lot of the yellowfin this week on flying fish, rigged on the kite, plus casting a #109 Mirrolure was very productive on the spinning tackle. A few more blue marlin shots and some pick-up in the white marlin department was reported this week. The wahoo were being a real nuisance: always cruising in the chum slick, cutting off the mono[filament] rigs set for the tuna and staying well clear of anything that even *looked* like wire. We did manage to trick a few into biting though! Weather remained great up till Saturday, but it's raining today and forecast to last till Tuesday.

23 May

The third week of May continued to produce lots of action, mainly yellowfin tuna and wahoo. As the season begins to settle in, the schools of fish keep growing in size, with a guarantee that everyone on board will almost surely land a couple. The blue and white marlin still haven't started to show in large numbers, but it won't be long before we report some good catches.

30 May

The last week of May saw little change, with continued good yellowfin tuna fishing and some bigger fish showing up (40–90 lbs). Catches of 10 fish a day was the average, with good catches up to 25 fish. Wahoo are still being caught in good numbers, but the size is falling. (It's summer lizard time!) In case you didn't know, a 'lizard' is a small wahoo (10–20 lbs). One thing's for sure: the marlins ain't small! A few more blue marlin encounters this week. The best, a 700 pounder, was released by my best friend, also named Alan DeSilva, on his boat 'Treasure Isle'. Congratulations, Alan!

6 June

First week of June brought great weather again. Seas are flat, wind speeds less than 15 kts, and lots of sunshine (80F). Yellowfin tuna catches are good, with the average size increasing to about 30 lbs with 40–70 pounders mixed in. Our best tuna catch of the week was 23 tuna, with the largest at 72 lbs. Wahoo fishing is still okay, with a

few dolphins showing up. The white marlin have arrived!! Quite a few have been seen and caught within the last few days, but the blues are still few and far between. Hopefully I can report better blue marlin fishing next week.

13 June

Second week of June and the weather & fishing are GREAT!! Seas are still calm, with light winds most days. Temperatures are in the low 80s. The yellowfin tuna fishing is first class, with catches of 10–20 fish per trip (25–65 lbs). The best fishing is the chumming, which we do with 30 lb stand-up gear (lots of fun). The wahoo and white marlin remain a bit slow, but the blue marlin are picking up every day. We tagged and released a 550 lb blue on Tuesday and pulled the hook on another fish about the same size. There were blue strikes every day this week, with some catches but mostly 'losts'. (You know. . .usual blue marlin fishing!!) On the reef fishing scene, the [headboat] 'Eureka' reports better catches with snapper & triggerfish, but no sharks yet.

20 June

Third week of June was interrupted by tropical storm 'Arlene', but there was some good tuna fishing before then and blue marlin fishing picking up on the weekend. Our best catch of the week was Tuesday, with the O'Briens, who managed to catch 28 yellowfin tuna plus 3 wahoo, as well as an assortment of rainbow runners and bonitos. The biggest blue of the week was a 700 pounder, released on the [boat] 'Chaos' (Good job, Brooks!). Seas are back to flat calm, forecast to stay that way for some time. Temperatures on the climb, now in the mid-80s.

27 June

For a while I thought I wasn't going to have anything to write about this week. Fourth week of June was quiet, very little tuna, wahoo, or marlin to report . . . until the weekend. Saturday and Sunday brought some of the best marlin action we've seen so far this season. Finally, boats reported seeing 2 or 4 fish in a day, instead of the one here and one there. Hopefully the marlin season is finally off to a start. Better late than never! WATCH OUT WORLD CUP TOURNAMENT! Bermuda's blues are still running BIG!! Most fish seen are over 400 lbs. We were 1-for-3 today, releasing a 450 pounder in the morning, then losing a 700 pounder just 30 feet from the boat in the afternoon. Plus, raising another blue. That's not all too shabby a day! Well, I can't wait till next week: it's the week of the full moon, so it'll be HOT!!

4 July

Blue & white marlin bites have been good this week, plus the yellowfin tuna have returned. As many as 20 tuna a day were caught this week. 'Sea Wolfe' had a great week with the blues, but catch of the week goes to Kathine, on the 'Reel Action', for her 600 lb plus blue marlin release. (Great job, Kathine!) Sixteen boats fished the World Cup Tournament in Bermuda today, but no big blues caught, just 7 small blues (150–250 lbs). Oh well, we'll give it our best shot again next year! Seas are still flat, and it's hot, temperatures in the mid-80s. Seems that August weather has come early . . . and I love it! That's all for this week. I'm going to bed early, planning on terrorizing a few blues tomorrow . . .

11 July

Second week of July: calm seas, lots of tuna & marlin! The yellowfin tuna bite was good this week. Our best catch of 22 tuna went to Mr. Scully & crew (Great Day!!). Most days averaging 10 or more tuna. Blue marlin fishing was okay, but still room for improvement. Our CONGRATULATIONS go to Mr. Barnes for his first blue marlin release . . . Great job!

18 July

This week's report is MARLIN, MARLIN, MARLIN! Yes, the blues have arrived, with as many as 5 fish a day seen and still a good number of large fish (400–700 lbs). . .a special congratulations to 13 yr old Daniel

Dickinson for his 550 lb blue marlin release. Tuna and wahoo fishing is slow with very spotty catches reported by the fleet. Weather is still great and we have fished every day this month (I love it!). The marlin fishing will be the ticket for the rest of this month, plus all of August.

25 July

The week's fishing was interrupted by some wind for a few days. Rest of the week saw mainly blue marlin fishing, with still spotty wahoo & tuna action. Visiting boat 'Chaos' from Virginia had the catch of the week, on Tuesday, with 5 blues out of 7 shots, and one fish over 700 lbs. The rest of the fleet all reported stay marlin action for the week. With the full moon coming this Wednesday, next week should be RED HOT!! for the blues. (Don't waste any time fishing for anything else!) Next week is also the local Marlin Tournament and, with the extra effort focused on marlin, it promises to be the best marlin week of the year.

1 August

BAD WEATHER was the main even this week, stopping most of the fishing on the full moon week. Today there was a break in the winds and good action from the blue marlin. Most boats reported 3, 4 and even 5 shots at the blues. CHAOS was the name of the day today, with the visiting boat from Virginia ('Chaos') going 2-for-5 on blues. Plus the local boat 'Chaos' released a 400 pounder (one of many shots today), the last blue caught in the Marlin Tournament and enough to give them the win. 'Mako's' best marlin day was Thursday. We went 2-for-5, missing a shot at an 800+ pounder and releasing a 180 lb and a 325 lb. Also had some luck with the yellowfin tuna this week, no big catches but stay bites. 'Chaos' is going back home tomorrow. Sure going to miss all the 'Chaos' crew and wish them a safe trip back to Virginia. Looking forward to their return next July.

8 August

The week started off great, good marlin action and good weather. We had the privilege of having Dr. Eric Prince, from National Marine

Fisheries, on board Monday and Tuesday, and were successful in tagging 3 blue marlin with 5-day satellite tags. Unfortunately the weather didn't last: winds of 15–25 kts, and lots of rain, kept most of the fleet at the dock. Ourselves and a few other diehards fished the rest of the week in rough conditions, with some success: a few yellowfin, wahoo, and marlin.

15 August

WAHOO!! That's right, the wahoo have started to bite already. Catches of 4–6 a day are common, with 6–12 a day by the wahoo experts. Where have all the tuna gone? Everyone's on the hunt for the elusive yellowfin. Sure hope they show up soon. We had to cancel our trips on Monday & Tuesday, due to bad weather, but rest of the week was fine. Had some good fortune with the blues this week. Mr. Bentley Fondren was our luckiest angler, with 3 blue marlin releases in two days of fishing. Bentley's best catch was the 700 lb blue released on Friday.

22 August

Pretty quiet week, with some yellowfin tuna, some wahoo, and some marlin. No great catches reported by the fleet. Our best day was Friday, with Mr. Ed Murphy releasing three blues (180 lbs, 200 lbs, 270 lbs). Weather still great, calm seas & hot (85F water temp). We are happy to report that all marlin tagged with satellite tags on the 'Mako' (five fish in all) have reported back and are doing well!! Next week is full moon. Let's hope the weather stays fair so the fleet can get a good crack at the blues.

29 August

What a week! Surrounded by storms, but the fishing and the weather is great! Good wahoo fishing reported by the whole fleet. Our best wahoo catch was with Karen & Steve Smith: 16 wahoo plus a 46 lb

dolphin . . . The yellowfin remain slow, with a 70 pounder being the 'Mako's' weekly best. Not a lot of effort put into the marlin fishing, with the wahoo fishing so good, although we did manage to release a few. The catch of the week goes to ME!! That's right: on Friday we had a last minute cancellation so what do I decide to do on my day off? GO FISHING! I went out by myself on my 23 ft Seacraft, 'Rabbit Hunter', and while live bait fishing for wahoo, I hooked a 400 lb blue marlin on 30 lb test line. Well, after 2 hrs 20 mins., I grabbed the leader, held the fish alongside the boat, then released her and proudly watched her swim away. With the start of the live bait season, look forward to lots of great catches by the fleet (wahoo, yellowfin, dolphin, and marlin). Catches of 10 to 20 fish a day should be common.

5 September

Just another great week of fishing! The yellowfin tuna are back, adding to the fun. Blue marlin are thinning out, with just a few encounters reported this week. Congratulations to Michael & Roger for their combined effort to release a 250 lb blue on Monday, on light tackle. Great catches: on Thursday, Big John, Colin, and Steinar, fishing all day in the rain and thunder, managed to catch 10 wahoo, 6 tuna, 1 dolphin, & a few dragons (barracuda). On Sunday the Bennett's catch of 5 wahoo, 8 tuna, a 46 lb amberjack, &, yes, more dragons, was a fine end to the week for the 'Mako'. With the end of [hurricane] Dennis, we are seeing improvements in the weather and the swell flattening out. Live bait fishing will be the ticket for success the rest of the month. Expect great fishing right through this month, regardless of the weather.

12 September

Wahoo!! Wahoo!! and more wahoo!! That's this week's report. Wahoo catches in the double figures were commonly reported by the fleet this week. Some yellowfin & dolphin catches, but wahoo are the main game in town. Weather has been fine all week, even though the

Wahoo Tournament was cancelled today (Sunday) because of forecast 12–18 kt winds. A bad call: many boats fished today with good results (wahoo & yellowfin). The 'Mako' crew (Ricky, Lala & Feeds) had a sizeable side bet with the 'Challenger' crew for the boat that caught the most wahoo today. Even though the tournament was off, the bet was still on! AND THE RESULTS: 'Challenger' lost, 4 wahoo to 'Mako's 11. It was definitely Ricky's week as he fished with us on Wednesday and caught 8 wahoo, 3 yellowfin, 5 barracuda and a trusty old shark . . . great catches, Ricky! Blue marlin reports are slow, with all efforts focused on wahoo, but 'Challenger' did manage to release a 150 lb [blue marlin] while wahoo fishing, and there were a few other hook-ups reported around the fleet this week.

19 September

Hurricane Gert brought this week's fishing to an early end. There was some great yellowfin tuna fishing early in the week reported by the fleet (some fish up to 100 lbs), plus the usual good wahoo fishing (5–15 wahoo a day). Our best catch goes to SUPER Jeff Radke who caught 17 yellowfin (20–60 lbs – total gutted weight 540 lbs) all by himself on 30 lb stand-up tackle. (How's those blisters, Jeff? Great catch!!) Because of Gert, we probably will not fish again till mid-week. Well, let me go tie 'Mako' down . . .

26 September

Hurricane Gert missed us, but it did stop us fishing most of the week. First day of fishing was Friday, and I'm glad to report there's still some fish out there. Some good wahoo catches (5–12 fish) with some bigger wahoo showing up (40–60 pounders). The yellowfin tuna have shown up on the north side of Challenger, with fish ranging from 15–70 lbs. Lots of them jumping, but a little tricky getting them to bite! On Sunday, Brooks, on his boat 'Chaos', decided to go marlin fishing and hooked 3 blues. Not bad for late September. Weather is still great and seas have been calm for the most part, with temperatures still in the mid-80s. Water temperature continues to be 82F.

3 October

October is here, and with it some choppy seas & cooler air, but some good fishing. Catch of the week goes to Ricky's gang, Saturday, with 10 wahoo, 6 yellowfin & 5 dolphin (not bad!!). The biggest wahoo, 62 lbs, goes to Jeff Radke (nice one!!). We got blown out on Friday but managed to fish the rest of the week, with good results most days. Conditions, and the fishing, should remain the same for the rest of October, tapering off into November.

10 October

Lots of wind this week. We only fished Monday, Saturday & Sunday. Juan's trip on Monday saw some good wahoo fishing, with 8 wahoo, the biggest (70 lbs) caught by Juan himself. Plus, we even had a 150 lb blue marlin come and eat one of our live baits. Unfortunately the light wire leader broke after 15 mins. We fished with Richard Carrie on Saturday, and, even with an 11:30 AM start, he managed to catch 7 wahoo and some barracuda by himself (The Lone Angler!).

17 October

This was a tough week! The fleet struggled to catch some fish to keep clients happy. Mainly just a few wahoo & yellowfin caught. Weather's not bad for October, but the fishing is definitely not up to par! I hope the rest of October improves but, with the normal slow fishing of November just around the corner, I have my doubts.

24 October

No change! Fishing is still slow, with some good catches here and there, like Ricky & Lala's twin wahoo, at 69 lbs each. Plus, a few yellowfin around. Lucky Bermuda missed another hurricane (José). There's some advantage to being small! With the peak of the fishing season ending, and fewer boats fishing, it'll be difficult to get a true perspective of the fishing in the coming months.

7 November

It's the end of Bermuda's busy season, but there's still some good fishing offshore. Some good yellowfin tuna catches to the northeast as well as on Challenger. Wahoo catches are up and down with some dolphin caught at the same time. Believe it or not, there's been some blue and white marlin spotted . . . I guess they haven't left yet! The weather this time of year is more rough (15–25 kt) than calm.

14 November

STILL SOME GREAT FISHING HERE!! And to prove it, Hanish chartered the 'Mako' on Thursday, for his sister (who had never fished before), to show her some Bermuda fishing before her return to England. After good success with 4 wahoo & 11 yellowfin tuna, I decided to try our luck with the marlin (YES, in *November!*). My mate, Bigger James, set up the two 130s for the ride home, while Hanish made the piña coladas! After trolling just 10 mins., we got a double hook-up: one 40 lb yellowfin & one 200 lb blue marlin release by Allan DeSilva (no, not me, another Allan). A great day any time of the year! The rest of the fleet have all reported better tuna catches than in previous weeks.

24 December

With the holiday season upon us, you know there's not much fishing taking place! For those of us lucky enough to get out, there's still some good yellowfin tuna fishing. Forget any trolling as the seaweed is thick . . . everywhere! So, if you get out, plan to chum either to the northeast of the island or on the southeast of Challenger. Hopefully the seaweed will clear out by the New Year, as January can be a good month for the wahoo, but it'll be hard work if the seaweed persists. So, until next CENTURY: Have a very HAPPY HOLIDAY from 'Mako'.

Commercial Fishing in Bermuda

7

There's only two kinds of people who feed the world. Farmers. And fishermen.

A Somerset fisherman

As in the case of most small offshore islands with a growing resident population needing to be fed, Bermuda has, since its beginnings as a colony in the early seventeenth century, acknowledged the importance of fish as a source of food, and artisanal fishing as a source of full-time employment.

While the impact of World War II on Bermuda clearly launched major changes in the fishing industry. . .the year 1972 marked a turning point for Bermuda's marine resources when a new Fisheries Act was passed which led to an updating of Fisheries Regulations.

It was during this period of time [after 1972] that Bermuda's commercial fishery underwent a remarkable transition. Within just a bit more than one generation, what had been a traditionally artisanal, labour intensive, open-entry form of self-employment was changed into a competitive, efficient, capital intensive, limited entry system of small fishing businesses often family run vertical enterprises with high cash flows from direct wholesale and retail sales, eliminating most middlemen altogether.

Report of the Commission of Inquiry (about Bermuda's fishing industry), February 1991

Men have been taking fish from the waters around Bermuda for nearly 400 years. Soon after the first permanent inhabitants from England aboard the *Sea Venture* were shipwrecked off what is now St George's in 1609, fish became a commodity for sale to other islanders as much as fishing became a common activity. A nascent commercial fishery thus spawned in Bermuda almost immediately upon its settlement and colonization.

Lefroy's *Memorials* recording the events of Bermuda's early discovery and settlement between 1515 and 1685 include 'A Letter sent in to England from the Summer Islands [Bermuda] written by Mr. Lewis Hughes, Preacher of God's Word there, 1615': 'For the present Tobacco is the best commoditie, and for victuals, if men have boates, nets, lines, hookes, and striking irons, they may have good fish at all times, as Rockfish, Angellfish, Hogge-fish, Amberfish, Cutlefish, Pilotfish, Hedgehogfish [probably spiny pufferfish/porcupine fish], Cunnyfish [cunners? also known as sea perch, a type of wrasse], Old wines [?], Stingraies, Snappers, Groopers, Cauallies [jacks], Moraies, Mullets, Mackerels, Pilchers, Breames, Lobstars, Turtles, Sharks, etc.'

Whatever other deprivations the early settlers may have suffered, a lack of fresh fish was clearly not one of them. An extract from Silvanus Jourdan's Narrative of 1610, in Lefroy's *Memorials*, notes that there was 'such store of mullets that with a single seine [net] might be taken at one draught one thousand at the least . . . of tray fishes very great ones, and so great store, as that there hath been taken in one night with making lights, EUEN [even] sufficient to feed the whole company a day'.

The 'store' of fish around Bermuda in the early 1600s gives some indication of the virginity of those then unexploited waters. That happy condition occurs today in very few island locations, either where fish have abounded or because the human population is small or the fishery protected.

Fishing might have sustained the small Bermuda population for hundreds of years without putting pressure on the fish stock. As early as 1620, however, the government enacted legislation 'against the killing of over young Tortoises [turtles]'. It legislated an 'Act to prevent the destruction of fish' in 1687. Environmental concerns about the impact of even such a small community on Bermuda's marine resources were apparent from the earliest years.

It is impossible to ascertain how much of the fishing in the first few hundred years of Bermuda's colonization was on a commercial basis and how much was simply for subsistence. There would naturally have been a combination of both, in varying degrees. As more settlers arrived, it is likely that some were fishermen by trade, and that they continued their trade in Bermuda. They would have handed down the practices of their craft to offspring and disseminated their skills among other individuals. Gradually there evolved a community of more or less full-time fishermen constituting a local fishery.

This report from the magazine *Forest and Stream* (now *Field and Stream*), from 16 March 1876, offers evidence that there was a thriving commercial fishery in Bermuda at least by the middle of the 1800s. The author of the article was G. Brown Goode, an eminent American authority in the field of natural history. At the time of publication of the article, Goode was assistant curator of the US National Museum (forerunner of The Smithsonian Institute). 'The only [fish] market is the water's edge. In the large towns, Hamilton and St. George's, the quay is lined nearly every morning at sunrise by a long row of fish-boats.'

Goode's brief account of the commercial fishing scene in Bermuda around the mid-1800s indicates, first, that a local commercial fishery was well established by then. The docks of Hamilton and St George's had clearly been used by many fishermen for many years as their natural marketplace. Moreover, the basic characteristics of the trade he describes would prevail for another three generations or so, until the mid-1900s. They may well not have changed greatly for three generations or more *before* his account.

Goode identifies a kaleidoscopic variety of fish being sold in Bermuda. Almost all the species were demersals, fished mainly by handline both from the reef and the outlying banks.

An old Bermuda postcard from the late 19th or early 20th century showing 'A Fisherman's Home' (probably at Devonshire Dock). In the right foreground, a typical fishing sloop is anchored near the mouth of the bay, with two small rowboats in the centre of the picture.

The **angel fish** (*Holacanthus ciliaris*)...perhaps the most highly esteemed ... The **gray snapper** (*Lutjanus caxis*) ... very difficult to capture with either hook, pot, or grains [a kind of fishing spear], and has gained it the sobriquet of 'sea lawyer' ... The **yelting**, or **glass-eyed snapper** (*Lutjanus aya*), the **red snapper** of the Florida Keys ... The name 'yelting' is very puzzling ... The **rock-fish** (*Trisotropis undulosus*) ... one of the choicest of table fishes ... The **grouper** (*Epinephelus striatus*) ... Great numbers are caught off the islands, and are brought in the wells of the smacks to the artificial ponds along the shore, where they are kept for the market, and are fed on fish and lobsters. The young fish are called **hamlets**; but, after reaching a length of eighteen or twenty inches, are known as **groupers** ... The **hind** (*Epinephelus guttatus*) is readily sold in the market, where specimens two feet in length are sometimes seen ... The **butter-fish** [**coney**] is often seen, and is of much interest, although its small size and the softness of its flesh render it of little economic value . . . The **chub** (*Sargus variegatus*) is very abundant, occurring in large schools in company with the following species . . . The chub is seined in vast quantities in Hamilton Harbour and other secluded bays . . . The **bream** (*Pimelepterus Boscii*) . . . easily distinguished from the chub, as far as it can be seen underwater, by the large black spot just behind the dorsal . . . The **goat's-head porgy** (*Calamus megacephalus*) and the **sheep's-head porgy** (*Calamus arbitarius*) are taken with the hook in large quantity . . . The **squirrel [-fish]** (*Holocentrum sogo*) is common . . . They are not often eaten . . . The **Bermuda bonito** (*Zonichthys fasciatus*) . . . is an excellent table fish . . . Large schools of the **'mackerel'** (*Orcynus alliteratus*) were observed in March . . . though rather oily, I think it superior to many of the Bermuda food-fishes . . . The **round robin** (*Decapterus punctatus*) is very common . . . 'Jigging robins' is a favourite amusement . . . The **goggler** or **goggle-eye [jack]** (*Trachurops crumenophthalmus*) . . . is found with the preceding, and is used for food . . . The **jack**, or **buffalo jack** (*Paratractus pisquetus*), is common . . . Two species known as the **shad** (*Eucinostomus gula*) and the **long-boned shad** (*Eucinostomus Lefroyi*) are seined in quantity in the harbors and sold from boats along the wharf . . . The **hog-fish** (*Lachnotaemus falcatus*) is very common here . . . The **cow-fish** (*Ostracium quadricorne*) is, I was told, much esteemed for food, and is frequently baked whole in its shell . . . The **barracuda** (*Sphyraena spet*) is frequently found in the markets, and is eaten with impunity, as far as I could learn . . . The **sennet** (*Sphyraena picuda*) is common . . . The young may be seen basking in the sun in the shallows, where they are seined in large numbers . . . The **mullet** (*Mugil liza*) is very common . . . **Anchovies** (*Sardinella anchovia*) occurred in great schools during the month of March, and were seined together with *Decapterus punctatus* [**round robin**], and sold in quantities

along the quay . . . Great quantities of **pilchards** (*Harengula macrophthalma*) were seined during the month of March, and sold from row-boats at the water's edge.

This postcard from about 1909 shows a big catch of mainly groupers, ready for sale to customers from a fishing boat alongside the dock in Hamilton. Motorized fishing boats gradually began to replace sail from about the 1930s.

Goode describes the typical craft used by Bermuda fishermen in mid-19th century: 'The fishing-boats are built in the English style, drawing five or six feet of water, deep-keeled, sloop or schooner rigged, and usually provided with a large well in the hold, in which the fish are brought in alive.' By inference, these would be heavy, beamy, long-keeled sailing vessels drawing five to six feet and 30–40 feet in length.

The similarities to a later account of fishing in Bermuda in the early 1900s are striking. Dr Raoul Andersen provides a seminal recollection of those days, illuminated by his interviews in 1976 with an old time St David's fisherman and boatbuilder, Geary Pitcher, Sr, 'Bermudian Handline Fishing in the Sailing Sloop Era: a Fisherman's Account'.

PITCHER: 'I've been around or at fishing for about 62 years. When I was a kid going to school, I used to go with the fishermen in the summertime. Handline fishing. No traps those days. No motor. Everything was sail. Either sail or row boats that averaged about 30 feet. They used to have a well in the boat like a tank; the water used to circulate automatically...And this well was built up and made like a tank. The walls were of wood with cement on the inside just like you cement a house. They would hold about three or four hundredweight of fish. They used to bring it [the fish] home alive.'

By the mid-1900s the days of exclusively sail-powered craft in the fishing trade in Bermuda were almost extinct. Like the early steamships that still carried masts, however, the vestiges of sail overlapped into the era of engine power.

Louis S. Mowbray, curator of the aquarium at the time, noted in a report about 'The Commercial and Game Fishing Industries of Bermuda', in 1949, that: 'There are a few row boats used, but most of the craft are power driven with gasoline engines of from five to sixty horse power. *A high percentage of them also carry sail.*' Within a generation, however, even those last remnants of the sailing era would give way entirely to an exclusively motorized fleet.

Up until quite recently, fresh fish for sale in Bermuda included both live fish, whole fresh dead fish, or fillets. Frozen was not an option until the second half of the 20th century. As Goode noted:

The fish swim in the wells [of the fishing boats] until customers are found for them; when one is selected [a fish, not a customer], it is taken up in a landing-net or by a gaff-hook, and quickly killed by thrusting a sharp awl into the base of the brain; it is then bled, skinned (rarely scaled), eviscerated,

and delivered into the hands of the purchaser, a loop of palmetto fiber always being attached for convenience in carrying.

Dockside selling of fish from the fishing boats prevailed well into the second half of the 20th century, although, by the later years, there might be no more than two or three boats alongside compared with the dozen or more in earlier years. In 1949 Louis S. Mowbray observed that the dockside trade was still alive and, apparently, thriving, if on a reduced scale. 'Fishermen who operate on a very small scale generally dispose of their catch at the dockside, and there is never a lack of customers. The fish is invariably fresh, due mainly to the fact that most boats are fitted with live wells and that nearly all ply their trade within about two hours run from the docks.'

By the beginning of the 20th century, fishermen were beginning to take their catch around the island in horse-drawn wagons as well as selling directly from their boats at the docks. The fishermen would blow conch shells like horns as the wagons moved around the island, to announce fresh fish for sale, a practice still in use today on some West Indies islands.

A common practice that has since disappeared was to keep fish (mainly groupers and rockfish) in man-made ponds built on the rocks along the shore. Fishermen brought in the fish alive and left them in the ponds until they could sell them. Geary Pitcher describes how this was done:

You'd bring the rockfish ashore alive. Some wouldn't live. Some would go in the boat and give up. They used to take and either put it right in the market, or if it was too late for the market, they'd tie a piece of rope in its mouth, and tie it out over the side and slack him down so he wouldn't touch bottom . . . Next morning, when the market opened at 7, they'd be there at the market, sometimes with the rockfish and things cleaned up.

You could keep the groupers if you couldn't sell them right away. You could put them in the pond. Say the grouper weighed 10 pounds or bigger. When you pulled him up to the boat, you used to hang him over the well. Just put his side on the edge of the well. You'd take your thumb and find his third rib, and just below the point of this third rib you'd punch a hole. You'd hold the edge of that scissor in the fish 'til the air come out. And you can't touch his liver. If you do, he's booked. You hold it there and just keep the hole open 'til all the air is out. Out would come the air – Sssss. When you took all the air out, you'd just dump him back in the well. And he'd go to the bottom of the well.

. . . Today they couldn't do that. They wouldn't know how to do it.

I've had 'em down at the pond for years. After you get 'em in the pond, they turns black. The fish is greyish, though some of 'em is red. But after he's in the pond about a month, he turns black, you know you've got him hooked. He's good and seasoned then, and he begins to eat. See, he won't eat when you first put 'em in the pond.

The fishermen would feed the live fish regularly with fresh bait such as grunts.

The ponds were built up along the shore with blocks of stone and mortar. Some were covered with wood slats, 'to keep it cool' by natural ventilation. At the bottom of the ponds, on the water side, a 'keyhole' was left as an opening. Water came in through the keyhole as the tide came in and flowed out when the tide went down, keeping the pond water in continual circulation, 'and the fish kept good'.

At the end of the season the fishermen cleaned out the ponds, hoeing, shovelling and raking out mud and debris. 'Then you'd put the keystone back. That's what they had going before the deep freeze came around.'

The use of fish ponds was well established by the 1800s, as Goode describes them in 1876. 'During the winter months, recourse is had to the fish ponds, which are stocked with the surplus of the summer's catch. These are of simple construction, usually natural pools in the rocks, or protected coves, inclosed by loosely-laid stone walls. Hundreds, sometimes thousands, of large fishes are here stored up for seasons when the severity of the weather is such as to prevent the usual visits to the fishing-grounds.'

Devil's Hole is one of Bermuda's earliest tourist attractions. This postcard is from the late 1800s or early 1900s. Originally Devil's Hole was a natural fish pond used by fishermen to keep surplus live fish that they did not sell in the market. The eminent American naturalist G. Brown Goode, Assistant Curator US National Museum, wrote about Devil's Hole in 1876 after he had visited Bermuda in February and March 1872. 'During the winter months, recourse is had to the fish-ponds, which are stocked with the surplus of the summer's catch. . .The largest of these, the "Devil's Hole", is a large natural pool near the centre of the main island, and about one hundred feet from the south shore of Harrington Sound. Several hundred large Groupers and Hamlets (Epinephelus striatus) are usually confined here, and the place is much visited by strangers.' (Extract from Bermuda and its Fish Markets, *by G. Brown Goode, published in* Forest and Stream *magazine, New York, on 16 March 1876, from the 'advance sheets' of Goode's* A Catalogue of the Fishes of the Bermudas.)

Goode then describes what might have been Bermuda's first tourist attraction still surviving to this day. 'The largest of these [ponds], the "Devil's Hole", on Harrington Sound, is visited by almost all the strangers on the islands, a small fee being charged for the privilege of seeing the fishes feed. Several hundred large Groupers and Hamlets (*Epinephelus striatus*) are usually confined here; and, when bait is thrown into the pond, the visitor can see only a close array of widely-stretched hungry mouths, each six or eight inches in diameter.' Fishermen stocking another pond, by Black Horse Tavern in St David's, also used to charge the occasional tourist visitor to watch them feed their fish.

Keeping live fish in ponds was a crude form of fish farming, or, at the very least, fish husbandry since the groupers probably did not spawn and reproduce in the ponds. The fishermen were able to manage the balance of supply and demand by keeping fish alive in ponds until they could take them to market. Supplies accumulated when the fishing was good (in the warmer months). Stocks would satisfy demand in lean times when the fishing was bad (usually the winter months).

In later years when the ponds fell into disuse, unsold fish might have been cut up for bait, given away, or harrowed into the earth by farmers for fertilizer, providing little or no income to the fishermen.

Fish ponds provided a buffer of supplies to give fishermen a more even spread of income throughout the year. They also eased the pressure on natural fish stocks since fishermen did not need to fish so intensively. Fishing grounds would lie fallow, to allow the resource to regenerate, just as farmers leave fallow fields.

Despite their economic and ecological value, the husbandry of live fish in fish ponds became extinct by the mid-1900s. The introduction of chilling and freezing facilities obviated their necessity. Abandoned ponds eventually became derelict. Remnants of some old ponds are still visible around the shoreline of Bermuda. Few are recognizable for the purpose they once served.

Louis S. Mowbray wrote in 1949 that some fishermen had by then begun to establish wholesale marketing ties with hotels and retailers. 'As there is no marketing centre, the more enterprising individuals have

a contract for their catch direct with one or more hotels or guest houses, a meat market or one of the United States bases.'

When there was bad weather (especially in winter), the fishermen could not go out, which disrupted their supply of fish. 'This forced the importation of fresh fish, particularly from the United States. When the better weather comes along the fishermen can make good catches, but then many of the hotels and markets inform them that as they have been unable to fulfil their contracts previously, other arrangements have been made. This meant that the fisherman was then faced with the great problem of disposing of several hundreds of pounds in weight before dark, or accept a total loss.'

Nevertheless, by the mid-1900s at least fishermen had more mobility (road transport) to take fish for sale elsewhere. Cold storage was by then an option, but only to a limited degree. 'There has never been a really satisfactory cold storage plant to which fish can be taken for quick freezing and preservation. What facilities there were closed down promptly at 5 p.m. and this caused many a catch to be thrown into the sea or given away after a market had refused it . . . In addition, the fisherman can now rely on motor transportation [cars were introduced in Bermuda in 1946] to shift his catch elsewhere to a buyer with less fear of spoilage, as it is possible to travel from one end of the island to the other in little over an hour.'

The Fisheries

Three local fisheries make up the commercial fishery in Bermuda, broadly divided by targeted species: off the platform for pelagic floating fish; on the platform and the banks for demersal bottom fish; and the lobster fishery. The lobster season (1 September to 31 May) coincides with the more turbulent winter months when fishing, and incomes for commercial fishermen, are diminished by bad weather and fewer fish supplies.

The reef fishery has been Bermuda's only fishery for most of the island's history, whether by pot, net, or line. There was no need to catch offshore species such as tuna and wahoo. Groupers, snappers, hogfish, and other bottom fish provided for everyone, until recently.

Commercial fishing for pelagics offshore expanded after the Second World War, as recreational gamefishing grew. Commercial fishermen cultivated the pelagics fishery to diversify away from the reef fishery. It remained mainly a recreational fishery until overfishing of demersal species became an issue in the 1970s.

Concerns about the overfishing of demersal fish stocks intensified in the 1970s and 1980s. The fisheries became more regulated and more restricted. Government intervention and legislation usurped the role of communal governance of the fishery by the fishermen themselves.

In 1988 commercial fishing licences (first introduced by the 1972 Fisheries Regulations) were divided into three categories of vessel: the charter fleet (boat registration numbers preceded by a 'C'); the fish pot fishermen ('F' numbers); and non-pot fishermen ('N' numbers).

Each category had certain distinctions. 'C' registrations, for example, required the fisherman to pay duty on the vessel when he imported it into Bermuda. 'N' and 'F' registered vessels brought into Bermuda were exempted from import duty. *Legally* they were obliged to pay the import duty on their boats if they subsequently wanted to get a charter licence to take occasional passengers (though, in practice, few would be likely to do that). Charter boats could carry passengers. 'N' and 'F' registered vessels could not. 'N' vessels could not use fish pots and were restricted to fishing by handline and rod and reel.

The 'N' and 'F' distinctions were eliminated when pot fishing was abolished. Vessels registered and licensed for charter fishing constitute an independent and separate group.

Fisheries Division issues licences to commercial fishing *vessels*, not to commercial *fishermen* (which makes them easily transferable). Anyone in Bermuda may catch fish without a licence. A fishing licence is actually a licence to sell fish. Licences are for one year, from 1 April in any year. Issuance of a licence obliges the fisherman to comply with certain Fisheries Regulations, such as the rule that he must spend a minimum of 100 days at sea, that he must report his catches (and other fishing data) to Fisheries Division, and that he must be 'wholly devoted to the [fishing] industry'.

Apart from vessel licences, the government maintains a register of commercial fishermen resident in Bermuda. These include not only vessel owners and captains but also the crew of any vessel who might sell the fish. Some 'fishermen' on the register are family members of fishermen who do not themselves fish but may sell the fish in the absence of the fishermen. In order to sell any fish in Bermuda taken from the waters of Bermuda's Exclusive Economic Zone, the 'fisherman' must be registered, and the fish must be from a licensed fishing vessel. (Supermarkets and restaurants are exempt from this requirement.)

Anyone in Bermuda may fish without a licence provided that it is not for 'commercial gain'. There is no restriction either on the sale of imported fish (such as some species of grouper) or marine molluscs (such as conch) which are protected species in Bermuda.

Fish Pots

Older generations of Bermudian fishermen were brought up almost exclusively on pot fishing. Use of the Antillian (arrowhead design) type of fish pots in Bermuda dates from the early part of the 20th century. Captain Geary Pitcher recalls in his interviews with Raoul Andersen in 1976: 'When I was a kid going to school, I used to go with the fishermen in the summertime. Handline fishing. No traps those days . . . When I was fishing in late years, potting years . . .'

Bermudian fishermen did use pots earlier although they were of a different design. Goode describes such traps as used in the mid-1800s.

The *Sparidae* [porgies, bream, chub], *Labridae* [wrasses], *Scaridae* [parrotfish], the smaller *Serranidae* [groupers], and many others, with great quantities of the large crustaceans so much in demand for bait, are captured in basket-work fish-pots constructed of split cane. These are built on the same principle with the lobster-pots in use on the New England coast, but are very peculiar in shape. A fair idea of one of them may be gained by imagining two crockery-crates placed together, with the ends at an angle so as to form a very thick capital letter V, with arms about four feet square, the entrance being through a funnel-shaped aperture placed in the inner angle. Smaller and more portable pots, made after the same model, in annealed wire, are also in use. Such pots are baited with fish or lobsters, and anchored in two or three fathoms of water.

Pot fishing at that time was mainly in shallow water, and line fishing in deeper water. In the 1900s fishermen using the Antillean style trap often dropped pots in 100 fathoms of water, and sometimes deeper.

Legislation in 1791 ('Act to prohibit the setting of Fish-pots, etc.') confirms that Bermuda's fishermen have used fish pots of various types for over 200 years. Their effect on the marine environment has concerned legislators for at least that long.

Gene Barrett, in his 1991 paper 'The Fish Pot Ban: Reef Overfishing and State Management in Bermuda', wrote that 'There were 88 vessels with a pot fishing licence in 1988 [two years before the fish-pot ban] . . . While the number of legal pots per boat was highly regulated, fishermen reported a varying range: small-scale fishermen from 8 to 10 [pots]; most averaged 20 to 30; a few had more than 50. In addition, most boats would have hook and line gear either for trolling, drift fishing, or handlining.'

In the early 1980s new regulations forced some pot fishermen out of the fishery. Restrictions included the minimum 100 fishing days a year rule to qualify as a full-time commercial fisherman, as well as a freeze on the number of pots in use.

The 1984 Fisheries Management Plan imposed further restrictions. 'Maximum sizes for fish pots were established and only full-time fishermen who had historically used pots were licensed to use them providing they met the qualifications of full-time fishermen [namely, by fishing a minimum of 100 days a year]. The number of pots used by these fishermen was reduced from 3,160 to 1,600.' (From Minister for the Environment Ann Cartwright DeCouto's statement at the time of the fish pot ban, in January 1990.)

The 1984 Fisheries Management Plan aimed to reduce the number of pots allocated to each full-time fisherman, scaling down over a period of six years (to 1990). It did not aim to reduce the number of pot fishermen themselves (although it did eliminate part-timers from the pot fishery). Nevertheless, 'the number of pot fishing vessels, about 130 in 1985, decreased to 71 in 1990' ('The Bermuda Fisheries: A Tragedy of the Commons Averted?').

Before 1984 the largest number of pots allotted to any individual had been 100. The Management Plan aimed to reduce that maximum to 30 pots by 1990.

The 1984 Plan also introduced a moratorium on new licences generally. Vessel licences could be transferred, but no new licences were issued again until 1999. (Licences traded among fishermen were valued at an average $10,000 each, according to the most recent [January 2000] government green paper on the fishing industry.)

The 1984 Plan, which aimed to alleviate stresses on reef fish stocks by reducing the use of fish pots, was not a success. Abuse of regulations was commonplace. Fishermen worked more pots than they were allocated, concealed the location of pots, and stole other fishermen's pots. Many fishermen openly admitted that they broke the law, because their smaller pot allotments caused them economic hardship.

At least part of the failure of the 1984 Management Plan owed to the fact that the commercial fishermen were not involved in its development to the same degree that they contributed to the 1972 Fisheries Regulations. The extent to which they flaunted the terms of the Plan mirrored the extent to which they were excluded from its creation, as well as the antipathy they felt towards fisheries officials by the early 1980s.

Barrett pointed out that the pot fishery was much more important, economically, than the hook and line fishery. 'Fish pots had been the preferred technology in Bermuda for nearly a century and utilized by 64% of Commercial fishermen . . . This fishery [pots] accounted for approximately two-thirds of total food fish landings and, if one includes the winter catch, nearly three-quarters of fishermen's income.'

Sales by pot fishermen averaged $3000 a month in the best summer fishing months. That compared with just $600–800 a month for hook and line fishermen. Winter sales for the pot fishermen averaged much less, between $1000 and $1500 a month, and were corespondingly lower for hook and liners.

The 1990 Fish Pot Ban

In 1990 the government banned the use of fish pots in Bermuda to protect endangered reef fish stocks. The ban immediately eliminated the pot fishermen's higher income type of fishing, diverting them to the lower income hook and line fishery. The pot ban was considered, at the time, the main solution to the overfishing problem. Its effect was to compel fishermen either to put more effort into the hook and line fishery to make a similar income as pot fishing provided, or to sustain a lower level of income, or to get out of fishing altogether.

The aim of the closure of the pot fishery had been to address the problem of overfishing by eliminating the use of fish pots, 'in order to immediately effect a significant reduction in [fishing] effort', as one of the 'drastic measures' the government considered necessary 'to ensure that the fish stocks are enhanced'.

Minister for the Environment Ann Cartwright DeCouto acknowledged that, 'Although closure of the pot fishery as the main thrust towards reducing fishing effort on reef fish stocks is a simple measure in concept, it will have far-reaching effects on all facets of the fishing industry. I fully recognise that the cost of exit from the pot fishery for many of the fishermen will be high. Fishermen who have been licensed to use pots have been rigidly controlled by a complex set of conditions, nevertheless, they have formed the backbone of the commercial fishery.'

Some fishermen, especially the older ones, did indeed quit fishing altogether. Others diverted to hook and line fishing where 'double to three times the amount of [fishing] effort has to be expended for relatively small catches and that fishery is now characterized by excess entry [i.e. too many fishermen]'.

The pot ban removed the traps, but rather than 'reduce fishing effort on reef fish stocks', it forced fishermen to *increase* their effort by hook and line fishing to maintain an acceptable income.

Fisheries Diversification

Since 1990, the commercial fishermen in Bermuda have fished in three ways: by handline or longline for mainly demersal species; by trolling or chumming for pelagics; and by nets for seasonal inshore runs of mid-water species such as jacks and yellowtail. The lobster fishery allows a catch of two lobsters per day ('during any continuous period of twenty-four hours', by the book) for any individual with a lobster licence (not restricted to commercial fishermen).

Most fishermen combine all three ways of fishing in varying degrees, depending on the weather, availability of different species at different times of the year, their experience in a particular method, personal preferences, and general fishing conditions at any one time.

Few fishermen concentrate exclusively on the offshore pelagic fishery which requires specific skills and experience in trolling, chumming, the use of specialized gear, and the marketing of larger whole fish such as tuna and wahoo. Most fishermen go for pelagics when those fish appear at times in abundance, or if their more conventional bottom fishing is poor. Having been brought up mainly on pot fishing, most fishermen feel they understand the demersal fishery better, even if it requires more effort by hook and line.

The reward from pelagics *seems* more profitable than the reef fishery: the income from two or three 60 lb wahoo and a few tuna caught in a day offshore may be envied by the reef fisherman who might not see 100 lb of fish in his boat from a week of fishing. On the other hand, the pelagic fisherman has considerably more invested in specialized gear and technology. Fuel costs are higher because trips off the platform are generally longer. The offshore fisherman needs to catch more pounds of fish per hour of fishing time, because the pelagics fishery is a more costly enterprise.

The availability of migratory species offshore such as wahoo and tuna is generally more reliable than demersal species from the reef fishery, which is to the advantage of the offshore fisherman. The fish nevertheless still have to be caught. The profitability from the pelagics fishery therefore depends as much on the skill and experience of the fisherman as on the relative costs and revenues from it.

Fisheries Development

The so-called Bardach Report in 1958 was the first formal initiative to organize Bermuda's commercial fisheries into a professionalized industry. The report, the 'Bermuda Fisheries Research Program', was undertaken by John E. Bardach, Associate Professor in the Department of Fish and Zoology at the University of Michigan, with collaboration by C. Lavett Smith and D. W. Menzel (research assistants), and Louis S. Mowbray, curator of the Bermuda Aquarium.

The Bardach Report aimed, for the first time, to create a professional, organized fishing industry as a specific government ambition.

The report's main recommendations to upgrade Bermuda's fishery included improved storage facilities, organized marketing and distribution procedures, the establishment of fisheries management and administration systems, biological research, and government sponsored funding to assist fishermen in the mechanization of boats and gear.

The brief of the report was to recommend ways in which the organization of commercial fishing in Bermuda could be more effective and efficient, in part 'to insure a continuing and maximum yield to the fisherman'. It encouraged fishermen to invest in more sophisticated technology, assisted by subsidized financing from a 'government loan scheme'.

Whether a modernized industry was compatible with the health of the fish stock around Bermuda was a moot point: environmental concerns at that time were negligible, as was research and formal knowledge about the resource. Fish pots then were the mainstay of Bermuda's fishery and were expected to remain so indefinitely. There was not the least indication that they might be contributing to the depletion of demersal fish stocks around the Bermuda reef platform.

Bardach even recommended ways to make the traps more efficient. 'Since trap setting will never vanish from the Bermuda fishing scene, these replacement motors [diesel engines to replace gasoline engines] should include a power take-off for the hauling of traps.'

Bardach's assessment of the reef fish stock around Bermuda was, with hindsight, highly optimistic, because it lacked reliable data (a deficiency the report addressed, with the recommendation for 'reliable fishery statistics about all fishes caught').

Bardach made 'a very rough estimate' that 'the weight of legal sized groupers which could enter the fishery every year [was] between 2.9 and 4.3 million lbs (10–15 lbs./acre/year on 450 square miles of fishing grounds at 640 acres/sq. mile)'.

It would be possible, in other words, according to Bardach's 'very rough estimate', that fishermen could take up to 4.3 million lb of groupers from Bermuda waters every year, under optimum conditions.

Conditions, however, were far from optimum. Since the distribution of groupers around Bermuda was uneven, and given the inefficiences of local fishing methods, Bardach recognized that it would be 'virtually impossible to tap this resource to the fullest', and that it would be 'unlikely that a yearly take of two million pounds of groupers will be exceeded by much in Bermuda waters'.

It is unlikely that Bermuda fishermen ever took more than one million pounds of groupers in any one year, much less two million, and probably much less. When formal fishing statistics were first compiled, from 1975, grouper landings by commercial fishermen totalled just over 450,000 lb. With restrictions to protect them, and with the fish pot ban in 1990, the grouper catch has now declined to less than 100,000 lb/year.

A comment in the second Progress Report of November 1955, leading up to the Final Report of August 1958, hinted with some prescience at potential environmental liabilities in the future. 'The two most highly preferred types of fish – preferred far above all other species – are the several species of rockfish and hamlet or Nassau grouper. They sell more easily and in some instances at a higher price than other species. Consequently, there is more intense fishing for them than for other Bermuda fish. *If there were dangers of overfishing for any species, a further intensification of the fishing effort would be felt by these first* [author's italics].' As, indeed, turned out to be the case.

The preliminary (1955) report also identified 'the most frequently cited market difficulty by all categories of consumers [individuals, hotels, restaurants, and retailers]', namely, inadequate supplies of local fish in terms of quantity, quality, and 'timing of supply'. This at a time when local fishermen were catching an estimated 1.2 million lb of fish a year, slightly more than today, for a population (42,640 in 1960) considerably smaller than today's (60,000). This finding would reinforce the report's recommendation that fishermen harvest more 'unexploited fishery resources', to meet the expected growth in demand with a more diverse range of fish species for sale to consumers.

It should be remembered that Bermuda in the mid-1950s was still a quiet place: staid, stable, and slow paced. Cars had been introduced just a decade before (1946). The only regular cruise ships were *The Queen of Bermuda* and the *Ocean Monarch*. The average price of fish was '2/6' (two shillings and sixpence) a pound. This was Bermuda in its pre-development phase.

Bardach recognized that fisheries in Bermuda was at a transition phase of early development. The report's recommendations suggested how it could be advanced into the next phase. To its credit, it even warned of a later stage of too intensive exploitation, although it may not have acknowledged how much its own recommendations contributed to that.

Most fisheries go through three phases in their development. At the beginning of the exploitation of the area or the species the accumulation of old and large members in the population [of fish] will work very much to the advantage of the fishermen.

The second stage of the fishery. . .is one in which the stock is under moderate to heavy exploitation. During that time more and more of the younger fish will have been harvested. The oldest and largest members will disappear from the population and the fishermen will tell you that 'fishing isn't what it used to be; I don't catch any big ones anymore.' What he does overlook in most cases, though, is the fact that the total poundage harvested is far greater than when the slowly growing big fish were caught. At this stage the thinning out of the stock has enabled the sometimes starved members of the population to catch up and achieve, in some cases, phenomenal growth.

The third stage is one in which stocks are over-exploited, and the growth of fish is further accelerated by removal of too many individuals. The catch per unit effort (that is, the catch per hour or day) goes down in spite of the fact that more fishing units [fishermen or boats] may be employed. Management procedures should be applied at this point to save a resource from being destroyed, or to facilitate its recovery.

The Bermuda fishery is probably [in 1958] just passing from the first to the second stage and in many regions, especially on the banks, is still in the first stage.

In the wake of Bardach's Report, commercial fishermen gradually invested more capital in their business. They replaced gasoline engines with diesel. New boats were bigger. Echo sounders, fathometers, and other electronic gear became commonplace. Boats were fitted with winches to facilitate pot hauling. This higher level of investment had to be maintained over time, to keep abreast of new technology.

Although fishermen invested more in their business, the fishing industry itself did not become more efficient or more profitable. The structure of the industry did not change after Bardach. There was still approximately the same number of people fishing as there had been before, but fishermen had much greater costs according to their individual investments in new technology.

After Bardach, fishermen fished more effectively and more intensively, but this diminished the resource. Fishing capacity (the number of fishermen fishing) even increased. As a result, investment by each fisherman was a costly investment in increasingly surplus capacity. Although it was not necessarily surplus capacity at the time, there was no contingency for flexibility if and when surplus capacity evolved in the future.

The number of fishermen in Bermuda has never diminished significantly enough to make it a rationalized, more profitable industry. If anything, quite the contrary has happened, even after the introduction of fisheries management techniques and regulations which have only indirectly advocated limited or reduced access to the fishery.

Bardach nevertheless proposed at some length that his recommendations would be virtually useless unless the fishing industry achieved a higher degree of organization as a unified force to complement a more mechanized industry. While never specifically proposing a reduction in the number of fishermen to counter the problem of diminished fish stocks, Bardach recognized the need for greater cohesion and cooperative effort among fishermen.

It may be argued that fishing is a very individualistic trade which does not lend itself to organization and that government assistance of any shape or form is undesirable. The fact remains, however, that maximum production per unit such as a boat day or netting hour, at a truly mechanized level, cannot be achieved without some organization either from within the ranks of the fishermen themselves or from without. Some attempts by the Bermuda fishermen were made over the years to form fishermen's societies. These disintegrated sooner or later for lack of interest, but mainly for the want of leaders with suitable organizing talent.

Fisheries Consolidation

Since the late 1960s there have been various initiatives by fishermen, and by the government, to consolidate Bermuda's commercial fishermen into a more unified force, to transform commercial fishing into a more profitable and professional industry. W. R. Evans, a former director of the Department of Agriculture, established one of the first fishermen's organizations as early as the mid-1950s.

Sean Ingham, an ex-fisherman who today sells fish that he imports into Bermuda from his operations in Turks & Caicos Islands, funded the constitution and establishment of the Bermuda Commercial Fishermen's Association in 1969. The Association is still alive but more or less dormant.

Sargasso Seafoods

At the beginning of the 1980s Sargasso Seafoods was a fish processing project funded by the United Nations Development Programme (UNDP) and the Bermuda government, and promoted by the Fisheries Division of the Department of Agriculture and Fisheries. Investment by UNDP and by the Bermuda Government totalled $2 million. The FAO provided technical assistance.

Sargasso Seafoods operated from a site at the US Navy Annex (NOB), a secure location for its operations from 1980 until 1982. A prime objective of the project was 'to increase fish landings, *particularly those which are at present under-utilised*'. ('Under-utilised' was a euphemism for what most people would call 'trash' fish.) Its other objectives were 'to improve the quality of fish available to the consumer', to develop new processed fish products, and to train fishermen in the most effective methods of catching species of fish targeted for use in the plant.

Whether the project also had an ulterior motive, namely, to get funding to develop the government's Fisheries Division, is a moot point. After the company's demise, however, the Fisheries Division personnel involved with Sargasso Seafoods moved to Coney Island premises where they remain to this day.

One of the objectives of Sargasso Seafoods was that it should have been taken over by the fishermen and run as a cooperative. 'This was proposed at the end of the project, but did not find wide acceptance among those fishermen who might have formed the cooperative. A lack of apparent economic viability was one factor which appears to have dissuaded fishermen from participating in the proposed cooperative.' (Commission of Inquiry)

Very few industrial processing operations are viable in Bermuda: operating (and especially labour) costs make them uncompetitive with imported products. Whatever reasons may be given to explain the demise of Sargasso Seafoods, the bottom line was that it was not commercially viable. The company was shut down after three years. Some of the plant was sold off. The rest was abandoned to become derelict.

The 1991 Commission of Inquiry about Bermuda's fishing industry cited a number of reasons why Sargasso Seafoods failed.

> First, there was no formal commitment on the part of fishermen to sell their fish to Sargasso Seafoods. Consequently, it appears that when fish was scarce, they sold directly to consumers and retailers, selling to Sargasso Seafoods only when there were surpluses, or those species which were not easily marketed directly, such as chub. Furthermore, it appears that purchasing policy and prices for Sargasso Seafoods were set by a Marketing Sub-Committee of the FAC, which included several fishermen. Thus it appears that the pricing may have been oriented more towards the needs of fishermen, than towards the establishment of an economically viable operation . . . **In the light of the points presented above, the Commission considers that it may be premature to conclude that a processing and marketing facility such as Sargasso Seafoods is not economically feasible in Bermuda.**

In a 1983 interview, Teddy Tucker commented on the project. 'The idea of a fish plant and research is, I think, an excellent idea, and they couldn't find a better place to put it. But the only way it could ever be successful is if it was run as a private enterprise.'

If, in other words, Sargasso Seafoods had been operated by a management focused primarily on making the plant economically viable, rather than on developing the local fishery *per se*, it might have survived.

Fisheries Transition

Gene Barrett noted in 1991, 'Bermuda was characterised up to the late 1960s by a traditional fishery: technology was simple, incomes were low, and effort was limited by the part-time nature of fishing.'

The principles of the local fishery until then were self-regulation, mutual respect for other fishermen's customs and, especially, territories, and *pluralistic employment* whereby fishing was a subsistence activity for fishermen in conjunction with other occasional forms of employment (especially during the winter).

Since fishing was mainly a part-time occupation, incomes from fishing were low. 'Prices and income were so low that that fishermen were hard-pressed to modernize, this prevented technology and [fishing] effort from reaching disruptive levels . . . Prior to the [subsequent] professionalization of the fishery, diversification within the fishery was greater, and had a similar latent conservation effect by providing certain areas and species a regenerative period each year.'

The Bermuda fishery was more viable when it was also more simple, less sophisticated, and based on respect for fishing customs, mutual trust among fishermen, and fishing etiquette evolved over generations. But, although the system seemed to work well, it had a critical weakness: poverty. According to Barrett 'The downside of traditional conservatism was its relationship to low income . . . From an economic standpoint therefore the traditional fishery was far from idyllic. It was characterized by an underemployment–underinvestment cycle that perpetuated poverty.'

On the other hand, while the income of fishermen was relatively low before the 1960s, so, too, were the costs of living in Bermuda. In 1949 Louis S. Mowbray estimated that 100 men were employed full time in fishing, and that they had a combined income of £78,000 (including income from lobsters), an average of £780 per fisherman.

At the same time (1950), a two or three bedroom cottage in Bermuda cost £3500–5000. That was equivalent to *five times* the annual average income of a fisherman.

By 1960 the price of an average two bedroom house had only risen to £5500–6000. In a single generation, between the early 1930s when a two or three bedroom cottage cost £1250–1500 and the early 1960s, house prices increased by 350%.

Today, when the decent average income for a commercial fisherman might be $25,000, the cost of a three bedroom house in Bermuda is closer to $500,000 – an increase of over 3000% from the generation before (1950s/1960s), and *twenty times* the average income from fishing!

In a single generation, between the 1960s and 1990s, Bermuda's economy, costs of living, wealth, and overall development escalated astronomically by comparison with its previous 350 years of history.

Taking account of the escalation of house prices and all other costs of living in Bermuda since the 1960s, today's fisherman is relatively 'poorer' than his forefathers whose fishing costs and costs of living were more in line with their incomes.

In the mid-1800s the price of fish for sale in Bermuda was fixed. Goode noted at the time, 'The price of fish is fixed by law at fourpence a pound, an advance of one penny having been made within a few years.'

A century later Louis S. Mowbray observed, 'The wholesale price averages one shilling and sixpence (21c. U.S. [at the time]) and the meat markets retail it at around two shillings per pound. The price per pound at the boats is two shillings in the city areas (28c. U.S.) and in the isolated parts it is a sixpence or so less.'

Today, 50 years later, fishermen get $5–7 a pound on average for fish, depending on quality, the species, whether it is sold filleted or whole, as a mixed fillet combination or on its own, and whether it is for the retail or wholesale trade. Small species (coney, barber, porgy, turbot, etc.) are mainly sold filleted direct to customers. Larger fish (wahoo, tuna, dolphin, groupers) are sold in steaks or fillets for the retail trade, and mainly as whole gutted and cleaned fish for the wholesale trade (supermarkets, restaurants, and hotels).

The average price of fresh Bermuda fish fillets or steaks in supermarkets today is $9–12 a pound. Fishermen sell $10 or $20 bags of filleted, usually mixed fish alongside the roads from coolers, as well as whole fish by the pound.

Since the 1972 Fisheries Regulations first required licensed fishermen to log and report their catch, the catch of all foodfish from Bermuda waters has varied between 750,000 lb and 1.4 million lb a year. The composition of the total catch has changed significantly. Pelagics such as tuna and wahoo have largely taken over from groupers and rockfish (many of the latter having been banned or their catch restricted by regulation since 1972).

The annual catch of fish by commercial fishermen seems to have been about the same in the late 1940s as it is today. Louis S. Mowbray estimated that, in 1948 ('an average year'), 100 full time fishermen in Bermuda caught about 900,000 lb of fish (and another 160,000 lb of lobster). It is impossible to know exactly how much fish was caught before fishermen logged their catch officially, but Mowbray's estimate was very high, according to the fishermen fishing then and now.

What is not in doubt is that the number of people who eat fish in Bermuda has mushroomed over the past 50 years. Since 1950 the population has grown by over 60%, from 37,000 to 60,000. The number of tourist visitors to Bermuda in 1950 was about 60,000. Fifty years later the numbers are closer to 500,000.

Throughout most of the 1990s there have been around 300 registered commercial fishermen in any one year. In later years the number has fallen to fewer than 200. Only 45–50, however, work full time as fishermen and are 'wholly devoted to the industry'. Most fishermen on the register have other jobs that occupy them while not fishing, in the 'pluralistic employment' tradition of their craft.

Fisheries Viability

The economic viability of commercial fishing in Bermuda can be approximated in simple terms. Fishermen get an average of $5/lb for the *net amount of saleable fish* from the 800,000–900,000 lb *gross* of foodfish caught by them in an average year. Assuming that fish yield about two-thirds of their gross weight as saleable fish (fillets or whole fish), the *net* amount of saleable fresh fish available is approximately 600,000 lb/year. At an average of $5/lb, its value is $3m. Lobsters (say, 30,000 individuals sold for $20 each) add another $600,000. The net value of fish from the commercial fishery is therefore around three and a half million dollars a year.

Operating costs (for fuel, maintenance, gear replacement, and other running costs) absorb around two-thirds of that revenue ($2.3m). The remaining one-third ($1.2m) provides the total net income for all Bermuda fishermen.

The question is, how many *full-time* fishermen 'wholly devoted to the industry' would that $1.2m total income *viably* support, compared with how many it *actually* supports?

To achieve a relatively modest (by Bermuda standards) average income of $30,000 per fisherman, the total pot of $1.2m would support no more than 40 full-time fishermen ($1.2m divided by $30,000).

At an even more modest $20,000 a year average income, the $1.2m would pay for 60 full-time fishermen.

There were actually 189 registered licensed commercial fishing boats in Bermuda in 1998, and 276 fishermen on the fishermen's register.

If all 276 registered fishermen had to depend entirely on the total pot of approximately $1.2m annual income from fishing, their average income would be less than $5000 a year each. Even if the pot was doubled to $2.5m, the average income would still be less than $10,000 a year.

The simple arithmetic is supported by empiric reality: there are just about the 'right' number of full-time fishermen (40–50) as the fishery supports economically. The rest either survive at the margins of subsistence or, most commonly, derive additional income from other work. The majority are part timers who do not devote the minimum 800 hours/year to fishing required by their licence (which begs the question of why they are granted a licence in the first place).

According to the Fisheries Division's own statistics, the average time spent at sea *per fishing boat* in the 1990s was less than 600 hours/year. The average sea time *per fisherman* was 300–325 hours/year, less than half the 800 hours/year stipulated by the licensing regulations.

Fisheries in the Balance

In earlier times the convention was for most if not all fishermen to be part employed in fishing and part employed in other work. This was possible because Bermuda was a much less sophisticated, less professionalized economy than it is today. Mobility between different types of employment was easier, and commonplace. A fisherman could fish as well as be engaged in boat building, or carpentry, or even farming during non-fishing months.

At the beginning of the 21st century, however, the Bermuda economy is specialized, competitive, and professionalized. This greatly reduces the potential mobility of workers between professions, crafts, or trades. A fisherman heavily invested in his main occupation, namely, fishing, is a specialist in his own right. He must pay for the investment in time, capital, and equipment by the activity for which those investments are intended (namely, fishing), or else be subsidized by other non-fishing activities (as an electrician, or plumber, or construction worker, for example).

The difference between 'then' and 'now' is that, today, there is a core of full-time, professional, specialized fishermen who derive their livelihood exclusively from fishing. Before the mid-1900s, virtually every fisherman was only engaged part time in fishing. 'Then', most fishermen needed to derive only a part of their income from fishing, because they usually had various trades to supplement their fishing income. Today, most fishermen (even part timers) depend on fishing for a relatively large part of their income, because they are specialized and have a substantial investment in their business.

Legitimate full-time fishermen in Bermuda today put more effort into fishing, and they expect, and need, to derive more income from it. They cannot afford to treat fishing as a casual occupation, because they have much greater investments in it than 50 and more years ago.

When almost everyone was a part timer in the fishery, it was a balanced effort. Nowadays, the coexistence of part timers and full timers upsets the balance of effort: full timers have to put more effort into fishing to compensate for income lost to the part timers whose fishing effort is less.

The question arises, would the commercial fishery be more viable if there were no part timers at all, and their effort and income redistributed to 50 or 60 specialized, professional full timers?

This question first arose in a formal way in the early 1970s when the industry began to experience its first signs of unrest. Gene Barrett noted, '. . . through a newly formed fishermen's association [in 1969], fishermen successfully lobbied with the government for professionalization. "Amateur" fishermen were seen by fulltime fishermen as cutting into their retail market. By 1972 the state [government] had restricted the lucrative pot fishery to licensed commercial fishermen only.'

A licensed full-time commercial fisherman must spend a minimum 800 hours (100 days) a year at sea in a licensed fishing vessel. The fisherman must 'in the opinion of the Marine Resources Board [be] wholly devoted to the fishing industry', according to the Fisheries Regulations.

If the letter of the law was upheld, a commercial fisherman would not be permitted to derive income from any source other than fishing. In practice, however, most of Bermuda's commercial fishermen today *must* find income from other sources, or otherwise skirt the official regulations, because most would not otherwise be able to support themselves and their families. The fishery does not economically support the 276 registered fishermen who are licensed to be 'wholly devoted to the fishing industry'. Nor is their number compatible with reducing pressure on fish stocks.

Fisheries Control

Fishermen in Bermuda traditionally, in years gone by, regulated themselves and managed the fishery by customs based on mutual respect for each other's fishing practices and husbandry of the fishing grounds.

Since the 1970s, government intervention, regulation, and legislation have gradually taken over the fishermen's role of self-management. In the process, the fishermen have become increasingly alienated from the management of their fishing grounds, and intensely distrustful of their custodianship in the hands of political and scientific interests outside fishermen's control.

Resentment, conflict, and tension have now replaced long time traditions of fishermen managing themselves in relatively harmonious coexistence. The lack of cooperation and consensus between fishermen and government, as much as any other factor, has made fisheries management in Bermuda much more contentious over the last 20 to 30 years.

Regulation, legislation, and the recreational use of local waters by others has gradually disempowered commercial fishermen from control over their fishing grounds. Until shortly before 1950, the waters around Bermuda were populated almost exclusively by commercial fishermen who shared the resource, more or less equitably, among themselves. The fishery was their domain: they cultivated it communally, managed it (more or less) fraternally, and husbanded the fishing grounds with skill and pride.

Where once the waters of the fishing grounds were virtually the private property of commercial fishermen, they became, within the space of 50 years, common property for all. Recreational use by amateur fishermen and the tourist industry caused the commercial fishermen to lose power over their 'entitlement' to the resource.

Bermuda's commercial fishermen were never by law the landlords of the waters they fished. That simply appeared to be the case by dint of their 350 year monopoly of the resource. They were, however, more accurately, the virtual sole tenants of the fishing grounds around Bermuda for most of the island's history.

As other tenants came to use local waters, bureaucrats intervened increasingly to manage the use of the resource as a common property for everyone. Exclusive 'entitlement' to it devolved away from the commercial fishermen. A system of fisheries management, combined with political and economic interests, began to take over.

Commercial fishermen, who had managed themselves for generations and who had instigated the first formal measures to legislate fisheries conservation in the 1970s, gradually felt disenfranchised from decisions made by bureaucrats that affected their livelihood. Their frustrations intensified with the feeling that their contributions to fisheries management decisions (provision of catch and effort data, local knowledge of the fisheries) were neither satisfactorily acknowledged nor reciprocated by bureaucrats.

Commercial fishing is a masculine activity. Fishermen are independent and anarchic individuals. Insubordination is a natural consequence of their reluctance to be governed by bureaucrats of whom they are distrustful.

Some fishermen felt emasculated by a loss of control and power over their use of the resource, culminating in their exclusion from the decision to enact the 1990 fish pot ban. Abuses of the fisheries regulations since the early 1980s by commercial fishermen, nominally to protect their livelihood, may to some degree be an assertion of the power and control they have lost to fisheries managers and bureaucrats over the years.

Fisheries management in Bermuda since the 1970s has largely been for the benefit of the marine resource. Management has been based on regulations to stabilize reef fish stocks at sustainable levels, but also to protect the aesthetic qualities of the resource 'for purposes other than fishing, such as recreation'.

A programme of strictly conservative regulations to protect the resource may be regarded as the first generation of fisheries management in Bermuda. The challenge of the next generation will be to devise a more holistic management process to manage the entire fisheries system, by re-empowering fishermen, by more sophisticated surveillance of the resource, and by employing professional fisheries

Somerset commercial fisherman cleaning his catch.

managers in a collaborative effort with fishermen that respects and values the qualities of each. Without collective responsibility for their respective roles, the viability of the fishery itself is undermined.

Longlining in Bermuda

Every day around the world's oceans industrial fishing fleets lay out thousands of miles of longlines, each up to 60–70 miles in length. Thousands of hooks on long leaders, spaced up to 100 metres apart, are attached to each main line. Yellowfin tuna, albacore tuna, swordfish, and shark are the main target species. Fleets often voyage away from their home ports for a year or more.

Bermuda has never had a fishing fleet on a large enough scale to sustain industrial longlining of this kind (although one local vessel in Bermuda has been longlining since the mid-1990s). Apart from Taiwanese and other foreign vessels, the only longlining in the Bermuda area has been on an experimental basis, to attempt to diversify the local fishery.

(A 60 mile longline set to follow the 100 fathom contour line around the perimeter of the Bermuda Platform, starting at a point off Hungry Bay on the South Shore, would stretch up around the northeast (St George's) end of Bermuda, past North Rock, around the north and northwest edge of the platform, down towards the southwest, finishing at a point somewhere just above Sally Tucker's.)

The first experimental use of longlines off Bermuda was in May 1955. The trial adopted a shorter version of the Japanese tuna longline, modified for use by small fishing boats. The line was just two and a quarter miles in length, about the distance across Castle Harbour from The Causeway to Nonsuch Island. It was made up of 'ten sections each of 200 fathoms of one quarter inch Italian hemp fishing line'. (At the time it cost approximately £100 to make up the line which was bought from the Belfast Ropeworks, in Belfast, Northern Ireland, 'at forty-one shillings per 130 yard hank, or about 1.25 (U.S.) cents per foot'.)

The longline, with just 100 hooks, was set four miles offshore in about 1000 fathoms of water, off the South Shore of Bermuda. Each

Ark Angel longlines for swordfish. The only regular longline vessel in Bermuda. Moored at Dockyard.

size 9/0 hook was baited alternately with either garfish or pilchard. Hooks were set at a minimum depth of 21 fathoms and a maximum depth of 30 fathoms.

The first set of the longline caught two albacore tuna (one of 51 lb, the other of 56 lb). Subsequent catches included blackfin and yellowfin tuna, mako shark, wahoo, white marlin, and blue marlin.

According to aquarium curator of the time, Louis S. Mowbray, the best conditions for successful catches were in a moderate swell. Calm conditions, he reported, 'produced nothing'. Sets at the new moon produced the most, followed by dark phases of the moon, with full moon sets producing the least.

Optimum depth for the hooks was 20–30 fathoms in 1000–1500 fathoms deep water. 'Setting in less than 750 fathoms was not productive.' Optimum water temperature was in the range 70–80°F. 'Pilchards [as bait] caught fish most consistently.'

The results of these first experiments in longlining off Bermuda were sufficiently encouraging to conclude that there could be a local longline fishery for yellowfin tuna 'and possibly albacore'. This was in the days when commercial fishermen were fishing primarily for groupers, snappers, and other bottom fish. When they eventually started to target offshore pelagics like tuna and wahoo, however, it was, and continues to be, with the more conventional, and more manageable, small boat gear for trolling, chumming, and drift fishing.

The Department of Agriculture's Fisheries Division conducted its own longlining experiments between 1988 and 1990. In its research and development capacity, Fisheries Division was looking to see if longlining could be a viable year-round proposition for Bermudian fishermen.

The first longlining trials off Bermuda in the 1950s used hemp line. In the late 1980s trials, Fisheries Division used 500 lb test monofilament wound around a hydraulically operated drum, with 10 fathom leaders 'stored and deployed from a leader spool for ease of handling'. Leaders were monofilament rather than wire so that unwanted catches like shark could bite through the line easily and escape.

The first sets made during those trials were between three and four miles in length. An average of 120 hooks were deployed per line. Later sets were seven to seven and a half miles in length, with 175–200 hooks per line. The later sets were left for an average of 2.5 hours before being hauled back on board the Division's 48 foot research vessel *Calamus*. The average time taken to set out a line was just over an hour and a half. The average taken to haul it back on board was just under four hours, 'provided there are not too many hitch-ups'.

Over the course of the trials, Fisheries Division laid out almost 120 miles of longline with just under 3200 hooks. The catch totalled 48 marketable fish, an average of 1.5 fish per 100 hooks. The biggest fish taken was a 120 lb yellowfin tuna and the most valuable, a 100 lb swordfish. Fisheries Division concluded that albacore, fished at depths of around 50 fathoms, looked 'most promising' as target species.

The main impediment to a successful longline fishery at that time was considered to be not the availability of fish in deep waters around Bermuda but the lack of processing and handling facilities on shore. The high cost of diesel fuel in Bermuda was also a major disadvantage in creating a competitive longline fishery using relatively small boats.

Fishing Tackle and Methods in Bermuda

All you need to be a fisherman is patience and a worm.

Herb Shriner

Every day may be a fishing day but not every day is a catching day. You have got to be in the right place at the right time in the right conditions.

Danny Farias, ex-commercial fisherman; *The Royal Gazette*, **28 August 1998**

Throw a lucky man into the sea and he will come up with a fish in his mouth.

Arab proverb

A line attached to a fisherman at one end, and a bait camouflaging a hook at the other end, is the standard model around which innumerable permutations are devised to catch fish. Dressed as a lord or stripped to t-shirt and shorts, a fisherman lacking the knowledge to use a fishing line, hook, and bait might just as well whistle underwater as go fishing.

Left: Martin Dixon (right) and John Daughtridge (left) showing off a rather modest size wahoo. Dixon still holds the Bermuda 50 lb test line record for a rainbow runner, 25 lb 6 oz (from 4 August 1980). (Bermuda News Bureau. Photo courtesy of Captain Keith Winter.)

There are as many ways to fish as there are fishermen in the world. Bermuda is no different from anywhere else. Everyone has his own methods. Fishing knowledge is passed on from one generation to another, among siblings and relatives, from one friend to another, each according to his means, guided by his inclinations and diverted by his imagination.

Conditions for fishing are never exactly the same in Bermuda from one day to the next. Similar at times, but never the same. A successful fisherman observes the conditions. He takes note of what works or doesn't work, according to the tide, the phase of the moon, the time of day, currents, location, and the behaviour of the fish.

Some Bermuda fishermen – especially commercial fishermen – are highly innovative, constantly modifying their methods, trying new techniques, new technology, adapting old skills or new technology to local conditions, always refining their skills to improve the chances of success.

The variations of fishing in Bermuda also reflect the differences in fishing from the shore, around the reef, and offshore. Learning how to fish is as much about observing the differences of location, weather, tide, and fish behaviour as it is about knowing what tackle and methods to use.

The variables of what tackle and bait to use are virtually infinite, according to conditions, the fisherman's personal preferences, whether he's lazy or keen, skinny or fat, rich or poor, or just wants to be by himself for a few hours, dipping his toes in the sea, humming a tune, and watching the clouds go by.

The following observations give an outline of how fishing is *generally* practised in Bermuda, some of which might be instructive to know.

The only real way to learn how to fish, however, is to fish.

Line

The very earliest line used in Bermuda for fishing was made of twisted natural fibres such as strands of palmetto leaf, jute or hemp rope, or flax. Early records show that lines used for fishing included rope strands and even, in one instance, 'shoe-thread suitable for fishing lines, being of the cargo of the brig Caesar bound from Newcastle-on-Tyne to Baltimore, Md., and stranded on the reefs off the west end of Bermuda'.

Other natural fibres (such as hemp and cotton) were used over the centuries until the invention of plastic polymers in the 20th century.

(Nets were probably the most common means of fishing in Bermuda for most of the island's early history. From an account in the year of Bermuda's first settlement, 1609, via E. A. McCallan's *Life on Old St David's*: 'Likewise in Furbushers building Bay [Richard Frobisher, arrived on the *Sea Venture*] we had a large Sein, or Trammell Net . . . which reached from one side of the Dock to the other; with which (I may boldly say) we have taken five thousand of small and great fish at one haul.')

When sportfishing first took off in Bermuda after the Second World War, braided Dacron (an artificial fibre) was the most commonly used line for offshore gamefishing. Dacron braid was soft and thin. It could be joined to another line by splicing or braiding. It had minimum stretch and wound well around a reel spool under pressure from a hooked fish, making it eminently suitable for trolling.

Dacron was quite flimsy to handle, however, and the lightest classes of line (up to about 30 lb test) were not particularly easy to use. Strands could abrade, too, reducing the strength of the line. Exposure to the sun weakened the line further. Dacron nevertheless had the advantage of being clearly visible to the fisherman who could keep an eye on its trail through the water. Fish, however, could also see it easily, which rather diminished its advantage to the angler.

Nowadays virtually all the fishing line in use in Bermuda is monofilament, a single (*mono*) filament of extruded nylon that provides high strength, flexibility, resistance to abrasion, and good transparency. The last is an important factor considering that fish can see line more easily in Bermuda's clear waters than in most other parts of the world. Monofilament also sinks faster than Dacron.

Small angler, light tackle, game fish. (Photo courtesy of Captain Allen DeSilva.)

On the downside, monofilament stretches more than braided line, has a greater diameter than braided line of equivalent breaking strain, and knots joining monofilament lines are susceptible to slippage.

Any fisherman who tries to pull his line free from around a rock or some other piece of underwater Bermuda real estate will attest to the stretchability of monofilament.

It goes virtually without saying that the size (test strength) of the line to use depends on the size of fish the angler expects to catch. 'Light' tackle line is anything up to 20–25 lb test. Genuine 'heavy' tackle is from 80 to 130 lb test.

Anglers fishing around the shoreline of Bermuda usually need light line of no more than 12 lb test. Over the reefs, line up to 20 lb test would be adequate in most cases.

Offshore, lines might vary from light 8 lb test on a spinning reel for fishing in a chum, to 130 lb test on the outriggers. Flat lines trolled off the stern of a boat might be from 30 to 80 lb test, depending on the skill of the fishermen aboard (novices may be more likely to lose a large fish on lighter line), the varieties of fish expected, the number of reels rigged, and the personal preferences of the fishermen.

Experienced anglers looking for record fish, or to use their skill in playing the fish, might choose a relatively light test line. The less experienced might use heavier line for the greater security of boating the fish.

Commercial fishermen generally use heavy test line for the greater guarantee of catching fish for the market. Longlining for swordfish is not common in Bermuda, but at least one local boat (*Ark Angel*, usually berthed at Dockyard in Somerset) is specifically geared up for swordfishing by longline, with heavy monofilament of 800 to 1000 lb test spooled on a large drum near the stern of the boat.

Leader

In both saltwater and freshwater fishing, but particularly offshore trolling for gamefish, it is desirable to attach a short length of heavy leader line between the lighter main line and the hook in situations where the fish would ordinarily cut the lighter main line by its sharp teeth, abrasion, sharp shock from a strike, or breakage by the tail or fins of a large fighting fish.

Leader material is either monofilament or wire. Wire predominated when gamefishing off Bermuda first started, because heavy tackle monofilament was not generally available. Wire is still commonly used, but nowadays heavy monofilament predominates, because of its transparency in the water, among its other attributes.

Wire offers great security from breakage and loss of the fish that present the most danger from sharp cutting or raspy teeth, such as wahoo, barracuda, or shark, or from thrashing bulk, such as marlin. Wire is used more for a trolled line than for still fishing. Fish generally approach a trolled bait from behind and have less clear sight of the leader. The wake of the boat travelling at five to eight knots or more also reduces the visibility of the wire leader.

Leader wire comes as single strand and cable or twisted wire. Single strand is the least expensive, easiest to rig, and most commonly used type in gamefishing offshore of Bermuda. The main disadvantage of single strand wire is that kinks, which reduce its strength, form more easily than in cable. Unkinking wire, depending on the degree of deformity, can weaken the leader even more. The safest option is simply to replace kinked wire.

A single length of monofilament up to 300 lb test is a suitable leader for most gamefishing situations in Bermuda, including tough customers like wahoo and marlin.

A 6 to 12 foot length of 50–100 lb test monofilament for light to medium weight 20–30 lb test flat lines is likely to be adequate for smaller gamefish such as dolphin or small tunas. Twelve to fifteen feet of 100–300 lb test monofilament is a secure leader rig for most larger fish.

An even more secure arrangement would be a short (up to 24 inch) wire leader between the main monofilament leader and the hook, for resistance against sharp cutting teeth or the striking bill of a marlin. Baits such as ballyhoo or small bonito are also somewhat easier for non-professionals to rig with wire.

Most offshore fishermen in Bermuda rig leaders with lures or fresh bait in advance. When trolling commences, or when a bait and leader is lost to a strike, the coiled prepared rig, with a snap swivel on the end, is ready to attach quickly to a plain swivel fitted to the end of the main line.

Hooks

The Mustad company of Norway is the world's largest manufacturer of hooks and provides most of the hooks used by fishermen in Bermuda today. Mustad started up in 1832 and today produces hooks in tens of thousands of different patterns, sizes, and finishes. In many countries, including Bermuda, Mustad is by far the largest brand of fish hooks.

Fish hooks are made from extruded steel wire which is tempered for strength and shaped according to the size, pattern, and finish of the type of hook desired.

The structure of a hook is comprised of its shank, with an eye at the bottom end, the bend around the point (which may be barbed or, less typically, unbarbed), the space between the point and the shank (the *gap*), and the depth of the bend to the point of the hook (the *throat*).

Hooks are sized by a scaling system. Small hooks are scaled by straight numbers: the larger the number, the smaller the hook. The smallest hooks on this scale (less than $\frac{1}{4}$ inch long) are numbered around 20 or 22. The largest are number 1. Hooks larger than number 1 use a scale starting at 1/0, continuing up to as large as 20/0. A size 14/0 Mustad shark hook, for example, is about 8 inches long.

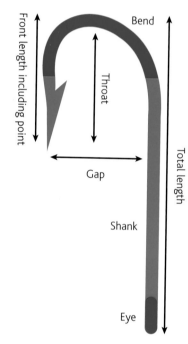

In the illustration the various parts of a fish hook are shown and labelled. The two most important dimensions of the hook are its gap and its throat. The hook shown here is a Mustad saltwater hook. Note the width of the gap, the distance between the point and the shank, and the depth of the throat of the hook. These generous dimensions make for a bigger bite, for deeper penetration of the point, and for better holding power. The weight of the fish is carried up on the centre of the bend.

Hook sizes are determined not only by length but by a range of other shape and style criteria, such as the size of the gap between the point and the shank. Different criteria apply to different categories of hooks. There is no particular standard for all hooks although the numbering system is consistent within a specific group of hooks and *generally* indicative for all hooks.

Hooks can either be straight (with the point aligned along the plane of the shank), or offset (with the point twisted slightly to one side of the plane of the shank). Both offset and straight hooks are suitable for any saltwater still fishing, although offset types seem to have a better hook-up rate. When fish try to throw an offset hook, the point tends to dig deeper into the fish's mouth. Offset hooks can, however, impair the trolling action of lures and live baits, and straight hooks are more usually preferred for use with trolled lines.

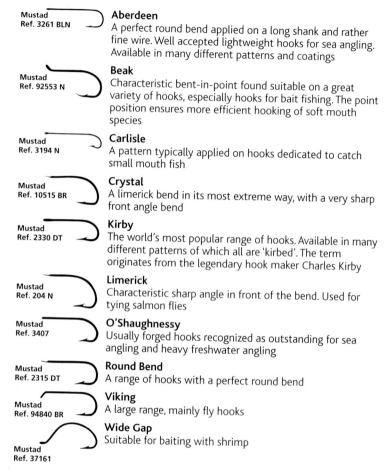

Aberdeen
A perfect round bend applied on a long shank and rather fine wire. Well accepted lightweight hooks for sea angling. Available in many different patterns and coatings

Beak
Characteristic bent-in-point found suitable on a great variety of hooks, especially hooks for bait fishing. The point position ensures more efficient hooking of soft mouth species

Carlisle
A pattern typically applied on hooks dedicated to catch small mouth fish

Crystal
A limerick bend in its most extreme way, with a very sharp front angle bend

Kirby
The world's most popular range of hooks. Available in many different patterns of which all are 'kirbed'. The term originates from the legendary hook maker Charles Kirby

Limerick
Characteristic sharp angle in front of the bend. Used for tying salmon flies

O'Shaughnessy
Usually forged hooks recognized as outstanding for sea angling and heavy freshwater angling

Round Bend
A range of hooks with a perfect round bend

Viking
A large range, mainly fly hooks

Wide Gap
Suitable for baiting with shrimp

Hook families and characteristics. Since fish hooks became an individualized product, fish hook manufacturers have divided the hooks into families with reference to the originator of the hook or the originating area. Occasionally, the family name refers to certain properties of the hook. Presented here is a selection of the families frequently used in fish hook terminology.

The shank of a hook may be different degrees of short or long. Long shank hooks are easier to pull out of a fish, but they are also more visible to fish. Hooks used in Bermuda tend to be either medium length or short (the latter especially in hooks where the shape is a round style with a wider gap than straighter styles).

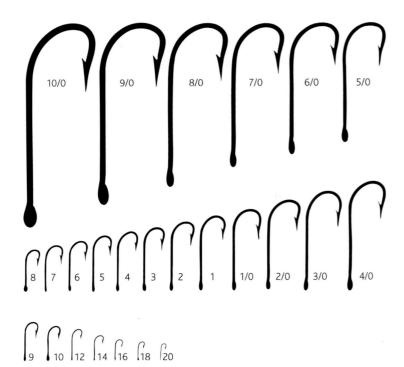

1665
A very popular all-round hook worldwide

1815
A light Aberdeen hook for all purposes

1980
Best selling eel hook

Different sizes of hooks.

A hook's eye may be ringed (that is, with the bottom of the shank bent around to form an eye), or needle type (that is, with an eye drilled through the flattened bottom end of the shank). Ringed eye hooks are generally used for most inshore fishing, as well as lighter tackle offshore fishing.

Heavy tackle fishing tends to use drilled hooks for great strength since larger fish can straighten out the ring type eye. Some big gamefish hooks with a ring eye have an eye brazed closed against the shank for great strength. The eyes may also be straight in line with the shank, or curved inwards towards the shank, or outwards away from it (the last mainly for fly fishing). (Some hooks actually have no round eye at all but are simply the flattened bottom of the shank.)

The point of a hook may be straight, roughly parallel with the shank, or it may be curved inwards towards the shank, or it may bend slightly out away from the shank. Tuna hooks and other styles used for big gamefish are often curved inwards. Small hooks with an inwardly curved point, used on light handlines for small fish, have gained in popularity in Bermuda. Sometimes only the point of the barb is curved inwards, like a beak (beak hooks), particularly well suited for catching live bait.

The common and garden variety of hook used by the occasional amateur fisherman in Bermuda is usually an all-round style, medium length, with offset point, ringed eye, front length bending slightly inwards towards the shank, and with a straight point.

Standard all-round style offset hooks sized 1/0 to 3/0 handle most species of Bermuda fish around the shoreline. For smaller fish (small grunts or bream), any size from about 5 up to 1 will do. With spinning tackle or for light handline fishing around the reef or inshore waters, hooks sized 3/0 to 6/0 would be appropriate for most species, from whitewater snapper to yellowtail. The size of hook used for gamefishing offshore may be anything from a 6/0 (for spinning tackle used in a chum) to 16/0 (for trolling on heavy tackle).

A good rule of thumb about choosing a hook is, when in doubt about the best size to use from a range of, say, three similar sizes, pick the smaller one. The clarity of Bermuda's water makes any piece of bright gleaming steel slung with bait very visible to fish. As with fishing line, the less hook the fish can see, the better.

Baits and Lures

Knowing the different types of food that different fish eat is an essential part of choosing what bait to use to catch those fish.

115

Squid, fry, anchovy, mussels, or the flesh of other molluscs or crustaceans (including small live crabs), alone or in combinations, will please the palate of most shore and reef fish in Bermuda. Small bream, grunts, squirrelfish, and other small shore fish (including pompano) will readily take bread, squeezed into a doughy ball on the hook.

Inshore fishermen in Bermuda often use a small live white grunt as bait to catch large grey snappers. The grunt is generally hooked through the back, thrown out on a weighted line, and left until a hungry snapper comes along.

Offshore baits used for chumming, trolling, and bottom fishing, including lures for trolling, constitute the widest range of possibilities. Anchovy, pilchard, fry and strips of other fish (mackerel or bonito, for example) are mainly used for still fishing (on bottom lines and in a chum).

Chumming has been a popular alternative to trolling around the offshore banks for many years. From an anchored (or sometimes drifting) boat, chopped up anchovy, fry, or other small bait fish, sometimes mixed with sand, is thrown out over the transom to create a chum line that drifts out with the tide to attract tunas, wahoo, and other gamefish. Anglers drift their lines out in the chum in the hope that a fish will strike as it feeds on the chum.

Trolled baits and lures are either dead whole fish (usually ballyhoo (garfish), bonito, other small tuna, or ocean robin), whole live fish (most commonly bonito or other small tuna), or feather or plastic artificial lures.

Because of their weight, whole fish are rigged on heavy tackle, usually from outriggers. Most small to medium size artificial lures are trolled from flat lines directly off the stern of the boat. Large heavyweight lures used for big gamefish like marlin are trolled from outriggers.

In the early days of gamefishing off Bermuda, feather lures were the most common artificial lures used for trolling. Today plastics in a wide range of formats and colours have taken over from feather lures.

The use of lures or baits from a trolled line is no substitute for knowing when, how, and where to fish, and what fish to catch. Finding

James Pearman with a small 40–50 lb white marlin. (Photo courtesy of Captain Allen DeSilva.)

the right lure for deep sea fishing in Bermuda as anywhere else is a matter of trial and error, asking other fishermen what seems to work best under certain conditions and at different times of the year . . . and luck.

The only certainty about artificial lures for trolling is that the magic one that attracts *all* fish to *all* fishermen in *all* conditions has yet to be created.

Some lures will skip in the wake of the boat like flying fish. Some will travel just below the surface in imitation of swimming jacks, ocean robins, or other pelagic bait fish. Others may be dragged 5 or 10 feet below the surface by downrigger.

There are no hard and fast rules about which types of lures work best in Bermuda conditions, although it is worth remembering that gamefish take a lure (or fresh bait) mainly because it appears to them like breakfast, lunch, dinner, or an in-between-meal snack. Any lure which best imitates the colour, form, or action of a delicacy commonly consumed by wahoo, tuna, dolphin, marlin, or the like (such as flying fish, ballyhoo, ocean robin, squid or small tuna) is most likely to attract their attention.

Large lures used for marlin fishing typically comprise a hard bright coloured plastic head with a trailing plastic skirt. Large 'konaheads' (lures with a slanted concave shape to the head, creating an erratic action through the water), developed in Hawaii, are particularly favoured for marlin fishing in Bermuda. Large flat headed lures, which run straight but make more of a surface disturbance than bullethead or concave lures, are also common in marlin fishing.

Bermuda's waters are very clear, especially offshore where there is no sediment, pollution, or runoff from the land. Sea conditions are usually wavy, keeping a surface trolled bait or lure skipping regularly in and out of the water. Any trolled lure or bait is therefore highly visible to fish in Bermuda waters.

Whether or not fish strike may be as much a reflection of their inclination to take a certain lure or bait as an indication of the absence or presence of fish. For that reason, a regular change of lures or bait until a good strike rate is achieved is a more highly recommended strategy for gamefishing in Bermuda than in other places where water clarity and visibility are of lower quality.

In the words of Jack Zinzow, author of *Saltwater Fishing*, 'Successful trolling requires having a variety of types of baits and a variety of colours available. You must offer a variety!'

In his *Guide to the Reef, Shore and Game Fish of Bermuda*, Louis S. Mowbray had this to say about the most effectively coloured artificial lures used in Bermuda (bearing in mind that the book was written in the early 1960s when feather lures predominated): 'Black feathers, or an all-black feathered lure give very excellent results. If the fish are not hitting at one colour, try another. All white, red and white, all red, yellow or yellow and green, and all black are tried and true lures for ocean trolling and an angler can seldom be wrong in using them.'

Of more recent vintage, the highly respected Australian angler Peter Goadby noted (in his 1991 book *Saltwater Gamefishing*) that success

This 431 lb 8 oz blue marlin was caught by Gary Rego (left) on 30 lb test line, 29 July 1976, during the marlin tournament that year. The catch set a new Bermuda record for the line class which stills stands. (Photo courtesy of Captain Allen DeSilva.)

depended on the constant observation of conditions, how the lures are performing behind the boat, and keeping a good record of which lures work best. 'Most success falls to skippers, crews and anglers who maintain concentration and constant watch on lures and what is happening in and on the sea. The factors that aid success in bait fishing are equally important with lures.'

Teasers are trolled behind offshore gamefishing boats. These devices, like lures without a hook, are used to create a disturbance in the wake of the boat, mainly to attract billfish. Teasers are attached by wire and swivel to a rope or other heavy line snubbed around a cleat on the transom and dragged up to about 20 feet astern.

Teasers used in Bermuda are usually large wooden plugs that may have some colour. Striking bills from marlin, attacks from wahoo and other gamefish, and wear and tear from constant use tend to endow teasers with a rich pattern of scrapes, scratches, and striations that enhance their function to create a lively surface disturbance.

Downriggers and Kites

Introduced in Bermuda in the late 1960s, the downrigger has been the single most valuable new technology used to improve the success rate of offshore fishing in Bermuda for pelagic species such as wahoo. Most sportfishing and commercial boats have at least one and more often two downriggers fitted on their transom. The rig is 'the most efficient tool ever designed for deep-trolling', as one gamefishing expert, Vic Dunaway, has noted. 'It is the only deep-fishing device that allows the angler to present his baits or lures at selected and variable depths, and to keep them there.'

The design of the downrigger is simple, consisting of a bracket base to mount the downrigger on the transom, a reel fitted with a cranking handle and spooled with wire, at the end of which is a lead weight, and an arm to extend the wire over the stern of the boat. The trolled line from the rod is clipped to the wire near the weight by a release snap.

When the wire, with the trolled line clipped to it, is spooled out just over the stern of the moving boat, the weight takes the line and lure to a depth of four to six feet below the surface. The wire will be extended out at a diagonal angle from the stern of the boat by the boat's speed. The total length of the wire payed out to keep the lure or bait at the desired depth will vary depending on the speed of the boat, the design of the weight, and sea conditions at the time. As much as 40 to 60 feet of wire may have to be payed out to keep the lure at a depth of six to eight feet.

Once the wire is payed out to the right length to keep the line and lure at the desired depth, the downrigger is locked. A fish striking the lure releases the line from the clip near the weight, the same way as a strike on an outrigger releases the line from the outrigger.

Some gamefishing captains in Bermuda use a kite (usually a box kite), an innovation of the early 1970s, to troll a flying fish. The kite takes a line from the back of the boat, leading down to a flying fish rigged on the hook so that its fins are set out in a flying position. As the bait is trolled over the water it pops in and out of the waves like a live flying fish. Gamefish, and large tuna in particular, find the skipping action of the flying fish irresistible. A strike on the bait detaches the line from the kite, and the fight is on.

Rods and Reels
Spinning

Two types of rod and reel are used predominantly in Bermuda: spinning tackle and trolling tackle. Spinning tackle lends itself particularly well to most fishing circumstances in Bermuda, including offshore. Deep sea gamefishing tackle is more specialized, although a rod and reel used for trolling around the banks can be used equally well to drop a weighted line to bottom fish on the banks or around the reef platform.

Bermuda is a light tackle fishing paradise. Spinning tackle is the most versatile gear to take advantage of its wide range of opportunities, from ultra-light 2 lb test line up to medium 30 lb test line. The optimum upper limit for spinning tackle is generally considered to be 20 lb test line. Depending on the circumstances, line of from 6 to 20 lb test is appropriate for most eventualities in Bermuda using spinning tackle.

Spinning gear is, by its nature, designed for light tackle fishing. In situations where heavy line may be desirable, a spinning rod and reel

Right: Well known international angler Jim Lopez, fishing off Bermuda in 1971. Note the long, whippy rod, common in the years when sport fishing was practised on lighter tackle, before the development of heavy 130 lb test tackle. Nowadays rods are shorter and stouter, to ease the pressure on the angler and increase pressure on the fish. Lopez still holds several fly tackle world records set in Bermuda in 1973.
(Bermuda News Bureau. Photo courtesy of Captain Keith Winter.)

would be inappropriate. There is simply not much point in using heavy line for heavy tackle situations with intrinsically light tackle gear. Above 30 lb test, in any case, when fishing from shore, the line becomes rather unwieldy to cast.

Spinning reels vary in size and capacity according to the amount and test strength of line they can take. Heavy duty reels can take up to 300 yards of 30 lb test line, but more with lighter test line. The capacity of the reel (yards of line by test strength) is usually indicated on the side of the reel.

In Bermuda rods are usually sold with the spinning reel already attached, facilitating the selection of a suitable size rod. Since reels are easily detachable from the rod, however, they can be mixed and matched according to the fisherman's preferences (and depth of his pocket). In general uses for fishing conditions around Bermuda, a fibreglass rod of six to seven feet in length will be most suitable.

Rods with a stouter, less flexible butt end are used for medium to heavier tackle. The more robust the rod, the heavier weight line (and size of fish) they will handle. The heaviest tackle spinning rods may be from seven to nine feet in length. Shorter rods with a sleeker construction, and more whippy, flexible action, are generally more appropriate for the lightest lines.

In whatever rod and reel combination, the size of the reel and robustness of the rod should be generally appropriate to the line size and fishing conditions anticipated. A small reel will not take very much heavy test line. Conversely, a heavy duty reel will take far more light test line than is generally needed in most light line fishing conditions in Bermuda. A heavy reel, or heavy rod and reel together, would be unnecessarily tiring and cumbersome for casting from the shore to catch small fish such as snappers or bream.

The exception would be in offshore conditions where the angler may be looking for relatively large and lively gamefish using very light line, in which case the larger capacity of the reel will be an advantage. An all-purpose rod and reel combination for Bermuda conditions would be an intermediate size reel with capacity to take 200–250 yards of 15–20 lb test line on a seven foot long rod of moderately robust construction.

Trolling

Any fisherman in Bermuda with ambitions to venture outside the reefs to troll around the edge of the deep or over the banks will need heavy duty tackle that can be set up to drag lures or baits behind a boat for hours at a time, take a strike from a fish anywhere in the range of 5 lb to 500 lb (and more), and resist the strain of the fighting fish for 10 minutes or 10 hours, with variable drag to put the most pressure on the fish and the least pressure on the angler. Whatever its fine light tackle features, spinning gear can never substitute for heavy duty trolling gear under those conditions.

A weighted and baited line dropped from 'trolling' gear is also useful for bottom fishing over the banks, the edge of the deep, or even over the reef platform, to catch larger bottom fish such as groupers, big snappers, or even sharks. It can be used as well for drifting a line out with chum to catch tuna, wahoo, and other pelagic gamefish.

There are two main types of gamefishing reels: the ones with a separate freespool lever and star-shaped drag mechanism (star-drag reels), and the ones that incorporate freespool and drag in a single mechanism (lever-drag or dual-drag reels).

On star-drag reels, the freespool lever, fixed to the side of the reel just above the handle, is flipped to its freespool position when letting line run out freely to the desired distance. The lever is then flipped back to its stop position which stops line running out. The star shaped mechanism at the base of the reel handle is adjusted to tighten or loosen the drag of the line.

Lever-drag reels, with the freespool and drag setting in the same lever mechanism, are operated by a single function: full forward position for maximum drag, full backward position for freespool, and all the degrees of drag in between which can be changed at any time. A separate mechanism pre-sets the range of drag (which is why they are sometimes called dual-drag reels).

In the early days of gamefishing off Bermuda, the only reels in use were the simple star-drag kind. These are still in common use as the least expensive but still dependable, all-purpose reels for the average fisherman in Bermuda with the modest financial means to suit occasional gamefishing or bottom fishing forays. Dual-drag reels are more expensive than star-drag reels, for their more sophisticated internal technology, higher performance standards, and generally higher quality workmanship than star-drag reels.

Penn Reels, one of the world's leading rod and reel manufacturers, has been the gamefish tackle brand leader in Bermuda for many years. Penn Reels started life in 1933, the same time as gamefishing in Bermuda emerged. The venerable Penn Senator range, introduced in the 1940s, features star-drag reels and has been a mainstay of the gamefishing scene in Bermuda since both were getting going in the early years. The Senator range, as with other star-drag makes, is an all-round, durable, workhorse reel that lends itself both to trolling and bottom fishing around Bermuda, for both the regular and the occasional weekend angler.

Penn's distinctive gold finished Penn International line of reels, introduced in the mid-1960s, is a classic example of high quality lever-drag reels used for high performance offshore gamefishing, especially for anglers fishing specifically to IGFA standards. The higher price of these reels, compared with the star-drag types, reflects their more sophisticated machining, technology, and wider range of models.

The main competitor to Penn now is Shimano, the Japanese manufacturer of reels and rods. Penn nevertheless continues to be the best selling brand in Bermuda, because of its long pedigree, all-round quality, and its availability from the local tackle supplier.

Trolling reels are labelled to show the optimum size or range of sizes of line they can take (20 lb test, 30 lb test, etc.). Flat lines trolled off the stern of boats fishing around Bermuda are usually from medium size reels taking up to 50 lb test lines. Outriggers are usually hooked up to reels with at least 500–600 yards of heavy 80–130 lb test lines. The occasional amateur will be adequately served in most situations with a medium size reel taking a minimum of 400 yards of 20–30 lb test line.

In the early days of Bermuda gamefishing, rods were whippy, bending to the weight of the fish and straining the lower back of the angler. Nowadays modern offshore gamefishing rods used in Bermuda are stouter, more rigid, and shorter poles which put less strain on the angler's back. These include stand-up poles and tuna sticks which keep the tip of the rod more upright when the angler is fighting a powerful gamefish.

Offshore tackle from the 1950s and 1960s in Bermuda was mainly light to medium weight. Many large fish (and big marlin in particular) were undoubtedly lost because the tackle then was inadequate to hold them. The widespread use of heavy 130 lb test tackle since the late 1970s has notably enhanced the success rate for boating these big fish.

Captain Alan Card landed Bermuda's first 'grander' marlin, of 1130 lb, in 1979, while 'fishing with two of the first Penn International 130s ever used in Bermuda'.

Before the 1970s, a marlin over 500 lb caught in Bermuda was an acclaimed achievement (particularly so considering the lack of heavy tackle). Nowadays 500 pounders seem to be no more than hors d'oeuvres. Fishermen have seen, and sometimes hooked, big fish around Bermuda for many years, but the tackle to catch them regularly has only become widely available in the past 20 years or so.

Charter captains and other full time commercial fishermen in Bermuda keep up to date about the latest fishing technology and equipment by direct links with suppliers outside Bermuda, since the range of equipment locally, especially new technology, is limited.

Some of Bermuda's charter captains have honed their skills by fishing around the Caribbean and elsewhere during Bermuda's off season in the winter months. Methods used in the Bahamas, Florida, and off Central America have all played a role towards the evolution of deep sea gamefishing techniques in Bermuda.

Access to showcase exhibitions such as the Miami Boat Show in February each year, specialist magazines and newspapers (*Sport Fishing, National Fisherman*, among others), and the Internet have widened the range of possibilities for dedicated fishermen in Bermuda to acquire more knowledge about fishing, and up-to-date fishing technology, than was the case just a generation ago.

Commercial Fishing

There are still fishermen in Bermuda who remember the early part of the 1900s when they only used locally built sailboats and rowboats to fish. Boats up to 30 feet long could either be sailed or, on calm days, sculled out to the fishing grounds.

Typical fishing boats of those years had a wide beam, long keel, and shallow draft (to clear the reefs). Fish wells in the bilges kept fish alive until the fishermen returned home. The wells were built of wood, finished on the insides with cement, and could accommodate as much as 500 lb of live fish. The walls of the wells were wider at the bottom and tapered up towards the top, to keep the water (and fish) from slopping out. Sea water circulated through the wells from as many as six openings (faucets) on either side of the keel.

Old fishing sloops were commonly rigged with a leg-of-mutton sail hooped or laced to a mast that could be set up and taken down easily since there were no supporting stays and no boom. A simple halyard raised and lowered the sail. Other boats had a more conventional stayed mast, with a Marconi (or Bermudian) rigged sail and long boom extending well past the transom.

The most common characteristics of the old sailing sloops were that they were heavily built from local wood, beamy with low freeboard, had ample cockpit space for the live-well, and had a long and shallow keel. Fishermen's boat races on non-fishing days were a regular event.

Rowboats (gigs, or dinghies) were used for netting (as some still are today), fishing by hook and line, or for hauling traps. Most fishermen were equally adept at sculling with a single oar set in the sculling hole on the transom, or rowing from either a forward or aft position in the boat.

In his 1948 book *Life on Old St David's*, E. A. McCallan describes the gear usually kept in sail or oar powered fishing boats:

Grains (or *staff-an'grains*): 'a two-pronged spear about 8 inches long fitted to a yellow-pine staff 16 to 18 feet long; used to strike or spear fish, lobsters, scuttles [octopus].'

Nippers: 'a pincer-like implement attached to a staff about 15 feet long, and operated by means of a light rope or line fastened to the movable half; used to nip or pick up shellfish and other objects under water.'

Water-glass: 'a water-tight glass-bottomed box from 10 to 14 inches square, and hopper-shaped as a rule; used to discern objects under water and often in association with nippers.'

Shark oil: 'sprinkled on the surface of the water to calm it, usually when nippers were in use.'

Killick: 'a stone weighing from 10 to 20 pounds . . . to which was lashed one end of an oleander stick about 5 feet long; to the stone and to the other end of the stick the mooring rope was bent or tied. This was used as an anchor, particularly on rough bottom where an iron anchor or grapnel might get hung or caught, and so lost. The stick of the killick kept the mooring rope off the bottom, and reduced chafing. When a boat was moored over rough bottom, in the absence of a killick, a trip-rope was usually bent on the anchor or grapnel.'

Creeper: 'a four-fluted implement much like a small grapnel; used to drag or creep for objects under water.'

Jack-iron: 'an eye-bolt about a foot long; used to clear a line hung or caught on the bottom.'

Dipping net: 'a few were of net, but most were of burlap . . . attached to forked sticks; used to dip fish from the well, and – if netted – to lift chubs from the water lest they break from the hook.'

Kibble: 'a club 12 to 18 inches long; . . . used to kill fish, to drive tight wooden thole-pins [early type of oar-locks], and like service.'

Hatchets: 'used for similar purposes as the kibble, and to trim fish.'

Other indispensable gear included sharp gutting and scaling knives, whetstones, chopping boards, strings made from palmetto fronds from which fish were strung for customers to carry the fish home, conch shells with their tip broken off and blown into, like trumpets, to announce fresh fish for sale, and bailers and sponges to bail out and wash down boats.

Fishermen used the water-glass to look for fish or likely holes where fish congregated around the bottom in shallow water.

In deeper water they could take marks from the land to position their boats at locations they had been baiting up for long periods, to attract and keep fish at those locations. Captain Geary Pitcher describes how fishermen took marks from the land to find their fishing locations ('scribes'), a navigational method still used by fishermen in Bermuda today (as well as by harbour and river pilots around the world to navigate vessels in and out of ports).

They used to make it [the 'scribe'] from the land. They used to take somebody's house, then another person's house, and an angle from St. George's. Say, you take a house here, another house here, and you bring that house right over this one; you take another house here, and another here, and bring that over. So these two [position] lines will come to one point. One line would be a 'running mark', a straight mark like the lighthouse over the battery.

If you want a 'stop mark', you take the hill on the flats over the oil dock, say. Or [the] tank and the oil docks. Or along one of the wireless poles. When you left here, you'd go out lighthouse over the battery quarters.

If your fishing place was within 3–4 miles, you could go right definitely on that spot. You can't go wrong. Pinhead it! You could go within, I'd say, 2 feet . . . Anything within 5 miles [of the land] you can get it pretty accurate.

In some places around Bermuda, off the East End for example, deep water is within a few miles of land. By following landmarks, fishermen did not need to see the bottom to find their fishing locations. They could bait up and fish locations in 25 fathoms, just on the edge of deep water, day in, day out, simply by following known position lines to those locations. (Grouper Ground, just to the southeast of Cooper's Island, was just such a location.)

Some fishing was regularly done around the breakers on the perimeter of the reef platform. Captain Pitcher recounts that 'the olden people', before his time, anchored between the breakers to fish in less than 10 fathoms of water. They would position the boat as near to the reef as possible by pulling up to it with anchors off the bow and stern. 'They used to use a very large line, big as my little finger. When they hook one of them fish [rockfish], it meant hook and hold. If you gave him any line he'd cut it off. When you held it, he'd mount with the tide and come to the surface.'

Fishermen used handlines up to about 100 fathoms long. They fished mainly for groupers and rockfish, in 10–12 fathoms inshore, and in 20–30 fathoms around the edge of the deep. They fished for snappers in the deeper waters sloping off the edge, up to 60–80 fathoms. Over the banks they fished mainly for groupers in 25–30 fathoms. Sometimes they set a trolled handline on the outward or return journey to the banks to catch a tuna, wahoo, or other floating fish. Generally speaking, however, fishermen fished only for the big three market fish in those days: rockfish, grouper, and snapper. Anything else was lagniappe.

Early fishing lines in Bermuda were made of natural cordage or hemp. Cotton line of 32–46 thread size was common by the 1940s. Now handlines used by commercial fishermen are typically 300–600 lb test monofilament. Piano wire is also used, especially in deep water fishing. A strong current, however, tends to set up a vibration along wire, which has a repellent effect on fish.

In past generations fishermen commonly wrapped a flat piece of lead around the line to weight it, a foot or so above the hook, tamping it up tight to the line with a hatchet. Most fishermen used a line with a single hook. They started the day's fishing with a small 'half-penny hook' to catch small groupers or other bottom fish, working up to large size hooks, and fish, during the day. A good all-round hook was the 'one-and-a-half penny' size, used for average size groupers and rockfish. Breaker fishermen used a big 'six-penny' hook.

These days a long vertical (or drop) line is weighted at the bottom end with five or six sash weights (the same as used in sash windows). A series of up to 15 leaders, each a few metres long, are rigged along the main line at intervals of similar length as the leaders so the hooks do not snag. Leader lines are light 30–60 lb test so they break free of the main line if the hooks snag on the bottom, therefore causing the fisherman to lose no more than a few hooks while the main line remains intact.

The line is payed out to the bottom, lifted a fathom or so from the seabed, and buoyed on the surface, left to drift. After a few hours the line is hauled back on board, any fish are removed, hooks are re-baited, and the line is set out again.

When old timers fished with a single hook, they squeezed up chopped bait into a handful size ball which they attached to the line near the hook by pushing a bight of the line through a ball of bait. Throwing the line overboard, they struck off the bait on the bottom by giving a slight tug on the line. The bait would spread out, falling around the hook (which usually also had bait attached), concealing it when the fish came to eat the bait. Too strong a tug on the line would spread the bait too far away from the hook for a fish to be hooked when it ate the bait.

While the line was down fishermen continued to chop bait on the stern of the boat, mushing it up and washing it overboard as a chum to attract fish on the bottom from a few hundred yards away. According to Captain Pitcher, 'Some calls it "chum", "charming", "washing in bait". Like "I washed in so much bait".'

Fishermen baited up their own fishing spots over long periods, to attract and hold fish at those locations. Fishermen respected each other's sites and would not, ordinarily, trespass on another man's spot. Baiting up a site gave a fisherman the right to fish that site exclusively. Nowadays baiting up is less common practice among commercial fishermen. Nor is there the respect for another fisherman's site as there used to be – because fishermen no longer have tenure over particular sites.

When live fish ponds were common around the shoreline of Bermuda, fishermen brought their catch home alive, to sell directly and keep surplus fish in their ponds. Fishermen caught bait to feed the fish in their ponds as well as for fishing. Around April the ponds were cleaned out (if all the fish had been sold) to prepare them for the next fishing season.

As Captain Pitcher has said, 'That's what they had going before the deep freeze came around.' And that's why there have been no live fish ponds in active use in Bermuda since the 1950s.

Commercial fishermen in Bermuda today still fish with relatively simple gear. The main difference between now and earlier years has been mechanization, including winches fitted on board boats to haul up lines (and, before 1990, fish pots) from as deep as several hundred fathoms. Vertical lines are rigged with up to 15 hooks per line now (the maximum permitted by law) and set in deeper water than in earlier years. Old methods such as striking off balls of bait against the bottom have consequently become largely redundant.

The demise of pot fishing in Bermuda has directed more fishermen towards the pelagic fishery, requiring the widespread use of rods and reels and other gear developed from recreational fishing that old timers never used.

Nowadays full-time commercial fishermen typically carry nets for catching bait fish (such as fry) and some schooling inshore food fish (such as jacks), handlines for drift or bottom fishing, and trolling gear including outriggers and downriggers. Few commercial fishermen specialize in the offshore pelagic fishery, but most carry the equipment they need to fish for wahoo, tuna, or other floating fish when it suits them to do so.

Commercial fishing boats in Bermuda range from small outboard powered skiffs (in the minority), to 30 to 40 foot boats with covered wheelhouses, a cabin under the foredeck to store gear, inboard diesels, and open deck space aft (sometimes equipped with a fighting chair or

Yellowfin tuna are an important staple of both commercial and recreational offshore fishing in Bermuda. (Photo courtesy of Andrew Card.)

two). Electronics such as depth-finders and fish-finders, as well as ship-to-shore radios, are now standard equipment. Some boats are fitted with powered winches to haul lines from deep water, a vestige of pot fishing days when winches were used to haul traps. (Ex-pot fishing boats often have a metal plate affixed to the outer hull of the boat, amidships, to protect against abrasion from the pots hauled in over the side.)

Commercial fishing boats used in Bermuda are now mainly brought in from the United States. Some older boats, however, were built in Bermuda and are still active today. They typically range from 20 to 25 feet long and are rather narrow beamed, with a simple covered wheelhouse and uncluttered afterdeck. An awning is sometimes rigged over the afterdeck when, at the end of the fishing day, the fishermen clean and fillet their catch on a wooden chopping board laid on the transom.

Mullet Fishing by East End Fishermen

Schools of mullet, a silvery grey cigar shaped fish, patrol the shallow waters around the shoreline of Bermuda year-round. Cruising along in small groups just below the surface, or snubbing around the bottom for food, mullet ignore baited hooks. Most commercial fishermen catch mullet by net and use them as a trolling bait, although garfish, which troll more smoothly, are preferred for this purpose.

On the fishing totem pole of desirability in Bermuda, mullet rate close to the bottom, not far above slippery dick. For East Enders from St George's and St David's, however, mullet are a prized prey for a few weeks every year in late October and early November. At that time spawning female fish yield up a natural treasure that East Enders covet as much as the finest Sevruga caviar: fresh roe.

Generations of East Enders have looked forward to the promise of a new batch of fresh cured mullet roe towards the end of every year. While the rest of Bermuda tucks into cassava pie at Christmas, across the Causeway they salivate at the prospect of a slice of mullet roe, richly flavoured by a simple curing process that belies its humble origins.

Mullet season is an annual tradition for a dozen or so East End fishermen. Early in November they set off in small boats to lay out gill nets close to shore, in the hope of trapping female mullets with their casements of soft roe intact. Nets are typically set at nightfall and checked the following morning.

For the dedicated mullet fishermen, the occasion is as much a social gathering as a fishing expedition, a chance for the boys to camp out together for a few days, to trade stories and reminisce about the past, generously fuelled by goodwill, soused with abundant camaraderie, and lubricated by liberal quantities of iced tea . . .

Mullets taken from the net with roes intact are handled gently. The roe sac is excised carefully from the belly to prevent spillage of the ochre-yellow eggs. After salting for about half an hour, to draw out water, the sac of roe is placed between two boards covered with wax paper. Weights are placed on the top board to flatten the roe, after which it is hung out in the sun to dry thoroughly for a few weeks.

By the end of November or early December, the roe sacs have dried to a hardened dark pod that yields up to 30 or 40 thin slices. A snick of roe can be chewed slowly in the mouth like beef jerky, or spread over toast, or used in recipes.

Nowadays the mullet, like many other fish species around Bermuda, are nowhere near as numerous as they used to be. The annual roe quest, however, continues, if not always blessed by a bounty of fish, in the spirit of a uniquely local East End social tradition.

Restricted Fishing Areas and Species

In a one-day fishing tournament recently, 3,800 lbs of hinds were brought in. . . about 80% of the hinds caught during the two month [spawning] period have been in spawning condition. . . The point in this being, of course, that if proportionally greater catches of a particular kind are taken before they have a chance to lay and fertilize their eggs in any given year, there is a danger of over-fishing the species. The only way to offset such catches during the spawning gatherings of these species is for the fishermen themselves to exercise practical common sense by wise restraint in order that their future livelihood in the fishing industry will be ensured. It would be morally wrong to legislate against the practice, but if the continued trend proves to be significantly detrimental to the annual yield, then it may become an economic MUST to restrict fishing for certain species during specific periods.

Louis S. Mowbray, Curator of the Government Aquarium, ZBM Radio broadcast, 16 July 1968.

Louis S. Mowbray's pointed warning about the dangers of overfishing, from a series of radio broadcasts he made in the 1960s, proved to be a prophetic insight into realities about the Bermuda fishery that would materialize in future decades. Mowbray, among others, had already discerned in the 1960s that a potentially serious imbalance was evolving between the marine resources of Bermuda, and fish stocks in particular, and the human population exploiting those resources.

Restrictions to control fishing in Bermuda had been enacted by legislation for almost 350 years. Parliamentary government in Bermuda was established in 1620. Between 1620 and 1916, when the first Fisheries Act was drawn up, more than a dozen pieces of legislation were enacted to control the local fisheries (including, in 1740/41, the first whale fishery legislation). Many of the various acts and orders were aimed at restricting the use of nets, to prevent overfishing and 'the destruction of fish'.

The first fish pot ban was enacted in 1791, almost exactly 200 years before the 1990 ban.

Modern fisheries legislation in Bermuda started with the first Fisheries Act, in 1916. After the Second World War, the Board of Trade (Fisheries) Regulations 1947 came into force. At that time the Board of Trade functioned as the authority to regulate all areas of commercial activity in Bermuda, including the fisheries. The Fisheries Regulations of 1953 were amended and revoked by the Fisheries Regulations 1963.

Much of Bermuda's fisheries legislation enacted between 1620 and up till the mid-1900s was characterized by its prescriptive nature, to ordain and delineate the parameters of what was permissible with the objective being to exert statutory control over the fisheries.

From the mid-1900s onwards the legislation has been increasingly proscriptive, to restrict or abolish altogether certain fishing methods and gear, circumscribe fishing areas, and prohibit the taking of certain species of fish. Environmental concerns abut the resource itself, rather than governance of the fisheries *per se*, have informed fisheries legislation since the 1960s.

In the 25 years between 1971 and 1996, about a dozen fisheries legislative orders and amendments were enacted as protectionist devices in defence of the resource and constraint of the fishermen.

One of the primary goals of contemporary legislation has been to reduce pressure on the resource. The parallel effect has been to reduce commercial fishermen's ability to fish the resource to an economically viable degree. Part of the reason is that, while the focus has been to restrict *fishing* access to the resource, legislation has so far not restricted the number of *fishermen* afforded access to the resource. Consequently there are more fishermen (including recreational fishermen) exploiting a diminishing resource, in terms of access to areas and species.

Coral Reef Preservation Act

The first contemporary statute aimed at protecting Bermuda's marine environment, The Coral Reef Preserves Act of 1966, established two coral reef preserves (The South Shore Coral Reef Preserve and the North Shore Coral Reef Preserve) which prohibited the removal or possession of, and damage to, all 'plants or animals, whether alive or dead, which are attached to the coast, sea-bed or any reef in the two preserves'. Line fishing was not prohibited in those areas.

This legislation, incidentally, included a prohibition against taking conch shells from the sea. Earlier generations of fishermen used conchs as a blowhorn while peddling fresh fish for sale from horse-pulled carts along Bermuda's roads. The trumpet sound of the conch announced the arrival of fresh fish for sale, in the same way that ambulating vendors all over the world use bells, horns, or musical jingles from their vehicles to announce the sale of their wares.

The Fisheries (Prohibited Areas and Prohibited Period) Order of 1971 was a seminal piece of legislation that restricted fishing in three protected areas during a closed fishing season originally from 25 May to 15 August but subsequently amended by the Fisheries (Protected Areas) Amendment Order 1996 to 1 May to 31 August.

By the early 1970s fishermen were becoming aware of the dangers of overfishing hinds and other grouper species. On their initiative, a series of regulations and restrictions were introduced by legislation, the first and most important of which were the Fisheries Act 1972 and related Fisheries Regulations 1972. The Act updated The fisheries Regulations 1963 and the Board of Trade (Fisheries) Regulations 1947. It also served as the authority for enacting The Fisheries (Protected

Species) Order 1978 and The Fisheries (Protected Areas) Order 1990, among other legislation.

The 1972 Fisheries Regulations, which today provide the benchmark for all fisheries legislation in Bermuda, included this provision:

> In any case where a person takes any fish which cannot lawfully . . . be taken, injured, sold, purchased or kept in possession, then in any such case it shall be the duty of the person taking the fish to return it forthwith into the sea; and if the person fails to do so he shall be guilty of an offence against these Regulations.

Since 1972 all fishermen who catch a species of fish which they are not lawfully entitled to keep have been required to throw it back in the sea, according to the above clause. No doubt some may do this, aware that they are throwing away part of their income to satisfy their conscience. At least as many, however, and probably more, reason that the fish is already dead, or likely to die when thrown back in the sea, and therefore is of much greater value to the fisherman for sale in the market than for conserving fish stocks. They keep the fish, fillet it into anonymous fillets, and offer it for sale as 'fresh Bermuda fish' – but otherwise unidentified (and unrecognizable in fillet form) as a protected species.

The humble fillet knife has thereby played a key role in Bermuda's fishing industry, in support of fishermen's revenues but to the detriment of protected species, since 1972.

A ban on selling mixed fillets, requiring all fishermen (and retailers) to present fish whole for sale, or as single species whole fillets, would go a long distance towards supporting the raft of legislation enacted to protect vulnerable species. It would also help to professionalize the marketing and distribution of fish by obliging fishermen to identify the fish they sell more properly to customers according to species.

Protected Species

The 1978 Fisheries (Protected Species) Order prohibited the taking of a number of species within Bermuda's 200 mile exclusive fishing zone (re-named the Exclusive Economic Zone in 1996) at any time, namely: marine turtles (all species), marine mammals (whales, dolphins, and porpoises), corals (all types), and certain molluscs (queen conch, harbour conch, Bermuda cone, netted olive, Bermuda scallop, calico scallop, Atlantic pearl oyster, helmets and bonnets, the calico clam, and the West Indian top shell).

Later orders giving protection to fish species are based on and refer to this original legislation.

Grouper and rockfish species have become among the most vulnerable fish species in Bermuda waters. Under the 1996 Fisheries (Protected Species) Amendment Order, revising the original 1978 Fisheries (Protected Species) Order, six grouper species and all parrotfish (as follows) were given full year-round protection:

Nassau Grouper (*Epinephelus striatus*), a.k.a. Green Hamlet, Grass Hamlet

Deer Hamlet (*Epinephelus morio*), a.k.a. Red Grouper

Mutton Hamlet (*Epinephelus afer*)

Yellowfin Rockfish (*Mycteroperca venenosa*), a.k.a. Red Rockfish, Prince Rockfish, Princess Rockfish

Finescale Rockfish (*Mycteroperca microlepis*), a.k.a. Gag Rockfish

Tiger Rockfish (*Mycteroperca tigris*), a.k.a. Gag

Parrotfish (Scaridae family)

Fishing for some species is restricted by *minimum fork length* (the total length of the fish from mouth to fork or end of tail), *weight*, and/or *bag limit* (number allowed to be caught per boat per day):

Salmon Rockfish (*Mycteroperca interstitialis*), a.k.a. Monkey Rockfish, Flag Rockfish. Minimum legal size 50 cm (20 inches) fork length; year-round bag limit of one fish per day per boat.

Black Rockfish (*Mycteroperca bonaci*), a.k.a. Runner Rockfish. Minimum legal size 75 cm (30 inches) fork length; year-round bag limit of one fish per day per boat.

Lane Snapper (*Lutjanus synagris*), a.k.a. Whitewater Snapper. Minimum legal size 25 cm (10 inches) fork length; year-round bag limit of 30 fish per *recreational* fishing boat per day.

Yellowtail Snapper (*Ocyurus chrysurus*). Minimum legal size 25 cm (10 inches) fork length.

Hogfish (*Lachnolaimus maximus*). Minimum legal size: 35 cm (14 inches) fork length.

Red Hind (*Epinephelus guttatus*). Minimum legal size: 35 cm (14 inches) fork length; seasonal bag limit of 10 fish per boat per day from 1 April until 31 August.

Minimum legal weights are in effect for the following tunas and swordfish:

Yellowfin (Allison) Tuna (*Thunnus albacares*): 3.2 kg (7 lb).

Bigeye Tuna (*Thunnus obesus*): 3.2 kg (7 lb).

Bluefin Tuna (*Thunnus thynnus*): 30 kg (66 lb) *or* 115 cm (45 inches) fork length.

Swordfish (*Xiphias gladius*). Minimum weight 25 kg (55 lb); minimum length 125 cm (49 inches), measured from lower jaw.

Fishing for **bonefish** (*Albula vulpes*) and **pompano** (*Trachinotus goodei*) is only permitted by hook and line.

Protected Areas

The Fisheries (Protected Areas) Order of 1990 (amended 1993, 1996, and 1997) includes three areas where fishing is prohibited from 1 May until 31 August to protect red hind, groupers and other demersal species during their spawning period. The three areas of seasonal protection are: The Southwestern Area, The Eastern Area, and The North Eastern Area.

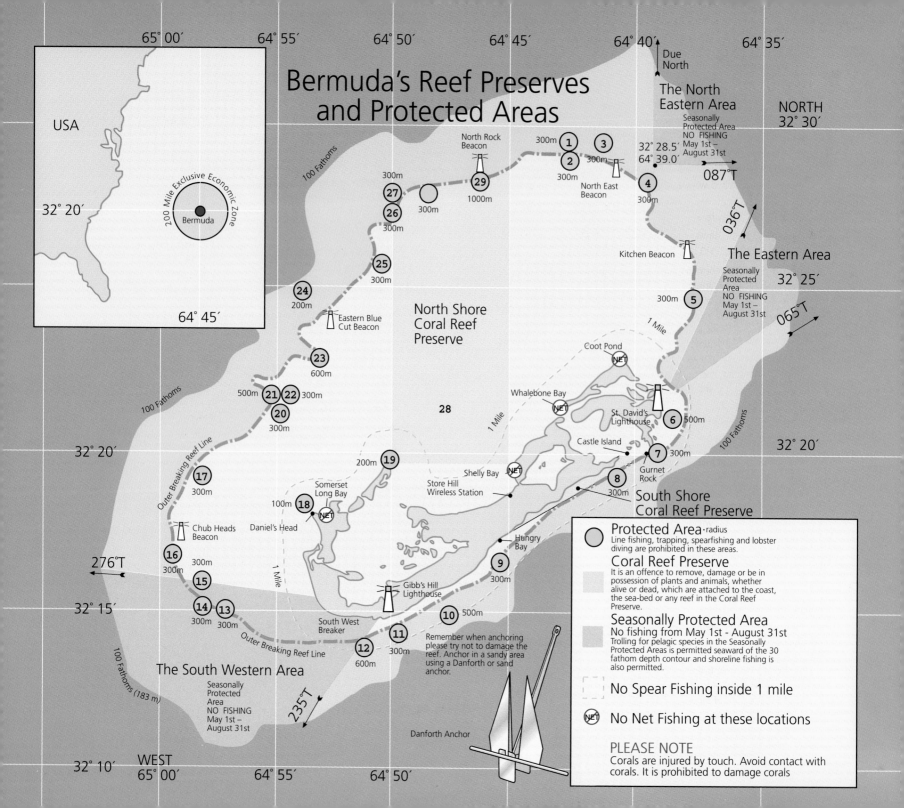

Bermuda's Reef Preserves and Protected Areas

USA

32° 20′

64° 45′

200 Mile Exclusive Economic Zone

Bermuda

NORTH
32° 30′

Due North

The North Eastern Area
Seasonally Protected Area
NO FISHING
May 1st – August 31st

32° 28.5′
64° 39.0′

087°T

036°T

The Eastern Area
Seasonally Protected Area
NO FISHING
May 1st – August 31st

32° 25′

065°T

100 Fathoms

North Rock Beacon

North East Beacon

Kitchen Beacon

North Shore Coral Reef Preserve

Eastern Blue Cut Beacon

100 Fathoms

Coot Pond

Whalebone Bay

St. David's Lighthouse

Castle Island

Gurnet Rock

Shelly Bay

Store Hill Wireless Station

South Shore Coral Reef Preserve

Somerset Long Bay

Daniel's Head

Chub Heads Beacon

276°T

Hungry Bay

Gibb's Hill Lighthouse

South West Breaker

Remember when anchoring please try not to damage the reef. Anchor in a sandy area using a Danforth or sand anchor.

Outer Breaking Reef Line

100 Fathoms

32° 20′

32° 15′

The South Western Area
Seasonally Protected Area
NO FISHING
May 1st – August 31st

100 Fathoms (183 m)

235°T

Danforth Anchor

WEST
65° 00′

64° 55′

64° 50′

1 — 300m
2 — 300m
3 —
4 — 300m
5 — 300m
6 — 500m
7 — 300m
8 — 300m
9 — 300m
10 — 500m
11 — 300m
12 — 600m
13 — 300m
14 — 300m
15 —
16 — 300m
17 — 300m
18 — 100m
19 — 200m
20 — 300m
21 — 500m
22 — 300m
23 — 600m
24 — 200m
25 — 300m
26 — 300m
27 —
28
29 — 1000m
300m (27/26 area)

Legend

Protected Area · radius
Line fishing, trapping, spearfishing and lobster diving are prohibited in these areas.

Coral Reef Preserve
It is an offence to remove, damage or be in possession of plants and animals, whether alive or dead, which are attached to the coast, the sea-bed or any reef in the Coral Reef Preserve.

Seasonally Protected Area
No fishing from May 1st - August 31st
Trolling for pelagic species in the Seasonally Protected Areas is permitted seaward of the 30 fathom depth contour and shoreline fishing is also permitted.

No Spear Fishing inside 1 mile

NET **No Net Fishing at these locations**

PLEASE NOTE
Corals are injured by touch. Avoid contact with corals. It is prohibited to damage corals

Protected Areas

The following areas of Bermuda waters are declared to be year round protected areas and are indicated on the map. Each site, except *Vixon, Commissioner's Point Area, Mills Breaker, The Cathedral* and *North Rock*, should be marked with a mooring buoy. Line fishing, spearfishing and lobster diving are **PROHIBITED** in these areas.

Contravening these laws carries a fine, upon conviction, of up to $5000 and/or imprisonment.

1   **'Cristobal Colon'** · *Located 32° 29.1'N, 64° 42.5'W* Area within 300 metres radius of a mooring buoy at the wreck of the *Cristobal Colon*.

2   **'North East Breaker'** · *Located 32° 29.0'N, 64° 42.5'W* The area within 300 metres radius of the *North East Breaker*.

3   **'Taunton'** · *Located 32° 29.5'N, 64° 41.5'W* The area within 300 metres radius of a mooring buoy at the wreck of the *Taunton*.

4   **'Aristo'** · *Located 32° 28.5'N, 64° 39.4'W* Area within a 300 metres radius of a mooring buoy at the wreck of the *Aristo*.

5   **'Mills Breaker'** · *Located 32° 24.6'N, 64° 37.8'W* The area within 300 metres radius of Mills Breaker beacon.

6   **'Pelinaion' & 'Rita Zovetto'** · *Located 32° 21.3'N, 64° 38.4'W* The area within 500 metres radius of a mooring buoy at the wrecks of the vessels *Pelinaion* and *Rita Zovetto*.

7   **'The Cathedral'** · *Located 32° 19.6'N, 64° 39.4'W* The area within 300 metres radius of the Cathedral.

8   **'Kate'** · *Located 32° 19.4'N, 64° 41.7'W* The area within 300 metres radius of a mooring buoy at the wreck of the vessel *Kate*.

9   **'Tarpon Hole'** · *Located 32° 16.2'N, 64° 46.6'W* The area within 300 metres radius of a mooring buoy at Tarpon Hole.

10 **'Hermes' & 'Minnie Breslauer'** · *Located 32° 14.4'N, 64° 47.4'W* The area within 500 metres radius of mooring buoys at the wrecks of the vessels *Hermes* and *Minnie Breslauer*.

11 **'Marie Celeste'** · *Located 32° 14.5'N, 64° 49.9'W* The area within 300 metres radius of a mooring buoy at the wreck of the *Marie Celeste*.

12 **'South West Breaker Area'** · *Located 32° 13.8'N, 64° 51.8'W* The area within 600 metres radius of a mooring buoy at South West Breaker.

13 **'North Carolina'** · *Located 32° 15.6'N, 64° 57.5'W* The area within 300 metres radius of a mooring buoy at the wreck of the *North Carolina*.

14 **'Airplane'** · *Located 32° 15.2'N, 64° 58.6'W* The area within 300 metres radius of a mooring buoy at the wreck of the airplane.

15 **'Blanche King'** · *Located 32° 16.3'N, 64° 58.5'W* The area within 300 metres radius of a mooring buoy at the wreck of the *Blanche King*.

16 **'Darlington'** · *Located 32° 17.2'N, 64° 59.0'W* Area within 300 metres radius of a mooring buoy at the wreck of the *Darlington*.

17 **'L'Herminie'** · *Located 32° 19.1'N, 64° 58.5'W* The area within 300 metres radius of a mooring buoy at the wreck of the *L'Herminie*.

18 **'Vixen'** · *Located 300 metres west of Daniel's Head, Sandys. Area within a 100 metres radius of the wreck of Vixen.

19 **'Commissioner's Point Area'** · *Located 32° 19.72'N, 64° 49.93'W* Area within a 200 metres radius of a stake at Commissioner's Point.

20 **'Lartington'** · *Located 32° 21.8'N, 64° 54.8'W* Area within 500 metres radius of a mooring buoy at the wreck of the *Lartington*.

21 **'Constellation Area'** · *Located 32° 21.8'N, 64° 54.8'W* Area within 500 metres radius of a mooring buoy at the wreck of the *Constellation*.

22 **'Montana'** · *Located 32° 21.7'N, 64° 54.8'W* Area within 300 metres radius of a mooring buoy at the wreck of the *Montana*.

23 **'Eastern Blue Cut'** · *Located 32° 23.4'N, 64° 53.1'W* Area within 600 metres radius of a mooring buoy at Eastern Blue Cut.

24 **'Xing Da Area'** · *Located 32° 26.5'N, 64° 50.3'W* Area within a 200 metres radius of a mooring buoy at the wreck of the *Xing Da*.

25 **'Snake Pit'** · *Located 32° 26.5'N, 64° 50.3'W* The area within 300 metres radius of a mooring buoy at the area called Snake Pit.

26 **'Hog Breaker'** · *Located 32° 27.5'N, 64° 49.8'W* The area within 300 metres radius of a mooring buoy at Hog Breaker.

27 **'Caraquet'** · *Located 32° 27.7'N, 64° 50.1'W* Area within a 300 metres radius of a mooring buoy at the wreck of the *Caraquet*.

28 **'Madiana'** · *Located 32° 27.5'N, 64° 48.5'W* The area within 300 metres radius of a mooring buoy at the wreck of the *Madiana*.

29 **'North Rock'** · *Located 32° 28.5'N, 64° 46.1'W* Area within 1000 metres radius of the North Rock beacon.

Using the buoys

A   When using a buoy, approach it against the wind or current. The mooring line will be pointing in the direction of the current.

B   Never tie your boat directly to the buoy mooring line. Always use a good length of rope from the boat to the buoy mooring line. Allow for extra scope during rough weather.

C   As you tie up to the buoy, inspect the mooring line to make certain the system is secure and lines are intact.

D   Someone should always remain on the boat and that person should know how to operate the boat.

E   When you are in protected areas, manoeuvre at idle speed only and watch for swimmers and divers.

F   If the buoy is in use and you must anchor, make certain you are anchoring in a sandy area within a Danforth or sand anchor. Be sure anchor, chain and rope do not touch the reef.

G   Buoys are for everyone on a first come basis. Please be considerate.

Flier sponsored by the UK Foreign and Commonwealth Office. Mooring buoys provided by public donations and the Bermuda Zoological Society. They are maintained by the Watersports Division of the Bermuda Chamber of Commerce and the Department of Agriculture and Fisheries. For more information call (441) 293-1785. NOTE: This is not a legal document.

The Southwestern Area

The area enclosed on the northern margin by a line originating at Gibb's Hill Light, running on a bearing of 276 degrees true to the 100 fathom contour (Gibb's Hill Light in line with the tripod at the southern end of the Western Boat Channel); on the southeastern margin by a line originating at Gibb's Hill Light and running on a bearing of 235 degrees true to the 100 fathom contour; and on the seaward margin by the 100 fathom contour.

The Eastern Area

The area enclosed on the northwest margin by a line originating at St David's Light and running on a bearing of 035 degrees true to the 100 fathom contour; on the southeast margin by a line originating at St David's Light and running on a bearing of 065 degrees true to the 100 fathom contour; on the seaward margin by the 100 fathom contour.

The North Eastern Area

The area enclosed on the western margin by a line originating at the Southwest corner (SWC) located seven nautical miles due north of St David's Light at coordinates 32° 28.5', North, 64° 39.0' West; running due north to the 100 fathom contour; on the southern margin by a line originating at SWC, running on a bearing of 087 degrees true to the 100 fathom contour (North Rock Beacon in line of sight with Northeast Breaker Beacon); and, on the seaward margin by the 100 fathom contour.

The seasonally protected areas are fundamentally to protect stocks of bottom fish species. Trolling for pelagic species (tuna, wahoo, barracuda, dolphin, marlin, etc.) is permitted *seaward of the 30 fathom depth contour* in these areas, as is shoreline fishing.

Year-Round Protected Sites

The fisheries (Protected Areas) Order of 1990 established 10 sites around Bermuda where anchoring, line fishing, spearfishing, and lobster diving are all prohibited year-round. Each site (with the exception of the wreck *Vixen*, near Daniel's Head, and Commissioner's Point) should be marked with a yellow drum mooring with the name of the site.

1. **Vixen**: Located 300 metres west of Daniel's Head, Sandys Parish. Area within a 100 metre radius of the wreck *Vixen*.

2. **Constellation Area**: Located 32° 21.8'N, 64° 54.8'W. Area within 500 metres radius of a mooring buoy at the wreck *Constellation*.

3. **Eastern Blue Cut**: Located 32° 23.04'N, 64° 53.01' W. Area within 600 metre radius of a mooring buoy at Eastern Blue Cut.

4. **Xing Da Area**: Located 32° 25.027'N, 64° 54.375'W. Area within 200 metre radius of a mooring buoy at the wreck of *Xing Da*.

5. **North Rock**: Located 32° 28.05'N, 64° 46.01'W. Area within 1000 metres (1 kilometre) radius of the North Rock beacon.

6. **Pelinaion** and **Rita Zovetta**: Located at 32° 21.03'N, 64° 38.04'W. The area within 500 metre radius of a mooring buoy at the wrecks of the vessels *Pelinaion* and *Rita Zovetta*.

7. **Kate**: Located at 32° 19.4'N, 64° 41.7'W. The area within 300 metre radius of a mooring buoy at the wreck of the vessel *Kate*.

8. **Hermes** and **Minnie Bressleur**: Located at 32° 14.04'N, 64° 47.04'W. The area within a 500 metre radius of a mooring buoy at the wrecks of the vessels *Hermes* and *Minnie Bressleur*.

9. **South West Breaker Area**: Located 32° 13.08'N, 64° 51'W. The area within a 600 metre radius of a mooring buoy at South West Breaker.

10. **The Commissioner's Point Area**: The area within a 200 metre radius of a stake located at 32° 19.72' N, 64° 49.93' W (Commissioner's Point) and bounded on the southwest and southeast by the shore.

Subsequent new legislation added another 19 protected sites around Bermuda where line fishing, spearfishing, and lobster diving are prohibited year-round (see map). These sites are protected for two reasons: first, and foremost, to establish safe and protected dive sites; and secondly, to reduce the pressure on fish stocks around the reefs.

Net Fishing

The use of nets for fishing in Bermuda waters is prohibited except, generally, to catch bait fish, and by licence to registered fishermen. The 1990 Fisheries (Use of Nets) Order allows the use of nets for catching bait fish (herring, 'chovies', blue fry, hogmouth fry, rush fry and half-beaks or ballyhoo); any jacks (except pompano); mackerel; and yellow-tail snapper.

The Order prohibits net fishing 'of any description to take fish of any kind' year-round in Somerset Long Bay, Shelly Bay, Whalebone Bay (Ferry Point Park), and in Coot Pond (north tip of St George's, west of Fort St Catherine).

Recreational fishing with nets may only be done with bait nets or cast nets. Bait nets may not exceed 75 feet (23 metres) in length and 9 feet (2.7 metres) in depth. There are also restrictions on the mesh size: $\frac{1}{8}$ inch (3.2 mm) minimum to 2 inches (50.8 mm) maximum (for both bait and cast nets).

Spearfishing

Spearfishing is prohibited all year round within one nautical mile of the shore of any islands in Bermuda. Use of spearguns (including the Hawaiian sling) is prohibited. Only pole spears are permitted. Spearfishing with SCUBA/aqualung equipment is prohibited.

There is a bag limit of two fish of any one species per person per day taken by spearfishing. Fish taken by spearfishing may not be sold.

Lobster Fishing

The generic term for lobster, for taking in Bermuda, refers to 'any crustacea of the family *Palinuridae*, including spiny, guinea chick or star lobster, or of the family *Scyllaridae*, including locust or sand lobster', according to the Fisheries Regulations.

To protect the local lobster population, there are a number of restrictions on taking them.

Recreational diving for lobsters requires an annual licence for that purpose, obtained from the Division of Fisheries at the Department of Agriculture and Fisheries. The licence imposes restrictions, as follows:

- Spearfishing of lobsters is prohibited, as is the use of SCUBA/aqualung equipment. Only a noose or snare may be used to take lobsters.

- There is a bag limit of two lobsters per person per day.

- Spiny lobsters (*Panulirus argus*) may not be taken during the five months closed season from 1 April to 31 August. It is an offence to be in possession of a spiny lobster, *whether alive or dead*, during the closed season. Other lobster species may be taken year-round.

- The minimum legal size for taking the spiny lobster is 92 mm carapace length (that is, measured from the ridge at the base of the horns to the end of the carapace (back shell) where the tail begins).

- Lobsters must be landed on shore whole. It is not permitted to remove the tails at sea. Lobsters taken by diving may not be sold. It is illegal for any person to take, injure, sell, purchase or be in possession of any lobster, *dead or alive*, at any time when the lobster is bearing eggs.

Chronology of Fishing Restrictions on Groupers and Other Fish Species in Bermuda

1972: The Fisheries Regulations 1972

Size limit of 14 inches for:

Hogfish (*Lachnolaimus maximus*)
Nassau Grouper (*Epinephelus striatus*)
Misty Grouper (*Epinephelus mystacinus*)
Red Grouper/Deer Hamlet(*Epinephelus morio*)
Rockfish (all *Mycteroperca* species)

Size limit of 7 lb (3.2 kg) for:

Yellowfin Tuna (*Thunnus albacares*)
Bigeye Tuna (*Thunnus obesus*)

Size limit of 14 lb (6.4 kg)for:

Bluefin Tuna (*Thunnus thynnus*)

1990: BR16/1990: The Fisheries Amendment Regulations 1990 (amending The Fisheries Regulations 1972)

Bag limit of two (2) fish per day of:

Nassau Grouper (*Epinephelus striatus*)
Deer Hamlet/Red Grouper (*Epinephelus morio*)
Mutton Hamlet (*Epinephelus afer*)
Yellowfin Grouper (*Mycteroperca venenosa*)
Monkey Rockfish/Salmon Rockfish (*Mycteroperca interstitialis*)
Black Rockfish (*Mycteroperca bonaci*)
Gag Grouper (*Mycteroperca microlepsis*)
Tiger Rockfish/Gag (*Mycteroperca tigris*)

Bag limit of ten (10) fish per day in period 1 May–30 September of:

Red Hind (*Epinephelus guttatus*)

> NB: This regulation (above) legislated the fish pot ban, prohibiting the use of 'fixed fishing gear' (i.e. fish pots) for taking fish or for any purpose other than under licence for scientific research, 'for the purpose of controlling the fishing industry', or for aquaculture. It also reduced the number of hooks a commercial fisherman could ordinarily (i.e. without special permission) use on a line, from 50 to just 15.

1993: BR46/1993: The Fisheries (Protected Species) Amendment Order 1993

All parrot fish species given full year-round protection.

1996: BR23/1996: The Fisheries Amendment Regulations 1996 (amending The Fisheries Regulations 1972)

Bag limit of one (1) fish per day of:

Monkey Rockfish/Salmon Rockfish (*Mycteroperca interstitialis*)
Black Rockfish (*Mycteroperca bonaci*)

Bag limit of thirty (30) fish per recreational fishing boat per day of:

Whitewater Snapper (*Lutjanus synagris*)

Fork length size limits for:

Black Rockfish (*Mycteroperca bonaci*): 75 cm (30 inches)
Monkey Rockfish (*Mycteroperca interstitialis*): 50 cm (20 inches)
Red Hind (*Epinephelus guttatus*): 35 cm (14 inches); also, bag limit of 10 fish per recreational fishing boat per day for period 1 May–31 August (amended from 30 September)
Hogfish (*Lachnolaimus maximus*): 35 cm (14 inches)
Yellowtail Snapper (*Ocyurus chrysurus*): 30 cm (12 inches)
Lane Snapper/Whitewater Snapper (*Lutjanus synagris*): 25 cm (10 inches)

Size limits for:

Bluefin Tuna (*Thunnus thynnus*): 30 kg (66 lb) or 115 cm (45 inches) fork length
Swordfish (*Xiphias gladius*): 25 kg (55 lb) or 125 cm (49 inches) for length measured from lower jaw

1996: BR25/1996: The Fisheries (Protected Species) Amendment Order 1996

Full year-round protection for:

Nassau Grouper (*Epinephelus striatus*)
Red Grouper/Deer Hamlet (*Epinephelus morio*)
Mutton Hamlet (*Epinephelus afer*)
Yellowfin Grouper (*Mycteroperca venenosa*)
Gag Grouper (*Mycteroperca microlepsis*)
Tiger Rockfish/Gag (*Mycteroperca tigris*)

Fishing Ecology and Conservation in Bermuda

The sea hath fish for every man.

Remains Concerning Britain, **Wm. Camden (1605)**

Also you must not be greedy in your catch, so as to take too many fish at one time, which you may do unthinkingly if you act according to these instructions, which will cause you to destroy your own sport and that of other men, as well.

A Treatise on Fishing with a Hook, by Dame Juliana Berners; printed in the *Book of Saint Albans*, by Wynken de Worde (1496); rendered into modern English by William Van Wyck (1933)

Overfishing occurs when more fish are taken from a population than can be replaced through natural reproduction. It results from excessive fishing as well as destructive fishing practices . . .

At its core, the crisis of overfishing stems from the fact that the world now has a substantial overabundance of fishing 'capacity' – the raw ability to catch and process fish . . .

The problem of overcapacity stems in part from the system of 'free and open access' to fisheries. Most fisheries of the world are open to all comers; whoever has a boat with a net [or other fishing gear] can go out and fish for the price of a license (if one is even required). Governments often wait to set rules until signs of trouble appear, by which time the size of the fleet often exceeds that needed to fish at sustainable levels. The rules usually focus on how and where fish may be caught, but most do not regulate the numbers of fishermen or boats or access to the fishery.

With no limits on the number of fishermen or overall capacity, fisheries managers are forced to come up with ever more inventive restrictions on such things as mesh sizes, the duration of the fishing season, closures of certain areas to fishing, and other measures to control the pressure on fish populations generated by burgeoning numbers of boats.

Excess fishing capacity also puts an enormous squeeze on fishermen. As competition among too many boats chasing too few fish escalates, the spoils go to those with the best technology and the most efficient gear. But keeping ahead costs money and adds to the economic pressure to catch more fish. Faced with the next mortgage payment, fishermen clamor for increases in the allowable catch. Managers, who struggle to keep the catch within sustainable levels, face tremendous pressures from fishermen . . . to keep catch levels high even when it is obvious that such levels are unsustainable . . .

Free and open access creates another problem: there are few incentives to conserve, as someone else will capture any fish left by conservation-minded fishermen. Unless everyone involved in a fishery acts with restraint, those who fish conservatively are not investing in the future; they are merely leaving fish behind for someone less responsible to take.

Hook, Line, and Sinking: The Crisis in Marine Fisheries, Natural Resources Defense Council (February 1997)

Until 1609 the fishing ecology of Bermuda was comprised entirely of the marine habitat and sea life of the surrounding waters. Soon after the first human settlers dragged their storm battered bodies ashore, fishermen (and fish consumers) became part of the fishing ecosystem for the first time. Fisheries in Bermuda started life when the first settler threw a line out to catch a fish, hauled it ashore . . . and threw his line out again.

Over the next 350 years there was sporadic legislation suggesting that the human population was tampering excessively with the marine environment, by the use of destructive fishing practices, or by excessive fishing.

In general, however, the local fishery evolved in relative harmony until the 20th century. Fishermen practised small-scale subsistence fishing, the human population remained relatively small, and the fish stock remained in good reproductive health. Fish, fishermen, and the small island community at large enjoyed a degree of mutual prosperity without serious imbalances.

(The docile cahow, a bird endemic to Bermuda, was not let off so lightly. Hogs landed off Spanish ships, rats, and human visitors to Bermuda in the 1500s and 1600s took their toll on an original cahow population that possibly numbered over a million. By 1620, less than a decade after Bermuda was first settled, the cahow was thought to be extinct, exterminated by man and other predators for food. In 1906, however, Louis L. Mowbray, who created the Bermuda Aquarium in 1926, found a single cahow on an island in Castle Harbour (although it was only identified as such 10 years later). In 1951 the birds were rediscovered. The government declared the islands where they were nesting to be a protected sanctuary. In 1960 just 20 pairs of cahows were identified. By 1995 their numbers were up to 50. One Bermudian, David Wingate, has spent most of his life dedicated to the conservation and regeneration of the cahows on the 14.5 acre Nonsuch Island sanctuary for the birds, the 'Living Museum' project, in Castle Harbour.)

Ecological pressures on the Bermuda fishery in the 20th century have grown out of the increase of Bermuda's population, the huge growth of tourism since the 1950s, the increasing affluence of Bermudians, the intensive development of the island itself (more roads, traffic, businesses, housing, hotels), the professionalization of the fishery, and the use of Bermuda waters for recreational purposes.

For hundreds of years Bermuda changed at the leisurely pace of a horse and carriage ride. Since the Second World War development has speeded up, first to a barely perceptible trot but finally to a gallop. Environmental effects of that dynamic development, especially compared with the stability and relative tranquillity of the previous 350 years, have upset the ecological balance between fishermen and fish.

The Arrowhead Fish Pot

Some time in the early years of the 20th century Bermudian fishermen started using the Antillian wire mesh fish pot. Before then, fishing was either by handline, nets, or smaller wooden fish pots.

The introduction of the arrowhead shaped Antillean fish pot, which could be half the size of a small car, meant that many more fish could be caught at one time than by handline fishing. Built of wire mesh and cedar or spruce wood frames, they lasted much longer in the water than the older style pots made traditionally from cedar tree roots. Wire mesh pots made life easier for the fisherman but stressed the fish population by increasing the amount of fish that fishermen could catch.

Depending on the season and weather conditions, a set of a dozen pots could bring in 300–400 lb of fish. With two hauls a day, a fishermen could bring to market over 500 lb of fish on a good day. Net fishing could sometimes bring that much, or more, if the fishermen happened to hit a good run of fish. Line fishing would rarely yield as much. In any case, line fishing required much more effort (including baiting a location for months). Pot fishermen were also able to do some handline fishing in between setting and hauling their pots, which added to their catch.

Pots were versatile in another way that allowed even more fish to be caught. Louis S. Mowbray noted, in 1949, 'At times, on days when the surface [of the sea] is reasonably smooth, a fisherman will often use a fish pot as an anchor when on the red snapper grounds. This may be in from fifty to one hundred fathoms, and it is not unusual to get an extra sixty or eighty pounds of snapper in the "anchor".'

Pots did not discriminate among which species of fish were trapped, although the size of the wire mesh was regulated to allow smaller fish to escape. The depth of water and location of the pots made them somewhat more specific about what they trapped, but pots nevertheless caught a wider variety of fish than handline fishing.

By the 1950s pots accounted for much more fish taken by commercial fishermen than handlining. Trolling offshore was still in its infancy. Pot fishermen were not restricted by closed fishing seasons until 1971. Until then spawning groupers and other species were vulnerable to pots set near spawning grounds. (There were inshore *areas* closed to pot fishing before 1971, but a closed *season* only applied to lobster.)

Until the 1970s no one seriously questioned the damage that pots could do by taking large amounts of fish indiscriminately. By then the fishermen themselves noticed that they were bringing in fewer and smaller fish. Alarm bells began to ring.

After the 1972 Fisheries Act and Fisheries Regulations, the 1984 Fisheries Management and Development Programme was the first serious attempt to reduce the use of fish pots which 'were found to have a far greater efficiency than was originally estimated', according to a 1993 paper by Fisheries Division researchers.

The 1984 Programme aimed to halve the number of pots allotted to full-time fishermen. From 3200 pots in 1985, the number was cut to 1600 by 1990. The largest quota of pots per fisherman before 1984 was 100 pots. By 1990 the maximum number of pots allotted to a fisherman was 30. The 1984 Fisheries Management Programme restricted pot capacity to a maximum of 7.2 cubic metres.

Environmental Development

Fish pots, however, were not the only environmental problem by the 1970s. Bermuda had started to become a mass tourism destination. New hotels were being built. Motor traffic on the roads increased. More small boats were in use for recreation. Population density was increasing: in 1900 the population density of Bermuda was about 810 people per square mile (high by any standards); in 1950 it was 1780 people per square mile; and in 1970 it was over 2500 people per square mile.

(By comparison, the population density of the United Kingdom now is 625 people per square mile, and that of the United States about 70 people per square mile. Only half a dozen places in the world are more densely populated than Bermuda.)

A big difference, too, between the early 20th century and the late 20th century in Bermuda was that fishermen had become professionals. Instead of using rowboats or sail powered skiffs, with the simple technology of handlines and fish pots, by the 1970s they had invested substantial amounts of money in larger boats, more sophisticated and varied gear, and, in some cases, onshore cold storage facilities. The overall technology of the fishery had ratcheted up, at considerable expense, and with considerably more economic pressure on the fishermen to pay off their investments.

With hindsight, the wonder is not only that the fishery was allowed to invest heavily, but that it was encouraged to do so following the recommendations of the Bardach Report in the late 1950s.

From an ecological point of view, intensive investment to professionalize the fishery was disastrous: it meant fishermen would have to fish more intensively in order to justify their investments. At the time, however, in the late 1950s, there were few indications of serious environmental stress on Bermuda's reef fishery.

The balance of power in the fishery ecosystem was dramatically tilted in the fisherman's favour by the 1970s, although the adoption of the wire mesh arrowhead fish pot 50 or so years before had already started putting pressure on fish stocks. Added to that was the steamrolling human development in Bermuda, compressed into a single generation from the 1970s. Its impact on the surrounding marine environment has only just begun to be acknowledged, much less understood.

Where Have all the Fish Gone?

Fish populations evolve over millions of years, through genetic changes, migration of larvae, climatic and oceanographic changes, among other phenomena. Left to themselves in their natural state, fish populations remain more or less stable over a dozen or so human generations (the time between Bermuda's first settlement in 1609 and today). Their habitat evolves more or less in harmony with the fish. A cycle of natural checks and balances maintains the stability of the system.

Abrupt changes, however, can upset that balance, with unpredictable consequences for both the fish communities and the surrounding ecosystem. Such has been the case with Bermuda in the second half of the 20th century.

In Bermuda, over just two generations, significantly more people have been squeezing into the same land area, more small boats are on the water, there is more intensive land development, more disturbance by massive cruise ships arriving every week, more recreational use of the marine resource, exhaust pollution from cars, trucks, buses, and motorcycles settling out of the air into the sea, and more runoff from the land of pollutants from construction, farming, waste incineration, and sewerage.

As if that were not enough, fishing has intensified.

Mr Harry Cox, in a speech from March 1990, observed that, 'No limited land area, let alone a sea area, can withstand, without material damage, that kind of . . . pressure [of development].'

The 1991 Commission of Inquiry on Bermuda's fishing industry noted:

> . . . in many inshore areas, the entire reef ecosystem appears to have been severely impacted by pollution. The Bermuda Biological Station testified to the presence of contaminants in most areas where these would be expected. For example, around urban areas, sewage outfalls, and solid waste disposal sites. Another major source of reef degradation appears to be the resuspension of fine sediments by ships passing through the ship channels [particles of seafloor sediment churned up by passing ships, re-suspended in the water, and finally re-deposited on the bottom]. These appear to have smothered reefs in the immediate vicinity of the channels, but there is no quantitative estimate of the extent of the damage.

A paper published in 1993 by Fisheries Department personnel referred to the problem of sediment dispersion adversely affecting the fishing environment.

> Castle Harbour still suffers from sediment raised when the Bermuda airport was built in the 1940s. That sediment overloaded the mucus production of the large brain corals (*Diploria strigosa* and *Diploria labyrinthiformis*), which are now almost certainly dead. These corals were succeeded by more sediment-tolerant branching corals, sponges, and algae. These changes in water quality certainly have affected the coral reef community in Castle Harbour and may have affected fish breeding, but there have been no studies to address this question.

Despite the lack of definitive information about the 'decline in quality of the nearshore environment', the Commission nevertheless concluded that, 'The Bermudian inshore environment is subject to environmental insult from sewage and cooling outfalls, water's edge trash dumps, thousands of boat moorings, over-the-side discharge from an equal number of boats, seepage from cesspits, overfishing of marine species, etc.'

The impact of the intensive development of Bermuda on its marine life, including more intensive fishing, has been apparent for some time. Divers, fishermen, and lay observers have noticed fewer and smaller fish around the Bermuda Platform (and offshore, for some species), as well as changes in the variety of species, since the late 1970s.

In *The Bermudian Magazine*, an article from May 1990 (just after the fish pot ban), 'Our Threatened Fish Industry', confirmed this phenomenon. 'It is not an opinion, it is a fact . . . Divers have noticed the sharp decline in reef fish populations over the past decade, along with tour boat operators, conservationists, scientists, and just about anybody who has spent time on or around the waters.' (Notice that fishermen were not specifically included in that list.)

Teddy Tucker, who has dived Bermuda waters for as long as anyone, recalled in an interview with *The Royal Gazette* in 1983:

> I can remember when you could go out on the banks and catch 25 to 30 of the big, red snappers. Now I doubt if a boat will catch a dozen of them all year. And the catch statistics will show you that what was absolute trash fish, is now fillet! . . . And the big misty grouper (*Epinephelus mysticinus*) – John Paws they call him is gone. In 1974 [referring to his records], I would anchor. Two of us fishing would catch nine of them in one day with a weight of 811 pounds. . .Out of all the fish we caught, less than five percent were below 30 pounds. While I'm not a scientific fellow, I think this tells you their mortality rate was very high and that those that did survive lived a long time.

Mr Cox called the destruction of the local reef environment a 'holocaust', leaving behind a marine ghetto populated by adaptable, hardy, but undesirable 'trash fish' (chub, grunts, triggerfish, turbot) where once the princely groupers and rockfish reigned supreme. Now, species once shunned as undesirable are sold as fillet for $20 a bag.

Why Have all the Fish Gone?

Fishermen and overfishing have largely taken the blame for the despoilation of Bermuda's reef fishery. The argument goes that fishermen have taken too much fish out of the platform waters around Bermuda for too long. This may be the most expedient explanation. Fishermen are certainly a factor. They may be the most critical *single* factor. But they are almost certainly not the *only* factor.

How do fish react to 30,000 tonne cruise ships churning through the channels over the reefs from April to October (during the fish population's most active spawning times)? And from weekly cargo vessels, and thousands of small pleasure boats, year-round? (The number of small boats in Bermuda, including sailboats, was estimated at 7000 in 1990, and is now probably closer to 10,000 – one for every six people resident in Bermuda.) How do fish react to the noise and disturbance of bottom sediment from this shipping intrusion; to the effluents deposited by marine engines; to emissions from road traffic settling slowly, microscopically, in the waters around Bermuda; to sediments from land runoff and sewerage; to electromagnetism from undersea power and telecommunications cables?

How *do* fish react to these disturbances? And to countless other unknown disturbances that we may still be unaware of? How does their behaviour change? Does spawning diminish? Do they reproduce less? Do they, like some land animals under stress, cannibalize their young? Do the fish move away to escape the disturbances? Are their migratory patterns affected? Is their mortality rate affected? Do they die younger? Do they change their diet? Are their biological systems stressed? Are the defence mechanisms of some species diminished, making them more vulnerable to other species? Are small prey fish (fry, anchovies, pilchards) affected, causing an imbalance to the food chain?

All of these factors might lead to diminished populations of fish, or to changes in the composition of fish stocks around Bermuda, aggravating the problem of intensive fishing.

The term 'overfishing' suggests that we know what the barrier is between fishing conservatively (at or below a sustainable level of fish stocks), and too much fishing that irrevocably diminishes the fish population.

In fact, we still have no idea of what is an acceptable level of sustainability for Bermuda's reef fish stock, because there is no satisfactory assessment of the stock. Although we know (roughly) how much fish is taken out of the water every year, we do not know much about the total size of the fish stock left in the water.

Conclusive assessment of the size of fish stocks, especially in reef environments, is a problem not only for Bermuda but in other fisheries around the world. Political decisions to regulate fisheries worldwide are influenced by stock assessments that may overestimate or underestimate depending on vested interests.

Is one million pounds of food fish taken from Bermuda waters every year 'overfishing'? Five hundred thousand pounds? Seven hundred thousand pounds? How much is tolerable, and sustainable, for different species?

Without a clear idea about the relationship – the balance – between how much fish is taken *out* and how much fish is left *in* the water, not to mention factoring in other environmental influences, population differences between different species, the interdependence of fish and the environment, and the balance of power between different fish species, 'overfishing' tends to become a guesstimate based on empirical observation.

The 'proof' of overfishing is that fewer and lower quality species are being caught. There is ample probable cause, however, if not indisputable evidence, to suggest that other environmental stresses have contributed to the depletion of fish stocks to some (unknown) degree.

Other man-made stresses may contribute as much to the diminished fish population around the Bermuda Platform as intensive fishing. Maybe more. Maybe less.

With the limited knowledge available, we can only make informed assumptions about the nature of the fish population based on observations of the fishing environment by fishermen, divers, and marine researchers.

The most convenient assumption now is that fishermen have been overfishing – whatever the role of other environmental influences. Media columnist Stuart Hayward, writing in *The Mid-Ocean News* of 2 February 1990, immediately after the fish pot ban was announced, concluded, 'There's not much difference between overfishing and over-development except that fishermen are easier to control and they don't ruin the Government.'

Fishermen don't bring in much money for the government, either. Development does. If there was a choice between restricting the practices of fishermen (a small constituency of nominal value to the economy) and curbing the environmental fallout from tourism, building works, and road transport (pillars of Bermuda's economy), the fishermen, rightly or wrongly, will take the hit every time.

Since fishermen are taking most of the blame for the depletion of fish stocks, and since they are an integral part of the fishery ecology, fisheries ecomanagement should be concerned equally with how decisions affect fishermen and fish.

The Fisherman's Burden

So far as the ecology and management of Bermuda's fishery goes, most of the attention to date has focused on the status of vulnerable fish and marine species. Fishermen, too, however, as much as the fish, have come under pressure, mainly from the economic stresses building up over recent years which have made it more difficult for them to balance their income from fishing with inflated costs of living.

Fifty years ago, when a small house in Bermuda cost £3000 or so, a fisherman sold fish at an average of two shillings a pound. In 1950, when a fisherman sold ten pounds of fish, he received one pound in money. It cost the 1950 fisherman, therefore, 30,000 lb of fish to buy a modest Bermuda cottage.

Today, the same house costs $400,000–500,000. Since a fisherman gets an average $5/lb for his fish, he has to sell at least 80,000 lb of fish to buy the house that cost a 1950s fisherman just 30,000 lb of fish.

If he wanted to buy the same $400,000 house with the same amount of fish needed by the 1950 fisherman to buy the same £3000 house then (30,000 lb of fish), he would have to sell the fish (wholesale) for over $13/lb to raise the $400,000. Retailers would have to sell it for over $20/lb. That compares with the $5/lb consumers pay for imported Florida grouper in Bermuda supermarkets.

Economics favoured the fisherman far more in 1950 than today. Fifty years ago fishermen had basic gear, relatively simple, low maintenance boats, hardly any marketing costs to speak of, and, commonly, other jobs.

Today fishermen typically have $150,000 and more invested in their boat and equipment, fuel at around $4 a gallon ($120–300 a day fuel costs, depending on the size of the boat and how far it goes), insurance ($2000–3000 a year), the costs of a van to transport fish for sale, slipping and maintenance costs, replacement costs for more sophisticated gear, and so on. And supplemental income from other types of work to offset the higher costs is less common than it used to be, especially for full-time fishermen.

The purchasing power of fishermen today is about two-thirds less than it was 50 years ago, measured by how much fish they have to sell to buy a house. And yet fishermen today have many times higher costs than their predecessors. Not only is their income worth less, their costs are much higher.

Intensive fishing effort by fishermen today is directly related to their need to catch more fish to support themselves than in generations past. Fishermen have to fish harder, catch more fish, and charge selling prices that are high by comparison with imported fish. And there is more competition from other fishermen.

All this puts pressure on the fish population and imbalances the fishery ecosystem. Ultimately it jeopardizes the long-term survival of the fishermen themselves: too much pressure on fish stocks by too intensive fishing leads to depleted fish stocks for the fishermen to exploit at an economically viable level, ending up, in the most extreme scenario, with no fishermen.

Conservation of the Fishery

When fishing in Bermuda was a part-time, less professional trade, fishermen husbanded the fish stock. They left fishing locations fallow from time to time. They respected each other's fishing territories. They used fish ponds to spread their fishing effort throughout the year, a simple form of fish farming. And they used gear (handlines mainly) that restricted the amount of fish they could take. The stress on fish stocks was minimal, tolerable, and sustainable for long-term reproduction of the reef fish population.

The ways of fishing that earlier generations of Bermudian fishermen practised, which maintained the stability of the fishing ecosystem by less intensive fishing, would not be possible today. The Bermuda fishery now is specialized, professionalized, and more highly capitalized. And yet *intensive* fishing may not have to mean *destructive* fishing.

If today's professionalized Bermuda fishermen are taking more fish out of the water than the fish population can regenerate, either the number of fishermen and amount of the catch has to be restricted, or the fish stock has to be replenished to maintain a healthy ecological balance. Or both.

Pressure on the fishery has to be eased. By reviving old methods adapted to modern circumstances, it may even be reversed.

The old custom of using fish ponds to keep fish for sale at non-fishing times of the year might be revived in a modified form. Instead of keeping fish for sale, fishermen might use rebuilt ponds as sanctuaries for certain vulnerable species that they could eventually release back into their natural habitat. Old time fishermen kept groupers alive for many months, sometimes years.

When fishermen catch endangered groupers and other vulnerable species, they might give the fish sanctuary by keeping them in dedicated ponds sited away from areas where the surge from large ships or pollution would disturb them. Fishermen might 'recycle' the fish by returning them, eventually, into the sea, rather than selling them on the market.

New, more sophisticated protected sanctuaries might even be constructed in the shallows around Bermuda, using fish farming technology for a variety of species. Cultivation of imported juveniles for re-stocking might be possible. Some fishermen might even be licensed to fish *exclusively* as a specialized sub-group of fishermen trained in fish farming techniques.

Fishing effort would be both economically rewarded and ecologically rewarding. Fishermen could be paid a certain amount from government funds for each fish caught and eventually released back into the sea, as an investment in the health of Bermuda's marine environment. The investment would also conform to the Bermuda government's legal responsibility to maintain, conserve, and protect marine resources within the 200 mile Economic Exclusion Zone (EEZ).

Apart from coastal sanctuaries along the shoreline, other sites might be husbanded by fishermen not only to protect fish stocks but to cultivate their growth. Around Bermuda's reef platform there are 29 protected areas where fishing is prohibited year-round. Most of these sites are around wrecks or at strategic points around the reef perimeter (North Rock, Eastern Blue Cut, South West Breaker) where fish are known to aggregate.

Some older fishermen might be employed to use traditional fishing methods (such as baiting up a site), not only to attract greater aggregations of fish to these offshore sanctuaries but also to guard and monitor their development. Pods of fish populations around the sites would be protected, cared for, and, ideally, their numbers expanded to migrate elsewhere around the platform.

The number of sites might be increased, too, with the deployment of fish attraction devices (FADs), to create a dispersed network of strategically located sanctuarial pods around the reef platform where fish stocks could be passively cultivated to help regenerate the entire reef fish population. Like seeding a field.

Fishermen who agreed to participate in such a scheme would be paid as agents in the field, assigned to a location, and employed to monitor, cultivate, and report on the development of their respective stations.

Funds for a fishermen's husbandry or aquaculture programme could come from fees for fishing licences levied on *all* fishermen, for both commercial and recreational fishing. Licence fees could be graded according to the type of fishery, from simple shore fishing ($10/year per licence, for example), to boat fishing for reef fish ($100/year per licence), to the offshore fishery for pelagic species ($500+/year per licence).

However the system was organized, it would recognize that the ecological cost of fishing in Bermuda waters must be paid for financially, ideally to benefit the marine environment as well as users of it.

The husbandry of fish in sanctuaries, either along the shore or offshore, would promote co-management of the fishery by fishermen, making them stewards of their own resource, as they used to be for generations. Appropriate remuneration would sustain the motivation of fishermen not only to practise regenerative fishing but also to regain more of a controlling interest in the fishery.

Fishermen paid to recycle live fish from shore ponds, or to cultivate offshore locations without fishing them, would have a vital economic interest in the stability of the fishing ecosystem as well as a source of income for themselves.

The problem of too many fishermen taking too many fish out of the sea might thereby be converted into a benefit for the Bermuda fishery rather than a cost to it. Their effort could be used to create a model system for regenerating and possibly even increasing the quality and quantity of the reef fish stock around the Bermuda Platform.

Some of these ideas might work. Others might not. Some might be feasible in a different form, or modified in different ways. They might all be, as one ex-fisherman once told me, 'in the right church but the wrong pew'. Even if they proved to be wholly impractical ideas in themselves, they might serve an equally dynamic function in the welfare of Bermuda's fishing ecology by stimulating further debate and other initiatives.

Fisheries Ecomanagement

Bermuda has already employed a gamut of 'inventive restrictions' on fishing to protect its marine environment, including 'mesh sizes [of nets], the duration of the fishing season, closures of certain areas to fishing, and other measures to control the pressure on fish populations generated by burgeoning numbers of boats'.

The challenge for the next generation of fisheries management in Bermuda will be to go beyond static and sporadic measures to protect the resource, towards a continuous process of managing the overall fishing ecosystem, including, perhaps most contentiously, the fishermen and others who use the resource.

Innovative conservation methods are not an easy option. They would take courage to consider in the first place and, subsequently, a lot of time, discussion, negotiation, finance, and changes in attitudes to fisheries management to bring about. Most of all they would take imagination and commitment to the responsibility of leaving the fisheries, and Bermuda's marine environment, better off for future generations.

Fisheries Management in Bermuda

11

Scientific uncertainty is the rule rather than the exception in fisheries management.

Hook Line & Sinking: The Crisis in Marine Fisheries, Natural Resources Defense Council, February 1997

Management is the organisation of people and resources to achieve an agreed result.

L. V. Phillips (1999)

Ideally, fisheries management should proceed as a collaborative effort between professional managers and fishers. Fisheries managers who have an intimate understanding of the people they are charged with managing, who know what management strategies these people are likely to invent, and what strategies they typically prefer, will have a far better chance of getting cooperation than will managers who keep their distance and remain focused mainly on conservation of resources. Likewise, fishers who are made aware of the culture of fisheries managers, who are given examples of successfully managed fisheries, and who are encouraged to actively engage managers in a cooperative dialogue can empower themselves to achieve greater control and sustainability of the natural resources they exploit.

Folk Management in the World's Fisheries, **C. L. Dyer and J. R. McGoodwin, eds, University Press of Colorado, 1994**

F isheries management is both ancient and new. Ancient, because fishermen have managed themselves – the way they fish, their relationships with each other, and their relation to the fishing grounds – from the earliest times, informally but effectively, and, until recently, without serious damage to the resource they have exploited. And new, because fisheries management has now become a science.

Management works best when it works by consensus towards a common goal. Fisheries management is no different. The system works most effectively when fishermen and fisheries managers (researchers, scientists, bureaucrats, politicians) agree about how best to conserve and enhance fish populations, the fishing environment, and the fishery overall. To the extent that they disagree, the system works less efficiently.

Disagreements in management arise when there are conflicting interests and differences of opinion about how to achieve common goals. Fisheries managers and fishermen may agree that the well-being of the fishery, including conservation of the fishing grounds and the fish populations, is the ultimate objective of their efforts (although there is often disagreement about what that 'well-being' means). Opinions usually diverge about the ways and means of pursuing, much less achieving, that objective.

The origins of formal fisheries management in Bermuda date from the late 1950s and early 1960s. The Bardach Report in 1958, which advised the Bermuda government on the way ahead for Bermuda's fishery, specifically recommended that, 'The fishing industry should be placed under the existing Department of Agriculture and the Director of Agriculture should become the administrative head for Agriculture and Fishery.'

The Fisheries Division of the Department of Agriculture was created in 1961, establishing a platform for fisheries research and development, and management, in the future.

Before that time fisheries management in Bermuda was not a technique. It was a behaviour pattern, a patchwork of fishing customs, traditions, and relationships that had been worked out and refined by generations of commercial fishermen. Individual and communal rights to fish around Bermuda were established and accepted (*legitimized*) by mutual respect and consent among fishermen. As fishermen managed themselves, they were, at the same time, managing the fishing grounds (the *resource*).

Since the 1960s the traditional, informal, communal management of Bermuda's fisheries has devolved away from the fishermen towards formal, centralized government control. As government has taken control of the fisheries, at the same time there has been an erosion of traditional fishing customs (by increasing pressures of competition) and growing concerns about the deterioration of the fishing resource, the so-called *tragedy of the commons* phenomenon as it was thought to apply to Bermuda's reef fishery.

Tragedy of the Commons

Garrett Hardin, a professor of biology at the University of California, Santa Barbara, described the tragedy of the commons theory in 1968. Hardin originally formulated his argument around the issue of population growth. It has since been applied mainly to problems about how to manage the use of natural resources open to the public for use by everyone (such as parklands, woods, open countryside, water resources, and fishing grounds). These are communal or common properties (the *commons* of the *tragedy of the commons*), natural resources open to all, and owned by no single individual or entity.

The problems of how to manage these resources for the common good have arisen as a result of the pressures of growing populations using the resources, especially when groups of users have different competing interests in the resource.

Hardin proposed that the users of any common property resource would inevitably dilapidate and ultimately destroy the resource because of universal human greed. He assumed that people would selfishly exploit the resource for as much profit as they could get out of it, either for their enjoyment or for economic interests. That selfish use of the resource would eventually culminate in its (tragic) destruction.

Hardin's example of the common property resource was a pasture, open to everyone. Herdsmen used the pasture to keep as many cattle as possible grazing on it. 'Tribal wars, poaching, and disease' first kept the number of herders and the number of cattle in check so that the pasture accommodated all the herdsmen and cattle using it. The so-called 'carrying capacity' of the land, its natural capacity to accommodate all the grazing cattle and their owners, the herdsmen, was not exceeded.

If one herdsman, however, began to ask himself how much more he could profit by adding one more animal to the pasture, he would expect to maximize his profits from doing so, according to Hardin. The more cattle he could graze on the pasture, the herdsman would think, the more income he would get.

The only disadvantage of adding one more animal to the pasture, in the herdsman's view, would be the additional grazing of the land by that single animal. According to the herdsman, one more animal grazing the pasture wouldn't matter much. It would have only minimal impact on the pasture's carrying capacity.

Hardin supposed that the herdsman would continue to believe that one more animal's grazing would have minimal effect on the land. The herdsman, rationalizing that just one more animal would not make much difference to the land's carrying capacity, would keep adding cattle to his herd, to increase his wealth.

'But this is the conclusion reached by each and every rational herdsman sharing a commons. Therein is the tragedy. Each man is locked into a system that compels him to increase his herd without limit – in a world [the pasture] that is limited.'

As each herdsman added 'just one more animal' . . . and one more and one more and one more, etc. . . . the land would become overgrazed and ultimately useless. It would eventually be destroyed because all the herdsmen were free to pursue their own best interests, each thinking to maximize their profits by adding 'just one more animal', incessantly.

By substituting the reef fishery in Bermuda for the pasture, and fishermen for herdsmen, this theory becomes the *tragedy of the reef commons* around Bermuda.

Since the 1970s, the policies of regulators, legislators, and fisheries managers in Bermuda have been shrouded by the threat of such an 'inevitable' process of destruction in their perception of how to deal with fisheries issues in Bermuda. In Bermuda's case the specific tragedy was the depletion of certain fish species, considered to be the result of overfishing (like Hardin's overgrazing herdsmen).

Unless restrained, according to Hardin's hypothesis, a fisherman will exploit the resource for all its worth . . . to *him*. And all fishermen will behave in the same way, leading 'inevitably' to the ruin of the resource by all the fishermen exploiting it for their own selfish gain.

Hardin recommended that the best course of action to avoid a tragedy of the commons was mutual coercion (for example, by taxation). 'The only kind of coercion I recommend is mutual coercion, mutually agreed upon by the majority of the people affected. . .We institute and (grumblingly) support taxes and other coercive devices to escape the horror of the commons.'

In fisheries management, 'other coercive devices' might include regulations and restrictions on fishing, and licences or permits to fish.

In a later essay on the origins and validity of his original work ('Extensions of "The Tragedy of the Commons"', May 1998), Hardin drew an example from the world's fisheries. 'In 1625, the Dutch scholar Hugo Grotius said, "The extent of the ocean is in fact so great that it suffices for any possible use on the part of all peoples for drawing water, for fishing, for sailing." Now the once unlimited resources of marine fishes have become scarce and nations are coming to limit the freedom of their fisheries in the commons [to avert the tragedy of the commons].'

Hardin's basic assumption was that all users of a common natural resource were identically selfish in their desire to exploit the resource for individual gain. They would, he said, do so at the expense of other users, and at the expense of the resource itself. He argued that individuals were trapped in this 'inevitably' destructive process, that they would always rationalize their actions in their own best interests, and that they could not change their behaviour.

An outside third party (the State) would need to impose restrictions on users, agreed by the democratic majority, to avoid the destruction of the resource by such self-interested exploitation.

Tragedy of the Commons Revisionism

Over the years critics have extensively debated the tragedy of the commons issue, challenging its underlying assumptions and re-assessing its conclusions. Critics have rejected the negative view that all users of a common natural resource are 'inevitably' selfish, that they are all locked into selfish behaviour patterns, and that they are intrinsically unable to manage or change their individual behaviour with respect to their communal use of the resource.

While Hardin, moreover, proposed a static example of *the* common resource (a pasture), it is now acknowledged that the characteristics of common property resources are diverse in the extreme. Each one has unique features that are, first, different from every other, and secondly, highly dynamic. Not only do solutions for each common resource need to be formulated specifically for that particular resource, they need to be constantly re-evaluated, modified, and re-formulated to reflect changing conditions.

Characteristics of CPRs [common property resources] affect the problems of devising governance regimes. These attributes include the size and carrying capacity of the resource system, the measurability of the resource, the temporal and spatial availability of resource flows, the amount of storage in the system, whether resources move (like water, wildlife, and most fish) or are stationary (like trees and medicinal plants), how fast resources regenerate, and how various harvesting technologies affect patterns of regeneration.

'Revisiting the Commons: Local Lessons, Global Challenges'

While not all environmental conditions can be managed, continual observation of how conditions change and appropriate ways to manage those changes are the responsibility of resource managers, in tune with the resource, in communication with users of the resource, and in harmony with goals to manage the well-being of both the resource and those who use it.

Knowledge about each of those attributes applies to Bermuda's fisheries. Managing the problem means managing all the conditions that make up the ecosystem that is Bermuda's common property marine resource: the local waters, the reefs, the fishing grounds, and the people who use them. Fisheries management of the resource should ideally comprise 'governance regimes' that take into consideration not only all features of the fishery specific to Bermuda (the fish, the reef, the marine environment, other users, etc.) but the dynamic interaction and relationships between those features as well, including the fishermen themselves.

The reef fishery of Bermuda is, like all common property resources, a complex system of interconnecting phenomena, in a continuously dynamic state of flux, influenced by natural and artificial changes, as it has evolved over the aeons since its beginnings. The main features of the resource include, most visibly, its physical attributes: fish, water, coral, and the myriad other flora and fauna of the reef environment.

The fishing ecosystem also includes less tangible features such as the knowledge and experience of fishermen using the resource for many generations, their individual and communal patterns of fishing behaviour, and their economic interdependence on the resource.

Managing the Bermuda Fisheries Commons

Intervention by government to manage the reef fishery in Bermuda was originally a direct consequence of concerns about what it perceived to be an unfolding tragedy of the reef commons.

The 1991 Report of the Commission of Inquiry about Bermuda's fishing industry noted:

The inevitability of overexploitation of common property resources, such as fishery resources, to which users have unlimited access, is well recognised, and is known as the tragedy of the commons. It is understood that without control, there is no reason for any user to exercise self-restraint, since there is no guarantee that any other user will do the same. Consequently self-restraint does not equate to conservation, it equates only to yielding resources to other users. Thus it is unreasonable to expect any user to exercise voluntary restraint so long as exploitation is economically feasible . . . In the face of the tragedy of the commons, regulation by consensus or by an agency with a mandate to regulate is the only possible solution.

Government took over the mandate to manage the fisheries in Bermuda when it perceived that a tragedy of the reef commons was underway. It assumed, by implication, that fishermen could no longer be trusted to manage the fisheries responsibly on their own. It considered that fishermen were the main cause of irresponsible overexploitation of the resource. It supposed that self-regulation of the fisheries by the fishermen was out of date, and probably well along the road to extinction anyway. Centralized regulation by the government was considered not only necessary but the only option available to avoid further damage to the reef fishing environment and avert, potentially, its ultimate destruction.

Another assumption, clearly stated by the Commission of Inquiry, was that fishermen could not be expected to exercise self-restraint in the fishery 'so long as exploitation is economically feasible'.

Fishermen, in other words, would behave exactly like Hardin's rational herdsmen. They would take more and more fish from Bermuda's reef waters until so few marketable fish were left that it became uneconomical to fish for them. Or until their freedom to do so was curtailed by government decree, for the common good.

Bermuda Fisheries Management

Responsibility for the management of the three broadly defined fisheries in Bermuda (reef, offshore pelagics, and lobsters) overlaps various government agencies: the Fisheries Division of the Department of Agriculture and Fisheries; the Ministry of the Environment; and, for marine issues generally within Bermuda's 12 mile territorial sea area (which includes the entire Bermuda Platform), the Water Authority.

As the fisheries Commission of Inquiry has pointed out, 'shared responsibility [for the fisheries] is not necessarily bad if roles are well defined and there is a central plan in place to lead all parties forward'.

As it stands, roles are not well defined, there is no universally agreed central plan ('The 1984 Fisheries Management and Development Plan does not include an explicit policy statement.'), and the management of Bermuda's most valuable natural resource has been orchestrated largely on the basis of centralized regulation and legislation but with *ad hoc* devolution of responsibilities.

Nominally, the Department of Agriculture and Fisheries has had overall responsibility for Bermuda's fisheries since 1961. By the 1990s, however, there was still no clearly formulated statement that outlined the division of responsibilities, or even objectives, for the implementation, enforcement, and development of policies related to the management of Bermuda's fisheries. Whether there are even clearly defined policies, apart from the conservation of the resource, is arguable.

The 1991 Commission of Inquiry was moved to state that 'there should be fishery specific management plans which identify management objectives, options and actions.' It went on to make a number of recommendations, most of which have not been pursued to any effective degree, if at all.

There is, in short, no comprehensive, sustained plan of action for the effective implementation of fisheries management policies in Bermuda, because there is no comprehensive fisheries management policy to begin with (except for a series of fisheries regulations that is aimed primarily at controlling fishermen in order to protect the resource).

The lack of a comprehensive fisheries policy plan, the disintegration of fishermen's trust in fisheries managers at least since the 1980s, and the lack of a sustained initiative by fishermen to organize themselves into a unified group since the 1960s and 1970s, in harness with fisheries officials who are generally not adept at managing fishermen much less the consent of fishermen to be regulated, has created an impasse that has made it virtually impossible to formulate consensual decisions relating to local fisheries management.

Gene Barrett, in his 1991 monograph *The Fish Pot Ban: Reef Overfishing and State Management in Bermuda*, offered his appraisal of the reasons why fishermen had come to distrust fisheries officials.

> Fishermen in Bermuda actually began lobbying for legislation to protect the resource when customary norms [of fishing] started to break down. One can see this in the formation of the Bermuda Commercial Fishermen's Association in 1969 and the various efforts and representations fishermen made to the government from the late 1960s onwards.
>
> However, the thrust of efforts by fishery managers to include fishermen in this decision-making process has been limited by the very structure of the process itself. In retrospect one can see it resulting in the polarization of fishermen and state interests. The process effectively delegitimized fishermen in the eyes of the managers and vice versa.

Barrett noted that the structure of formulating fisheries policies in Bermuda was based on

> a consultative process whereby statutory advisory committees composed of representatives of various interest groups and community leaders make recommendations to the Minister on licensing and effort regulations and arbitrate disputes . . .

In effect the Fisheries Advisory Committee, created in 1972, and the Fisheries Commission, created in 1984, were groups that thrashed out and fine-tuned policies developed by bureaucrats and scientists.

Their primary purpose was to legitimate and administer policies by giving a façade of consultation. These Committees also ran interference for fisheries managers and politicians by taking the blame for practical decisions on cutbacks and licence cancellations once policies were in place. Policy-makers argued the general merits of regulations, but would not be culpable for their practical effects.

Boiled down to its bare bones, the criticism is that consultative bodies, commissions, committees, and conclaves set up to deal with *ad hoc* problems but without a long-term interest in the consequences of their decisions for the fishery, have assumed but dissipated responsibility for fisheries management decisions.

No one directly involved in the fisheries, that is, could be damned, praised, or otherwise held accountable for the effects of decisions made over the well-being of fish, fishermen, or the fishing environment of Bermuda. Even as power was concentrated at the top, responsibility throughout the ranks was diluted virtually to the point of evanescence.

While legislative power and legal authority over Bermuda's fisheries have crystallized out among ministerial functions, administrative authority has devolved downwards to fisheries management personnel who use it, quite properly and legitimately, to exercise their control over fishermen. This 'top-down' process of power devolution is a natural consequence of management by regulation: the more regulations and restrictions in place, the more authority must be exerted from above.

Another consequence of this situation is that fishermen, who used to have a high degree of self-determination and control over the fisheries, now have virtually none. The erosion of their sense of empowerment over the fishing grounds, their fishing practices, and their livelihood has been a fundamental source of their disaffection with government and fisheries officials.

Aggravating fishermen's disaffection over their loss of power is the fact that they do not recognize, to a large degree, the legitimacy of the authority imposed on them. This is because fishermen have gradually lost the power to contribute their own knowledge, opinions, and beliefs to fisheries management decisions. Part of the reason for this is because their disunity has diluted their authority as a group. The other reason is because government has removed that authority from them.

For whatever reasons, the perception by fishermen that the authority imposed on them is largely illegitimate has significantly weakened the potential for effective fisheries management in Bermuda, in terms of enforcement of regulations, collaboration between fishermen and fisheries officials, consensual decision making, and enhancement of, and long-term planning for, the future of the resource.

Evolution of Fisheries Management in Bermuda

In the early 1970s when government made its first significant steps to regulate the Bermuda fisheries, the main goals were 'to support and develop the fishing industry to exploit the harvestable resources to their maximum sustainable levels; to increase the efficiency of all facets of the industry and to increase availability of Bermuda fish to the consumers'. Development of the industry 'to maximum sustainable levels' was the priority.

At that time, as a Fisheries Division policy paper in 1975 confessed, 'Virtually all existing regulations covering the management or conservation of Bermuda's fishing resources have no firm scientific foundation.'

Research and development for fisheries then was severely underfunded. In 1973 the fisheries programme had a government budget of just $22,000. Even though the value of the local fishing industry was 'approximately half the value of the locally produced agricultural products of all kinds', agriculture had a support budget of almost $300,000, more than 10 times the budget for fisheries.

In 1974 Fisheries Division had just two officials: a scientist and an enforcement officer. Since it had just one small open boat to patrol Bermuda's 450 square miles of reef fishing waters, it had to enlist the assistance of visiting naval and air force units to investigate reports of fisheries violations in waters outside the reef area.

In those circumstances the priority of the Fisheries Division was to get adequate funding simply to establish a basic research and development programme to study and assess the resource. The policy platform in any case was development of the fisheries. It was not management *per se*, which was oriented towards supporting development of the marine resources, 'to realise their maximum sustainable yields, their sport fishing potentials and their natural beauty'.

The first priority for development of fisheries, then, was to find out more about the local fish population, and the reef fish stocks in particular.

> Once a knowledge of the stocks and fishing information has been obtained (the latter through statistics), it is possible to formulate the necessary conservation regulations. These must cover such things as closed seasons for selected varieties [species], restricted areas, size limits, fishing gear restrictions and overall control through licensing and limitations of licences. This, in turn, would allow the fishermen to formulate their own fishing policies as they relate to seasonal distribution of fish, types of vessels and gear used and associated fishing methods.

The Fisheries Division report also cited the need for a more efficient fishing industry, to increase productivity.

Since there are known under-utilised resources, it is presumed that local waters can support a larger catch than at present. If research confirms this, then there will be an additional requirement to increase productivity of individual fishermen to achieve larger yields and possibly lower prices. This, however, will require the development of more systematic processing and marketing of fish in order to meet the requirements of the consumer.

Most of the research effort of fisheries managers from the mid-1970s was directed towards getting better information about Bermuda's fishing resource, to develop the fishery into a 'viable industry'. Collection of catch statistics provided by licensed commercial fishermen since 1973, to build up a statistical database of species caught in Bermuda waters, was the first step towards that end.

Fisheries Division realized that catch statistics alone, however, would not be enough to substantiate management related policies based on factors such as the determination of the production potential and maximum sustainable yields of reef fish species around Bermuda. (At that time, the focus was exclusively on the reef fishery. The pelagic species offshore were considered to be 'useful as food, but which are being exploited locally mainly as sport fish, although some are sold for food'.)

> In order to assess the production potential of a particular species, it is necessary to have an estimate of the present numbers by class or age, together with such information as the rates and modes of reproduction, which in turn indicate whether there are age groups or spawning areas to be protected. Some biological data is also required for an understanding of full life cycle, such as growth rate, feeding habits, reproduction rates and maximum population size . . .

When such information is combined with the catch statistics discussed above, it is possible to make the required assessment of the production potential of the species.

Over the following years the concept of fisheries management in Bermuda was based on those premises: the collection of information about the fisheries to regulate the industry and conserve the resource, alongside administrative functions (such as licensing fishermen) and enforcement duties.

To that end Fisheries Division has focused on research and development, as it was originally established to do and continues, mainly, to do. However, as the plight of diminishing reef fish stocks became more evident throughout the 1970s and 1980s, the focus on development of the fisheries yielded to the more pressing need of protecting the resource. For that reason, research has, to all intents and purposes, become the mainstay of Fisheries Division's function since the 1980s. Development has become a secondary priority, largely oriented towards promoting the diversification of the fisheries into other areas (such as the offshore pelagics).

Reported fish landings and other statistical data supplied by fishermen constituted the basis for Bermuda's fisheries management from the 1970s. Fisheries managers were nevertheless equally aware of other environmental influences on the reef fishery. The focus, however, was on regulation of the fishery, because 'we can more easily and more quickly regulate fishing effort (i.e. the number of fishing vessels, number of fish pots, etc.) than we can reverse ecological changes brought about by pollution'.

Even though Fisheries Division acknowledged that catch and effort statistics were not entirely accurate, it satisfied itself that 'absolute precision [was] not required' in assessing long-term trends related to pressures on the fishery and potential overfishing.

The attitude of fisheries managers by the 1980s was that they were taking 'a conservative position of preventive management'. The view was that 'all cause and effect relationships within a fishery do not have to be unequivocally documented before protective measures are implemented'.

Turning that statement on its head, it begs the question, to what extent *does* cause and effect need to be documented to justify protective measures, and, for that matter, *which* causes and effects should be considered? Without a clear definition of those criteria, the implementation of 'protective measures' has a *carte blanche* authority based on criteria that may be legitimate but are none the less arbitrary.

The perception of a tragedy of the reef commons already under way has dominated fisheries management issues in Bermuda since the mid-1980s. Fisheries Division has used its catch and effort statistics showing reduced landings of certain species, and the groupers in particular, as the primary criteria for justifying restrictions and regulations to protect vulnerable species and conserve the marine environment overall.

Proscriptive regulations have thereby constituted the standard range of methods employed in the management of Bermuda's fisheries to date. These have comprised most conventional measures used in other fisheries elsewhere, including compulsory reporting of fish landings by commercial fishermen, restrictions on the types of gear used, restrictions on the size of some fish species caught, bag limits on some species, closed fishing periods to protect certain species at spawning times of the year, and closed fishing areas where no fishing is permitted.

As a 1993 paper by Fisheries Division personnel confirms, 'All of these regulations have the same intent: to reduce the number of fish taken until their populations can recover. The first priority is to reduce harvests of the species that are most depleted.'

The *management* of Bermuda's fishery has not actually been management of the fisheries overall but rather a series of regulations designed to *control* the fishing industry within a wider brief to protect the marine resource. Since the use of the resource has become oriented more towards recreational use than for commercial fishing, the

Bermuda government has had at least as great a vested interest in preserving its aesthetic qualities as managing its use as a fishery.

Tourism and recreational uses of the waters around Bermuda are actually valued far more now, in economic terms, than the fishery. According to the 1993 paper by Fisheries Division personnel, 'In 1988, snorkeling, diving, glass-bottom boat tours, and sport fishing grossed more than $9 million . . . Commercial fishing, on the other hand, including the harvesting of lobster and offshore species, generated annual gross earnings of some $3 million.' Reef preservation, it concludes, is clearly more valuable than the fishery. (The paper appeared to be using the economic argument to support, in part, the fish pot ban of 1990.)

Most things in Bermuda are ultimately measured in dollars and cents. Commercial fishing, being neither particularly aesthetic nor a big earner for the government, loses heavily on that balance.

In 1984 a Fisheries Management and Development Programme was drawn up. There was no 'explicit policy statement' in the Programme, but the implication was that there had to be a 'tradeoff between fishing and tourism', between the rights of fishermen to exploit the reef fishery and the rights of other recreational users to appreciate the undoubted 'inestimable' aesthetic qualities of the reef environment.

By the mid-1980s fisheries management in Bermuda was becoming increasingly skewed towards management of the marine resource for an increasing number of non-fishing users. Local residents were becoming more vocal in calling for action to remedy the degradation of reef fish stocks. A new organization, Friends of Fish, was formed in 1987/88 to add its voice, and lobbying effort, on behalf of non-fishing interests.

The Fish Pot Ban

Legislation to ban fish pots, which were considered the main cause of overfishing, was passed early in 1990. The fish pot ban was unquestionably the most controversial fisheries management decision of the 20th century and possibly in the history of Bermuda's fishery. The ban was absolute (no phasing out period), it was decisive, and it was non-negotiable, which the government had not only anticipated but intended it to be.

Government announced the closure of the pot fishery at the end of January 1990. No new pot fishing licences were to be issued after existing licences expired at the end of March that same year.

With virtually immediate effect, fishermen who had depended entirely on fish pots for their livelihood for most of their lives were prohibited from using them. In many cases this cut their annual income by half. Compensation of up to $75,000 to each pot fisherman was offered, according to their dependence on the pot fishery based on their catch and effort records from the previous three years.

In the 1970s fishermen played an instrumental role in fisheries management decisions. They were the first to advocate the closure of fishing grounds to protect vulnerable grouper species (red hind, originally) during spawning months. Their influence on the decision to ban fish pots, however, was negligible. Anecdotal evidence suggests that government assured at least some fishermen shortly before the ban that no such prohibition would be enacted.

It was only a matter of time before a ban on pot fishing, or some other draconian measure to rehabilitate the reef fishery, would be enacted, considering the economic and political climate in Bermuda at the end of the 1980s.

Pressures to protect the reef fishing environment had been mounting. Use of local waters for activities other than fishing had been increasing its value as a recreational resource. Earlier fisheries management measures had been unsucessful in restricting access to the reef fishery.

Pressures, in other words, were coming to a head. One swift stroke of legislative penmanship was intended to ease political pressures, as well as the pressures on fish stocks. Pot fishermen, however, expressed their angered frustration at the decision. Today, more than a decade later, that anger has still not entirely subsided, although most ex-pot fishermen accept that they will probably never again be allowed to use fish pots (at least not the traditional Antillean arrowhead design pots they had used for most of their lives).

Gene Barrett, an opponent of the ban, noted in his monograph *The Fish Pot Ban: Reef Overfishing and State Management in Bermuda*: 'Despite strong objections from fisheries staff concerning a total ban on pots, a new minister [Minister of the Environment Ann Cartwright DeCouto] and a new senior fisheries officer with strong ties to the recreational and charter fishery pushed through the legislation.'

Barrett argued that the real reasons for the fish pot ban were rooted, first, in the failure of fisheries management up till then, which necessitated a dramatic and draconian corrective measure, and secondly, in the hyper-development of Bermuda's economy since the 1970s.

Overfishing, he emphasized, was, by the late 1970s, 'very real and was recognized by fishermen and resource managers alike'. But the root of the tragedy of the reef commons was the collapse of traditional self-management practices by fishermen, 'not simply the predictable consequence of unchecked human greed' as enshrined by the tragedy of the commons hypothesis.

The fish pot ban was a response to 'unchecked human greed', according to Barrett, rather than a solution to the problem of collapsed institutions of traditional fisheries self-management.

To that extent the ban missed the point entirely: policies to control 'human greed', he argued, were limited to defence mechanisms of constraint and regulation, whereas policies to reconstitute traditional self-management practices in a modern fisheries management context offered a much broader range of positive, offensive options.

The fish pot ban was a severe constraint, a reprimand, a ham-fisted slap on the hand, to check the 'human greed' factor. Government not only overlooked but did not even consider the possibility of reconstituting traditional management mechanisms as a remedy for the overfishing problem, such was the climate of desperation at that time to halt further damage to the reef resource (as well as to respond to mounting political pressures).

Fisheries management, Barrett argued, had become 'illegitimised' by proscriptive government regulations and by the attendant decision-making process that increasingly alienated fishermen. Hyper-development of Bermuda's economy pushed fishermen to fish more intensively, putting more pressure on the reef fish stock at a time when the government was trying to reduce pressures.

The key to the whole problem was that, for many and diverse reasons, fishermen and fisheries managers, from both sides of the fence, were in continual confrontation. Neither side ever treated this confrontation as an issue in itself. Whatever the rights and wrongs of each side's case, the conflicting relationship between them was, and remains to this day, effectively unresolved.

If anything, the fish pot ban has soured the relationship between fishermen and fisheries managers, however it may have soothed the stress on the reef fish populations.

As a culmination of 'conservative preventive management', the ban forcibly and unequivocally spiked the tragedy of the reef commons issue. As a political decision, the ban satisfied the majority while leaving a tolerable minority (the fishermen) disgruntled. As a component of holistic, integrated fisheries management, it was a sledgehammer cracking one nut (albeit a rather large nut) in a field of acorns.

Either way, and rightly or wrongly, the pot ban was an inevitable consequence of the evolution of official fisheries management perceptions in Bermuda over the preceding 20 years.

Traditional Fisheries Management

The concept of fisheries self-management (also known variously as folk management, traditional management, and indigenous management) may be described as 'the ways in which fishermen perceive, define, delimit, "own", and defend their rights to inshore fishing grounds. That may include strategies for limiting fishing effort and enhancing the productivity of fish stocks. [It] often differs little in practice from biologically based, modern fisheries management' (Dyer and McGoodwin, *Folk Management in the World's Fisheries*).

An important but sometimes less recognized value of traditional fisheries self-management is that it often relates to the management of fishing *space* rather than levels of fishing *effort*. The concept of spatiality – fishermen's perceptions of communal and individual boundaries over their fishing grounds – dictates how fishermen manage their use of fishing grounds, reinforce their authority, and legitimize their territorial fishing rights. Spatiality is a precondition of where and how fishermen fish, and what they catch.

Up to about the 1960s, before Bermuda's waters came to be shared by many different users, commercial fishermen practised virtual self-regulation of their fishing activities. Self-management of the pre-1960s 'traditional fishery' in Bermuda, with much less sophisticated technology and less intensive fishing, was founded on principles of respect for the communal use of the resource.

The collapse of those traditional values occurred when competition for use of the waters around Bermuda increased, when Bermuda's economic development started to take off, and when government removed responsibility for management of the fisheries from the fishermen to itself.

The erosion of traditional self-management ethics in Bermuda's fishery came about when competitive pressures for use of the marine resource and in the land economy increased gradually after the Second World War, and precipitously from the 1970s onwards.

As competitive economic pressures grew, fishermen could less afford to respect traditional fishing ethics. Government intervention in the fisheries increased. The fishermen became increasingly alienated from their fishing grounds, particularly since government policy was oriented towards controlling their access for conservationist purposes.

The practices used by fishermen to manage the fishery among themselves evolved as a natural process over many generations. Families or individuals fished permanent locations which they marked, nominally, and recognized, by custom, to 'belong' to them. 'Owners' would defend their locations by cutting away the gear of intruders or by other hostile defence mechanisms.

Fishermen 'cultivated' specific parts of the reef around Bermuda for their own use. They marked territorial boundaries by dropping a regular supply of bait ('baiting up') over a location for long periods to keep groupers and other demersal species at or near the spot. Other locations were passed on to family members by inheritance, keeping them within the family from generation to generation.

By such means was the reef platform around Bermuda dotted with fishing locations nominally 'owned' by specific individuals or families, fished by them to the exclusion of others, and protected, ostensibly, by etiquette, courtesy, and honesty. Encroachment on another fisherman's ground was taboo, comparable to burgling his home.

The spatial perception by fishermen, in their mind's eye, of who fished where, was the only legitimate authority over territorial rights to the fishing grounds, in the absence of actual stone wall boundaries.

As Captain Geary Pitcher remarked in his description of handline fishing in the early 20th century:

> One man wouldn't go to another man's place. There was honesty in those days. A man would 'have' that spot. . .People was more honest in those days than they are today [early 1980s]. You could come home and tell people in those days what you saw on the bottom, fish and what not, and they wouldn't go there. Because they was honest. They figured, that's your fish. You baited it and found it; that's your fish. But today, if you got traps out, and you come in, got a good voyage, and the other fellow knows it, he's got you compassed the next day with his traps. He tries to catch the same fish you caught. Don't make sense to me. The fishermen today is not like they used to be.

The self-management system may seem to imply that fishermen in Bermuda used to be honourable, moral, and upstanding gentlemen, while fishermen today are ruthless, amoral, and dishonourable villains. In fact, the ethics of self-management related only to the fishing grounds and how men fished. How they conducted themselves otherwise and elsewhere may be as open to speculative villification or beatification as it is with any other individuals.

It is a curious irony that, when only fishermen used the reef fishing waters around Bermuda, the resource was more properly 'owned' by those individuals than it is today when many more different users are claiming entitlement to it as a common property. Now that everyone uses it, no one 'owns' it. So, who now has *responsibility* for it?

Some fishing locations were not tied to a single 'owner' but were fished commonly by all fishermen. Grouper Ground, off the southeast of St David's, fished heavily during groupers' spawning period in late May until mid-July, was one of the best known. Kitchen Shoals, the southwest hind grounds, and other locations around the reef platform where groupers and other species aggregated to spawn, as well as the offshore banks, were also open to all-comers. Generally speaking, any locations deeper than about 25 fathoms, which were off the edge of the reef platform, including Challenger and Argus Banks, were considered communal fishing grounds.

The Economic Imperative

Self-management was possible because, first, it represented a profitable investment in the way men fished, and secondly, there was less economic incentive to buck the system because it was a less competitive business than it is today.

An important aspect of self-management, alluded to by Captain Pitcher, was that fishermen used to 'bait up' a site for long periods to keep the fish at that site. The bait, and the time spent 'baiting up', constituted their investment in that site. The fishermen were not only seeding the site, they were fertilizing it, managing its growth and well-being, and cultivating it for harvest of the fish there. In those days of simple technology, the cultivation of the site was the fisherman's investment. *His* bait. *His* time. *His* site. *His* fish.

The competitive pressures to encroach on another fisherman's site were much less than they are today. For the most part it wasn't worth the risk of opprobrium, the social disgrace, of breaking the taboo of encroachment on another man's site, for the sake of a few more fish. There was relatively little economic return on that kind of poaching activity, compared with the much greater risk of ostracism by other fishermen in the community.

Cultivation of your own site was not only a more profitable investment in the long run, because you improved the yield of fish per

site by intimate knowledge and appropriate husbandry of each site, it also enhanced your standing in the fishing community. A successful fisherman was respected for how well he fished, which depended on how much he respected the rights of other fishermen.

Another aspect of the traditional management of the fishery was the use of fish ponds to keep surplus fish. Ponds were used mainly to stock fish to sell in non-fishing months of the year but sometimes for much longer periods. As Captain Pitcher remarked, 'I've had 'em down at the ponds for years.' The use of fish ponds as a fisheries management technique was like keeping money in the bank, using your surplus assets to protect your investment for future profits in leaner times.

The key to the success of self-management in the Bermuda fishery was that fishermen were managing both the resource as well as their fishing activities in harvesting the resource. Fishermen had a direct, tangible, material relationship with the fishing grounds they husbanded, because they had a proprietal interest, an investment, in those grounds. Self-management, as an investment in the cultivation of specific fishing sites, was therefore as much an economic necessity as a system of communal ethics.

One of the apparent benefits of self-management was that it was environmentally friendly and had what Gene Barrett has called 'a significant husbandry effect'. Property rights, in the context of the fisheries, gave fishermen collective and individual 'ownership' of the resource, in practice if not in law. 'Ownership' gave fishermen an incentive to invest in the resource by, for example, leaving fishing grounds fallow from time to time to let fish stocks regenerate.

Captain Pitcher explained: 'I've had them places and catched every fish there and you wouldn't see another fish there. I've fished out several fishing places. You leave it for 3–4 months or so and go back, and bait it again, and you get more fish . . . You take the fish when you can. In fishing, there ain't such a thing as leaving some for tomorrow.'

'Fishing out a place' and 'not leaving some for tomorrow' blatantly suggests that fishermen in those days were not guided by a deliberate conservationist ethic. Their aim was to catch as many fish as efficiently as possible, by leaving sites fallow when they were fished out, to regenerate stocks at those sites, and subsequently to bait them up again. The process was similar to a farmer seeding and fertilizing a field to cultivate a crop, over a cycle of as many months as was needed to attract fish back to the site.

It was imperative for a fisherman to conserve the fishing quality of his sites for economic, not ethical, reasons. Fishermen were, in that sense, no more ethical than the farmer who practised good husbandry of his lands. It was simply good fishing practice to conserve the resource by cultivating it in the most efficient way appropriate to his means, namely through a cycle of baiting up the site, fishing it hard, leaving it fallow, baiting up again, and so on.

The concept of conservation then was not laden with the burden of ethical or moral implications as it is today. Whether it was eco-friendly or not was hardly a consideration either. It was a practical system of fishing and management (another modern concept) of the resource that sustained both the fisherman and the resource in a mutually beneficial symbiotic relationship.

In those days fishermen fished hard around the grouper spawning grounds at spawning times of the year. In spawning aggregations, and in an excited state, the fish were easy money for fishermen. If there had been a deliberate conservationist ethic among fishermen in those years, they would not have fished the spawning grounds so hard, or even at all. The fact that they did, enthusiastically, suggests that they were primarily motivated by economic considerations, namely, to make money from as much fish as they could catch efficiently and sell accordingly.

Even in later years when pot fishing predominated, but 'prior to the professionalisation of the fishery', Barrett noted that

> diversification within the fishery was greater, and had a similar latent conservation effect by providing certain areas and species a regenerative period each year . . . Customary tenure ['ownership' of fishing locations by dint of custom] had the effect of limiting overall entry levels [restricting the number of

new fishermen], and ensuring that fishing practices followed established patterns . . . Positional tenure [marked fishing locations 'owned' and passed down by inheritance but used only seasonally] had an especially interesting conservation effect by encouraging 'fallow' cultivation of fishing grounds. The upshot of these factors meant there were more fish around. And, with more fish available, fewer pots and less effort was required to catch the fish.

The catch in all of this was that self-management in Bermuda's fishery was, for all its conservationist benefits, a static system. It benefited the fish populations because there was less stress on them. It worked for the fishermen because they had control over their working lives. But it was predicated on an unchanging cycle of fixed patterns of fishing within a closed system that perpetuated low income, a subsistence livelihood, and very limited capacity to invest in more sophisticated technology. Fishermen typically earned money from other trades, but fishing itself was, in economic terms, a subsistence activity.

The dynamics of traditional self-management techniques were largely directed towards the fishing grounds and the fish. While these thrived, the fishermen themselves could do little more than tread water to keep fishing. They expended most of their effort on maintaining healthy fishing grounds, rather than improving their own livelihood.

Fishermen made a trade-off between a high degree of control over their working lives, self-esteem, and job satisfaction, at the sacrifice of ambitions to achieve a higher standard of living. It is a moot point whether, in those simpler times in Bermuda, the accumulation of wealth and cultivation of social status was as desirable a commodity as it is today. Fishermen, by the nature of their vocation, were locked into a system that precluded them from the possibilities of advancement within their fishing lives.

For all of its economic deficiencies, self-management by Bermudian fishermen was nevertheless a system of functional, practical, and empirically tested methods and practices. Evolved over generations, it was rooted in the fishing grounds cultivated by fishermen, dignified by the moral authority of an honour system, and regulated by a code of ethics that reflected the independent nature of fishermen and their communal working class status.

All of which is not to say that the same system would work today in Bermuda's more complex environment, not least because the common property of the fishing grounds, previously monopolized by the fishermen, is today shared with numerous other users.

In past times when traditional self-management prevailed, Bermuda was a slower-paced, less dynamic, less wealth-oriented community than it is today. Old methods that worked *then* may not necessarily work *now*.

Dug up, brushed off, and refurbised, however, traditional practices might be adaptable to complement and enhance the techniques of contemporary fisheries management in Bermuda.

Current Status of Fisheries Management

Fisheries management in Bermuda since the 1970s has been characterized by: centralized decision making by the government; decreasing involvement of fishermen in decision making; focus on the use of regulations to protect the resource with an impositional regime to restrain fishermen's practices; the assumption by government and fisheries managers that fishermen are irresponsible and will, if left to their own devices, destroy the resource for their own gain ('tragedy of the commons'); the use of conventional mechanisms to *regulate* rather than *manage* the fisheries; and, a focus on managing the resource for the benefit of all users with a bias towards tourism and recreational use because it has a higher economic value than commercial fishing.

After 30 years of increasingly restrictive legislation and regulation, there is now a grudging stalemate between fishermen and fisheries managers. Regulations oblige fishermen to collaborate with fisheries officials (for example, by providing catch and effort statistics, and by compliance with licensing requirements). Fisheries managers need the contributions from fishermen (catch and effort statistics, mainly) to carry out research and development.

Beyond those official lines of communication, bridges between fisheries bureaucracy on the one side and the fishermen on the other are few and far between.

By and large, fishermen in Bermuda do comply with regulations. Infringements most often involve the use of illegal traps (still commonplace) and the sale of prohibited fish species camouflaged in either bags of mixed fillet or described as another species altogether. (This may occur less commonly now than before when 'snapper' on restaurant menus was often more likely to be parrotfish.) Imported fish, including species banned in Bermuda, is also sometimes sold as 'Bermuda fish'.

Passing off illegal fish is easy. Most people cannot tell a red rockfish (a fully protected species) from a red hind, much less whether it was local or imported — especially after the fish is cleaned, filleted, and broiled at 350°F with a sprinkling of paprika.

Fisheries managers have selective vision in their view of fishermen's infringements. Like policemen who pull in drivers only when they grossly exceed the speed limit, fisheries officers tend to look the other way or conciliate in matters where fishermen do not strictly comply with regulations but which may be tolerably within stretched limits.

Limited funds and facilities for enforcement also restrict the effectiveness of fishing wardens. Every fisherman in Bermuda alleges, for example, that many fishermen still use pots with sunken buoys to mark their locations. Wardens from Fisheries Division, however, rarely catch, much less prosecute, illegal pot users, because they have minimal resources to enforce regulations. Successful prosecution in the courts is rare.

Fisheries management in Bermuda has become a cat and mouse game. An implicit set of rules has evolved, stating, roughly translated; you fish on your side of the river, we fish on our side, and no one fishes in the middle. Conflict and confrontation between fishermen and fisheries officials is minimized by the equilibrium of balance of power.

Degrees of leniency in fisheries management in Bermuda have become the norm. Standards of compliance and enforcement have come to be scribbled as much around the margins of fisheries legislation as followed to the letter of the law. As with many things in Bermuda, the system works best when it works loose (but not too loose).

Future Options for Bermuda

Bermuda has ideal conditions to make it a model for cooperative fisheries management. The fishing grounds are a relatively small, localized area with well defined boundaries. There are only a few hundred commercial fishermen. Fishing is small scale and technology simple. Fishermen use similar fishing methods. Fishermen are knowledgeable about the fishing grounds and the fish around Bermuda. Government bureaucracy is small scale. And there is a fish depletion problem.

Cooperative fisheries management means that, instead of a coercive regime, instead of conflict and confrontation, instead of centralized decision making, there is a collaborative effort between fishermen and fisheries bureaucrats. Fishermen, other users of the local waters, and managers of the resource negotiate agreements to achieve management goals efficiently and effectively. Power, and responsibility, is negotiated by mutual consent and shared by mutual respect.

Elements of traditional self-management (for example, cultivation of specific sites, use of fish ponds to store surpluses, and communal governance and enforcement of fisheries regulations) can play an integral role in the co-management of the fisheries. Self-management methods have largely disappeared from use in Bermuda. They none the less exist as deeply rooted traditions that may be usefully regenerated as complementary forms of contemporary fisheries co-management.

Co-management agreements are most effective when they incorporate existing traditional management principles. They have a degree of legitimacy that fishermen recognize and, ideally, that fisheries managers value.

The next generation of fisheries management might aim for greater cooperation between fishermen and government, to manage the fisheries complex overall rather than simply controlling it by centralized decision making to conserve the resource.

Cooperative (co-management) principles combined with pre-existing self-management methods might be 'a creative way to break the impasse in government–fishermen conflicts over the most effective solutions to such crises', as Evelyn Pinkerton, a renowned author about fisheries management issues, has remarked. 'While [fisheries] self-regulation by itself is often insufficient, there may be elements of self-regulation that are highly significant in a co-management context.'

This is especially true when conservation of the fish stocks on the one hand and sustaining the viability of fishermen on the other are treated as interdependent, not separate, objectives.

The goal of fisheries managers in Bermuda so far has been to conserve the resource and defend fish stocks against predatory fishermen who will, apparently, eliminate all fish unless strictly regulated.

Overfishing and the tragedy of the reef commons have been the benchmark of fisheries management decisions in Bermuda for the past 30 years. Fisheries managers have assumed that they are powerless to control other environmental factors (pollution, sediment disturbance, etc.) that contribute, alongside intensive fishing, to the depletion of fish stocks.

Current fisheries management practices make no provision for uncertainty about the impact of 'other environmental factors' on fish stocks. Overfishing is targeted as the central problem, to be resolved to the exclusion of other less controllable factors.

In the future, fisheries managers might take a broader view of the problem. They might incorporate in their planning at least the acknowledgement of the influence of other environmental factors on fish stocks. A provision to consider the potential harmful influence of those factors would help plan to enhance, rather than just regulate, the resource.

An appropriate authority such as the Ministry for the Environment might be better able to control those 'environmental factors' than if their impact on fish stocks had not even been treated as a management issue in the first place.

By extending the scope of their focus, managers might take a more comprehensive view of managing the overall fisheries ecosystem, rather than narrowly focusing on controlling fishermen to protect the resource.

As much as good fishing is about observation, good fisheries management is about vision: the ability to see the whole problem in a changing perspective; the imagination to consider different options; the intelligence to value different types of information and information sources; and the resolution to see clearly the way ahead.

Fisheries Co-management

The virtue of co-management lies not only with its ethical implications (to safeguard the marine environment for future generations of users) but also with its practical applications. Efforts made to achieve consensus by collaboration among fisheries managers and fishermen pay dividends in reducing the effort, and cost, needed to manage the fisheries.

Enforcement of regulations is more effective, and less costly, when fishermen are actively involved in the decision-making process at the ground level, to establish regulations that the majority understand and agree to abide by. A higher degree of self-enforcement by fishermen is virtually inevitable to the degree that they have a contributory role in the management of the fisheries.

The restoration of a sense of economic self-determination by fishermen who contribute to the management process gives them a greater vested interest in maintaining the health of fish stocks. Managers and bureaucrats benefit by obtaining more reliable information from fishermen. Higher quality information increases their knowledge about fish stocks and the fisheries overall which enhances their research efforts, the fruits of which are communicated back to the fishermen.

Knowledge about the resource, communicated among fishermen, fisheries managers, and the general public, ultimately enhances the resource for all users who must also be willing to acknowledge, renegotiate, and resolve their differences. Otherwise the health of the resource is compromised.

Conditions necessary to pursue a co-management process in the fisheries include: the agreement by fishermen and fisheries managers that it is desirable to do so; the existence of an independent body dedicated specifically to fisheries management; the collective organization of all fishermen, to speak as a unified group; the agreement by all parties that co-management as a fisheries objective is a goal in itself; the acknowledgement either that the existing management system is not ideal and that co-management could be a more effective alternative, or that there are problems with the existing system that co-management might resolve; and, government commitment to finance the system.

One of the options for fisheries management in Bermuda is to do nothing. To maintain the *status quo*, imperfect as that may be. There is no compelling motivation to change direction towards co-management unless there is perceived to be a serious problem with the system as it stands.

If the objective continues to be to conserve the marine environment, and preserve fish stocks in particular, the existing regime of imposing regulations on fishermen might continue to be an acceptable approach. Fishermen would continue to grumble, as fishermen everywhere grumble at regulations that restrict them. But as long as they feel they can live with the irritation, their disquiet may never amount to a demand for change.

The use of regulatory mechanisms imposed by centralized authority, accepting a measure of tolerance around the perimeters of strict legality, may not be the most comprehensive means of managing the fishery overall, but it has proved to be an effective way to control fishermen in Bermuda so far. The increase of parrotfish around Bermuda's shores is evidence that the system has benefited fish stocks.

The weakest link in the system is that fisheries officials depend on fishermen for data, specifically the catch and effort statistics of their landings of fish and time spent fishing. If fishermen refuse to contribute that information, by a collective act of defiance against the management regime, or if they distorted the data, the conclusions reached by fisheries officials about the status of the fish stocks would be compromised. Without reliable data, the justification for fisheries regulations and legislation would be undermined, and probably unenforceable.

The trade-off between fisheries managers and fishermen now is that fishermen continue to contribute data and other fishing related information, in exchange for which fisheries officials keep their distance, allowing the fishermen some latitude in their fishing activity as long as the resource is kept in reasonably good condition. In many ways this is a truly Bermudian 'don't rock the boat' solution. It might not be strictly kosher, it might not whet the edge of enlightened thought about fisheries management, but if it doesn't cost much, doesn't take much effort, doesn't upset too many people too much, and works tolerably well, why change?

Fisheries management is a difficult task, fraught with tensions, complicated by political influences, biased by vested professional interests, shrouded by the uncertainty of scientific knowledge about the fishing environment, and overshadowed by greater economic interests from non-fishing (recreational) groups.

One thing is certain. It will take collaboration and cooperation, as well as shared responsibility and accountability, to achieve common goals, to enhance as well as protect both the resource and the fishery. Responsible fishing, responsible management, and responsible use of Bermuda's marine environment, with a personal commitment to its future well-being, are covenants to which everyone might aspire.

Appendices

Families of the Most Important Catch Fish Around Bermuda

Serranidae (groupers, sea basses)

Epinephelus striatus .... (Nassau grouper)

Epinephelus afer .... (Mutton hamlet)

Epinephelus guttatus .... (Red hind)

Cephalopholis fulva .... (Coney)

Mycteroperca bonaci .... (Black grouper)

Mycteroperca venenosa .... (Yellowfin rockfish)

Mycteroperca tigris .... (Tiger grouper/rockfish)

Mycteroperca microlepis .... (Finescale rockfish)

Mycteroperca interstitialis .... (Yellowmouth grouper)

Paranthias furcifer .... (Barber)

Sparidae (porgies, sea breams, chubs, spadefish)

Calamus bajonado .... (Blueboned porgy)

Calamus calamus .... (Sheepshead porgy)

Diplodus bermudensis .... (Bream)

Kyphosus sectatrix .... (Bermuda chub)

Kyphosus incisor .... (Yellow chub)

Balistidae (triggerfish, filefish)

Balistes capriscus .... (Common triggerfish)

Balistes vetula .... (Queen triggerfish)

Canthidermis sufflamen .... (Ocean triggerfish)

Labridae (wrasses)

Lachinolaimus maximus .... (Hogfish)

Halichoeres radiatus .... (Puddingwife)

Lutjanidae (snappers)

Lutjanus synagris .... (Whitewater snapper)

Lutjanus vivanus .... (Silk snapper)

Lutjanus griseus .... (Grey snapper)

Lutjanus apodus .... (Schoolmaster snapper)

Ocyurus chrysurus .... (Yellowtail)

Pomadasyidae (grunts)

Haemulon sciurus .... (Yellow grunt)

Haemulon plumieri .... (White grunt)

Haemulon album .... (Margate)

Holocentridae (squirrelfish)

Holocentrus ascensionis .... (Longjaw squirrelfish)

Holocentrus rufus .... (Common squirrelfish)

Albulidae (bonefish)

Albula vulpes .... (Bonefish)

Coryphaenidae (dolphins/dorados)

Coryphaena hippurus .... (Common dolphin/dorado)

Carangidae (jacks)

Caranx hippos .... (Steelhead jack)

Caranx latus .... (Horse-eye jack)

Caranx ruber .... (Bar jack)

Caranx lugubris .... (Black jack)

Caranx fusus .... (Blue runner)

Pseudocaranx dentex .... (Gwelly)

Uraspis secunda .... (Cottonmouth jack)

Seriola dumerili .... (Amberjack)

Seriola rivoliana .... (Horse-eye amberfish/almaco jack)

Seriola fasciata .... (Lesser amberjack)

Elagatis bipinnulata .... (Rainbow runner)

Decapterus macarellus .... (Ocean robin)

Decapterus punctatus .... (Round robin)

Trachinotus goodei .... (Pompano/palometa)

Scombridae (tunas, mackerels)

Thunnus albacares .... (Yellowfin/Allison tuna)

Thunnus atlanticus .... (Blackfin tuna)

Euthynnus alletteratus .... (Little tunny)

Katsuwonus pelamis .... (Skipjack tuna/oceanic bonito)

Thunnus alalunga .... (Albacore)

Acanthocybium solandri .... (Wahoo)

Istiophoridae (marlins, sailfish, spearfish)

Makaira nigricans .... (Blue marlin)

Tetrapturus albidus .... (White marlin)

Istiophorus platypterus .... (Sailfish)

Sphyraenidae (barracuda)

Sphyraena barracuda .... (Great barracuda)

Sphyraena picudilla .... (Sennet)

Carcharhinidae (sharks, rays)

*Carcharhinus galapagensis** .... (Dusky/cub shark)

Galeocerdo cuvier .... (Tiger shark)

Prionace glauca .... (Blue shark)

Sphyrna zygaema (**Sphyrnidae shark family**) ... (Hammerhead shark)

Isurus oxyrinchus (**Isuridae shark family**) .... (Mako shark)

* Known elsewhere in the world as the Galapagos shark; in Bermuda, until recently, the Dusky shark was identified as *C. obscurus* (see: *Fishes of Bermuda*, Collette, Luckhurst, Smith-Vaniz)

Chronology of Fisheries Legislation in Bermuda 1620–1997

Date	Legislation
1620	Act against the killing of over young tortoises
1626/27	Act against the drawing of pilchards and fry to make oil
1687	Act to prevent the destruction of fish
1703/04	Act to prevent the destruction of fish, by net-hauling
1722/23	Act to prevent any person or persons in the islands from making, having or keeping any [fishing] net or nets exceeding the length of three fathoms and a half
1727	Act to prevent any person or persons *whatsoever* in the Islands from making, having or keeping any [fishing] net or nets exceeding the length of three fathoms and a half (also: 1737/38; 1758; 1767)
1733/34	Act laying a duty upon the whale fishery of these islands, for the use of His Excellency the Governor
1740/41	Act to regulate the whale fishery of these islands
1777	Act to prohibit the taking fish in these islands with any seine [net] (also: 1782 [amendment]; 1802)
1789	Act to prolong an Act initiated 'An Act for the encouragement of the whaling and fishing business'
1791	Act to prohibit the setting of fish pots
1893	Act to continue the Act to restrict the use of fishing nets, and for other purposes (Repealed 1951.78)
1911	The Harrington Sound Fishing Act 1911 (Repealed 1921.69)
1916	The Fisheries Act 1916 (Repealed 1921.69)
1947	The Board of Trade (Fisheries) Regulations 1947
1953	The Fisheries Regulations 1953
1963	SR&O 11/1963: The Fisheries Regulations 1963 (revocation and amendment of 1953 Fisheries Regulations)
1966	Coral Reef Preserves Act 1966
1971	SR&O 32/1971: The Fisheries (Prohibited Areas and Prohibited Period) Order 1971 (first designation of prohibited areas [South Western Area, North Western Area, North Eastern Area] and closed fishing period in those areas)
1972	The Fisheries Act 1972
1972	SR&O 25/1972: Fisheries Regulations 1972
1973	The Fisheries (Protected Area) Order 1973 (prohibition of fishing within 300 feet radius of wreck *Vixen*, off Daniel's Head)
1976	The Fisheries (Protected Areas) Order 1976 (to protect spawning aggregations of Red Hind)
1978	BR 8/1978: Fisheries (Protected Species) Order 1978
1978	The Fisheries (Use of Fish Pots) (Argus Bank) Order 1978 (use of fish pots on Argus Bank restricted by permit)

1981	The Fisheries (Use of Fish Pots) (Challenger Bank) Order 1981 (use of fish pots on Challenger Bank restricted by permit)
1983	The Fisheries (Use of Fishing Nets) Order 1983 (prohibition of taking grey snapper (*Lutjanus griseus*) by nets)
1986	The Fisheries (Use of Fishing Nets) (South Shore) Order 1986
1988	The Fisheries (Protected Areas) Order 1988
1989	BR 20/1989: Fisheries (Anti-Fouling Paints Prohibition) Regulations 1989
1990	BR 17/1990: Fisheries (Protected Areas) Order 1990
1990	BR 18/1990: Fisheries (Use of Fishing Nets) Order 1990
1990	BR 16/1990: The Fisheries Amendment Regulations 1990 (fish pot ban, species restrictions)
1993	BR 28/1993: The Fisheries (Protected Areas) Amendment Order 1993
1993	BR 46/1993: The Fisheries (Protected Species) Amendment Order 1993
1996	BR 25/1995: The Fisheries (Protected Species) Amendment Order 1996
1996	BR 23/1996: The Fisheries Amendment Regulations 1996 (modification of restrictions on taking certain species)
1996	BR 24/1996: The Fisheries (Protected Areas) Amendment Order 1996
1996	Fisheries Amendment Act 1996 (amended articles re: Exclusive Economic Zone, previously Exclusive Fishing Zone)
1997	BR 29/1997: The Fisheries (Protected Areas) Amendment Order 1997

Directory of Charter Fishing Operators in Bermuda

Bermuda Sports Fishing Association
'Creek View House', 8 Tulo Lane,
Pembroke HM 02

Tel:	295 2370
Fax:	292 5535

Captain Keith Winter
Playmate Charters, 4 Mill Point Lane,
Pembroke HM 05

Tel:	292 7131
Cellular:	235 5172
Fax:	292 9598
Boat:	*Playmate*

Charter Fees:

Full day:	(7:00 AM–5:00 PM): $850
Half day:	$600
Booking deposit:	$200
Credit cards:	Visa, Mastercard, Amex

Captain James P. Olander/
Captain Hans Olander
Albatross Charters, PO Box DD 69,
St David's DD BX

Tel:	297 0715
Fax:	297 0299
Cellular:	234 9478
e-mail:	albatross@ibl.bm
Boat:	35 foot *Barong*

Captain Michael Baxter
Baxter's Reef Fishing, 15A Pinetree Lane,
Somerset MA 02

Tel:	234 2663/234 9722
Fax:	234 5958
Boat:	*Ellen B*

Rates:

$75 per person, half day (4 hours)	
Children under 12:	$40
Charter the boat:	$450, half day

Caters to small groups, personalized service.
Reef fishing for Bermuda chub, yellowtail,
snapper, small groupers, jacks, barracuda,
shark. All tackle and bait provided.

Captain Stephen Cabral
15 Mariner's Lane, Spanish Point,
Pembroke HM 02

Tel:	295 0140
Boat:	*Sea Scorpion III*

Captain Alan J. Card
PO Box SB 110, Somerset Bridge SB BX

Tel (home):	234 0872
Tel (boat):	237 2109
e-mail:	ajcard@northrock.bm
Boat:	*Challenger* (40 foot Gamefisherman)

Captain Blake West
Early Bird Charters, PO Box CR 103,
Crawl CR BX

Tel:	293 0813
Cellular:	234 9855
Boat:	*Troubadour*

Edness Fishing Charters
PO Box WK 9, Warwick WK BX

Tel:	236 3702

Captain Reggie Horseman/
Captain Andrew Marshall
Equalizer Charters, Suite 1043,
48 Par-la-Ville Rd, Hamilton HM11

Home Tel:	296 9158
Cellular:	237 3474
Boat:	235 4218
Boat:	*Equalizer*

Half day:	$600.00
3/4 day:	$700.00
Full day:	$800.00/

Early Bird Special leave dock at 6:00 AM
(10% of charter rate)

Eureka Fishing Ltd

11 Abri Lane, Spanish Point, Pembroke HM 02
Tel (office):   296 5414
Cellular (boat):   235 3836
Fax: 295 3620

Deep sea and reef fishing on 65 foot party boat *Eureka*. Private charters available for up to 60 persons.
Half day: adults $60, children (under 12) $40
Full day: $100 per person

Group and family rates available

Albert ('Peter') Fox Charter Fishing

28 Cashew City Rd, St David's DD 02
Tel: 297 1079
Cellular: 234 7456
Boat: *Elaine S. II*

Kelly Marie Charters

Somerset Bridge, Sandys
Tel: 234 1479/234 8335
Fax: 234 0356
e-mail: kellyfishing@ibl.bm

Steven Rance

Knock Down Charters, PO Box PG 177,
Paget PG BX
Tel: 236 3551
Cellular: 235 0792

Captain Rick Richards

PO Box SB 145, Somerset Bridge SB BX
Tel: 234 2378
Boat: *Traveller*

Captain Cliff Lambert

3 Aubrey Rd, Unit 1, Hamilton Parish CR 02
Tel (home):   293 4390
Cellular (boat):   234 9294
Cellular (mobile):   235 1691
e-mail: clambert@ibl.bm
Boat: *Striker I*

Captain Russell Young

2 Rushy Lane, Somerset MA 03
Tel: 234 1832
Cellular: 234 9819
E-mail: seawolfe@ibl.bm
Boat: *Sea Wolfe*

Captain Sinclair Lambe

Jamie C Charters, 5 Sound View Drive,
Sandy's MA 06
Tel: 234 3081/234 1071

Deep sea reef fishing in 35 foot *Jamie C*
Up to 8 people

Deep Sea Rates, 1–6 persons:
Half day: $650 ($100 each additional person)
Full day: $900 ($100 each additional person)

Reef Fishing Rates, 1–6 persons:
Half day: $550 ($75 each additional person)

For made up parties of 1–6 persons:
Half day deep sea rate: $110 per person
Full day deep sea rate: $150 per person
Reef fishing: $100 per person

Visa/Mastercard accepted

Captain Allen DeSilva

DeMako Charters, 11 Abri Lane,
Spanish Point, Pembroke HM 02
Tel (office):   295 0835
Cellular (boat):   234 8626
Fax: 295 3620
e-mail: mako@ibl.bm
Website: www.fishbermuda.com
Boat: *DeMako*, 57 foot Carolina Sportfisher,
             up to 6 persons, 30 kt cruising speed

Blue marlin specialist
Full day (9 hours): $1200; 3/4 day (6 hours): $1000; Deposit: $500 (refundable with bad weather (small craft warning) or 10 day advance warning cancellation of trip)

Amex, Mastercard, Visa

Captain David DeSilva

Princess Charters, 8 Tulo Lane, Spanish Point, Pembroke HM 02
Tel: 295 5813
Cellular: 234 8430
Fax: 295 4569

Captain 'Joe' Kelly

M.V. Messaround Charters, PO Box 107,
St George GE-BX
Home Tel: 297 8093
Boat: 234 8953
Fax: 297 1455

Half day: 4 hours
Full day: 8 hours
Up to 10 persons offshore
Rates only on request

Also: Caribbean Yacht Charters

Fishing Tackle and Marine Services Suppliers in Bermuda

Fly Bridge Tackle
Church St (opposite City Hall)
Hamilton HM 11
Tel: 295 1845
Fax: 296 1610

Main fishing tackle outlet in Bermuda, bait,
some outerwear

Robinson's Marina
Somerset Bridge
Tel: 234 1409
Fax: 238 3249

Fuel, marine services, bait, limited stock of
fishing lines, hooks, bait

Riddell's Bay Esso Marina Station
231 Middle Rd (Riddell's Bay)
Southampton SN 04
Tel: 238 8419

Fuel, marine services

**Pearman Watlington (P.W.'s) Marine
Center**
Pitt's Bay Rd
Pembroke
Tel: 295 3232
Fax: 292 5092

Fuel, marine services/maintenance, boating
supplies and equipment

Mill's Creek Marine/Darrell's Marine Ltd
17 Mill's Creek Rd
Pembroke
Tel: 292 6094
Fax: 295 8101

Fuel, marine services/maintenance

Meyer's Marine Services
Slip Rd
St George's
Tel: 297 8078
Fax: 297 0483
e-mail: meyerindus@ibl.bm
Website: www.meyer.bm

Fuel, marine services
Part of Meyer Group (travel, shipping, freight,
property, insurance, marine/auto, engineering,
steel supplies)

Bermuda Fish Recipes

Baked Bermuda Fish

1 six lb fish, scaled and gutted
2 sprigs thyme
½ cup Bermuda or sweet white onion rings, thinly sliced
6 tbsp. lemon juice
½ tsp. salt
½ tsp. freshly ground pepper
3 tbsp. butter

Stuffing
1 large onion, finely chopped
1 celery stalk, finely chopped
6 tbsp. canola oil
2 tbsp. fresh thyme, or 1 tbsp. dried thyme
2 tbsp. fresh parsley, or 1 tbsp. dried parsley
salt and pepper, to taste
2 cups breadcrumbs

To make stuffing, sauté onion and celery in 4 tablespoons of canola oil until golden. Remove from heat, mix in thyme, parsley, salt, pepper, and breadcrumbs.

To bake fish, place piece of foil large enough to be loosely folded around fish in roasting pan. Spread the remaining canola oil evenly under fish with half the onion and a sprig of thyme.

Insert stuffing into cavity so that it is easily contained with wooden skewer. Put the remaining thyme and onion and lemon juice over the fish. Season with salt and pepper.

Fold foil around fish, being sure to seal it so that no juices escape.

Put into pre-heated 350°F/175°C (moderate) oven, and bake about 45 minutes (7–8 min/lb). Fish is cooked when it flakes easily with fork.

Carefully lift fish from foil with large spatula, and place on platter. Garnish with lemon slices and herbs, and serve immediately with Hoppin' John (black-eye peas and rice) and salad or roasted fresh Bermuda vegetables.

From: *Traditions & Tastes*, by Judith Wadson

Baked Stuffed Bermuda Fish

1 whole fish (3–4 lb) (snapper, yellowtail, hogfish, etc.)
½ cup package stuffing
2 tbsp. parsley, chopped
¼ cup onion, chopped
¼ cup celery, chopped
¼ cup green pepper, chopped
2 tbsp. butter
Salt and pepper
Lemon juice
3 strips bacon

Wash fish and pat dry. Squeeze lemon juice over fish and inside cavity. Rub fish and cavity with salt and pepper. Sauté onion, celery, and green pepper in butter. Add parsley and mix well with stuffing. Spoon the stuffing into the cavity of the fish and close with toothpicks. Pre-heat oven to 350°F/175°C. Place fish in a greased roasting pan. Arrange bacon strips over fish. Bake for about 40 minutes. Serves 4.

From: *The Bermuda Cookbook*

Rockfish Almandine

2 lb rockfish fillets
Lemon juice
½ cup flour
Salt and pepper
½ cup melted butter
½ cup blanched almonds
2 tbsp. parsley, chopped

Squeeze lemon juice over fish fillets. Sprinkle with salt and pepper. Roll in flour and fry in butter until golden. Remove fish from pan to a warm plate. Add almonds to pan and fry until light brown. Add parsley. Spoon sauce over fish.

From: *The Bermuda Cookbook*

Baked Wahoo

5 lb wahoo
Juice of 1 or 2 limes or lemons
Salt and pepper
Butter (unsalted)
¼ tsp. rosemary leaves, crushed
¼ tsp. thyme leaves

Have wahoo filleted away from the bone in one long piece. Place wahoo in a large rectangular Pyrex dish with the skin surface down. Squeeze lemon or lime juice over the fish. Sprinkle generously with salt, pepper, thyme, and rosemary. Cover with plastic film and refrigerate for about 12 hours.

Preheat oven to 325°F/160°C. Turn fish over so that skin of the fish is uppermost. Sprinkle with a little more salt and pepper. Dot with unsalted butter. Bake for about 1 hour (12 minutes/lb).

From: *The Bermuda Cookbook*

Codfish Cakes

These treats have a crispy exterior, and are soft and creamy inside. Fresh herbs are the secret to superior cakes. A traditional dish, they are featured on holidays, but are served throughout the year for lunch and dinner, usually with a banana. Many locals eat a cake between a bread roll – with or without the traditional Bermudian smear of mayonnaise – or enjoy it solo with a squeeze of lemon juice. On Good Friday, many a kite-flyer puts one of these between a sweet hot cross bun and continues with the airborne task at hand.

1 lb salt cod, drained after soaking in water for 12 hours
(three water changes recommended)
4 lb red-skinned new potatoes, scrubbed, or large white variety, peeled and cut into 1 inch cubes
3 tbsp. fresh thyme, finely chopped, or 1½ tbsp. dried thyme
2 tbsp. fresh parsley, finely chopped, or 1 tbsp. dried parsley
freshly ground pepper
milk (optional)
1 egg, beaten (optional)
canola oil

In a large saucepan or medium stock-pot, add water to 1 inch below stainless steel steamer. Bring to boil, add potatoes, cover, and steam. They are cooked when skewer or paring knife can be easily inserted. Remove with slotted spoon. Put in large mixing bowl and mash well to eliminate lumps. (A food mill gives a finer consistency to the potatoes.)

Carefully remove steamer, and add more water to accommodate fish and bring to boil before adding cod. Poach fish in gently simmering water. When it flakes easily with fork, drain water and mash it as smoothly as possible. Add to potatoes with herbs and pepper, and blend well. If mixture is dry, add several tablespoons of milk, or egg. (Dryness depends on potatoes. Red skinned new potatoes are best, and these do not need to be peeled.)

To form cakes, roll about ½ cup of mixture into ball and gently flatten between palms to about 1 inch thick. Smooth edges of the patty, and put wax paper on a plate. Continue process, leaving at least 1 inch between each. These can be made a day ahead if stored in an airtight container.

To cook, put about ¼ inch canola oil in skillet over medium high heat. Test oil is correct temperature by putting small piece of fish mixture in skillet. If it cooks rapidly, oil is ready. Dredge patties through flour and gently place in hot oil without crowding pan. Cook about 5 minutes or until golden. With spatula, carefully flip patties towards far side of pan to prevent oil from splattering you. Cook second side until golden. Remove and serve.

From: *Traditions & Tastes*, **by Judith Wadson**

Bermuda Fish Chowder

There are many different recipes for this dish. It is best prepared a day ahead, to allow flavours to blend. It is usually served with Gosling's Bermuda black rum and sherry peppers (fresh hot peppers steeped in sherry for several months).

Fish Stock
2 large fish heads and bones, from a white meat fish [porgy, snapper, hind, etc.]
1 large carrot, chopped in 1 inch pieces
2 celery stalks, chopped in 1 inch pieces
2 medium onions, chopped in 1 inch pieces
6 peppercorns
2 bay leaves
2 gallons cold water

Put ingredients in large stock pot. Bring to boil and then reduce heat to gentle simmer. About every 5 minutes, skim residue and oil from surface with ladle. Cook 45 minutes. Pass contents through strainer and refrigerate if not using immediately.

Soup
1 large carrot, chopped in ¼ inch cubes
2 celery stalks, chopped in ¼ inch cubes
2 Bermuda or sweet onions, chopped in ¼ inch cubes
2 large potatoes, in ¼ inch cubes
6 fresh tomatoes, seeded and chopped in ¼ inch pieces
1 tbsp. curry powder

¼ cup fresh thyme leaves, minced
6 small cloves garlic, minced
½ tsp. cinnamon
1 lb fresh white fish fillets, preferably red snapper, yellowtail or grouper

Combine strained stock and all soup ingredients except fish and simmer gently in stock for 2 hours. Add fish and cook another 15 minutes. Serve immediately with warm rolls.

From: *Traditions & Tastes*, **by Judith Wadson**

Fourways Inn Fish Chowder

(serves 12)

Ingredients
1 gallon fish stock
1½ lb Bermuda fish (snapper, rockfish, etc.)
½ lb onions, finely diced
½ lb celery, finely diced
½ lb carrots, finely diced
1 lb tomatoes, finely diced
2 bay leaves
4 cloves garlic, finely chopped
4 oz tomato purée
4 oz parsley, chopped
4 oz butter
2 oz thyme
4 oz Worcestershire sauce
Salt and pepper to taste

In a heavy-bottomed pot, sweat all vegetables and garlic on low heat. Then add pulped tomatoes and tomato purée, fish stock and fish. Simmer for about an hour and finish with fresh herbs. Serve with a splash of black rum and a judicious dash of sherry peppers.

From: *Fourways Inn*

Current World and Bermuda Gamefish Records Set in Bermuda

Current Line Class World Records Set in Bermuda as of 1 February 1997

Common Name	Line Class*	Weight kg	lb	Place	Date	Angler
Amberjack	M–10 kg/20 lb	54.17	119 lb 7 oz	Bermuda	16/6/80	Willard R. Watson
Amberjack	M–15 kg/30 lb	67.58	149 lb	Bermuda	21/6/64	Peter Simmons
Amberjack (tie)	M–37 kg/80 lb	70.59	155 lb 10 oz	Challenger Bank	24/6/81	Joseph Dawson
	M–37 kg/80 lb	70.64	155 lb 12 oz	Bermuda	16/8/92	Larry Trott
Jack, horse-eye	W–6 kg/12 lb	10.20	22 lb 8 oz	Argus	17/7/90	Mrs W. Beauchamp
Runner, rainbow	W–2 kg/4 lb	6.46	14 lb 4 oz	Argus Bank	18/7/94	Mrs W. B. DuVal
Tuna, blackfin	M–3 kg/6 lb	13.15	29 lb	Challenger Bank	6/8/72	Keith Winter
Tuna, blackfin**	M–6 kg/12 lb	17.94	39 lb 9 oz	Challenger Bank	27/6/87	Francis H.P. Patterson
Tuna, blackfin	M–15 kg/30 lb	18.59	41 lb	Bermuda	19/9/90	James R.M. Parris
Tuna, blackfin	M–24 kg/50 lb	19.05	42 lb	Bermuda	2/6/78	Alan J. Card
Tuna, blackfin	W–10 kg/20 lb	14.57	32 lb 2 oz	Bermuda	23/10/68	Mrs Herbert Arnold
Tuna, blackfin	W–24 kg/50 lb	17.09	37 lb 11 oz	Northwest Edge	25/8/82	Denise O'Toole
Tuna, skipjack	M–10 kg/20 lb	17.80	39 lb 4 oz	Challenger Bank	13/7/78	Keith Winter
Tuna, yellowfin	W–3 kg/6 lb	17.74	39 lb 11 oz	Challenger Bank	5/7/80	Janet M. Lines
Tuna, yellowfin	W–4 kg/8 lb	28.43	62 lb 11 oz	Challenger Bank	28/8/87	Dylis Pantry
Tunny, little	M–4 kg/8 lb	9.97	22 lb	Challenger Bank	31/12/89	David D. Barber
Tunny, little	M–8 kg/16 lb	10.61	23 lb 6 oz	Challenger Bank	18/8/91	Bertie Lines
Tunny, little	M–10 kg/20 lb	12.81	28 lb 4 oz	Challenger Bank	2/7/94	Robert Charles Davies
Tunny, little	W–8 kg/16 lb	14.62	32 lb 4 oz	Challenger Bank	23/6/90	Susan D. Wilson
Wahoo	M–6 kg/12 lb	36.93	81 lb 7 oz	North Rock	22/12/84	Michael Midgett
Wahoo	M–10 kg/20 lb	52.16	115 lb	Bermuda	2/7/61	Leo Barboza

*M = Men's record   W = Women's record   ** New record of 39 lb 12 oz (by J. Guzman, Miami, Florida) since approved by IGFA

Current Fly Rod World Records Set in Bermuda as of 1 February 1997

Common Name	Tippet	Weight kg	lb	Place	Date	Angler
Runner, rainbow	3 kg/6 lb	2.72	6 lb	Bermuda	29/6/72	Lefty Kreh
Tuna, yellowfin	6 kg/12 lb	30.61	67 lb 8 oz	Bermuda	7/7/73	Jim Lopez
Tuna, yellowfin	8 kg/16 lb	36.74	81 lb	Bermuda	28/6/73	Jim Lopez

Bermuda Gamefish Association Current Record Catches

Amberjack (*Seriola dumerili*)

Line test				
2 lb	Vacant			
4 lb	Vacant			
6 lb	30 lb	13/9/80	Raul Miranda	
8 lb	47 lb 12 oz	20/7/90	W. Du Val	
12 lb	76 lb 10 oz	8/9/63	J. H. Stubbs	
16 lb	Vacant			
20 lb	119 lb 7 oz	16/6/80	W. Watson	
30 lb	149 lb	21/6/64	P. Simons	
50 lb	92 lb 4 oz	30/6/96	Warren McHarg	
80 lb (tie)	155 lb 10 oz	24/6/81	J. Dawson	
	155 lb 12 oz	16/8/92	L. Trott	

Bonefish (*Albula vulpes*)

Line test			
2 lb	7 lb 4 oz	18/5/92	Graeme Dick
4 lb	9 lb	11/11/91	William Frith
6 lb	11 lb 4 oz	17/8/78	Douglas Marotta
8 lb	12 lb 3 oz	5/5/83	Norberto Herrero
12 lb	13 lb 9 oz	7/2/52	W. R. Higgs
16 lb	Vacant		
20 lb	14 lb	29/12/50	Dr H. R. Becker

Dolphin (*Coryphaena hippurus*)

Line test			
2 lb	Vacant		
4 lb	17 lb 8 oz	7/11/89	David Pantry
6 lb	16 lb 12 oz	22/9/73	Dr Robert Brien
8 lb	27 lb 6 oz	15/7/93	Lisa Booth
12 lb	38 lb 8 oz	1/9/73	John Berg
16 lb	30 lb 12 oz	20/9/92	Charles Robinson
20 lb	60 lb 8 oz	6/10/91	Francis Patterson
30 lb	63 lb	22/5/78	Jeffrey Cobb
50 lb	Vacant		

Jack, Horse-eye (*Caranx latus*)

Line test				
2 lb	Vacant		
4 lb	Vacant		
6 lb	Vacant		
8 lb	19.1 lb	14/7/94	G. B. Sowers III
12 lb	23 lb 6 oz	30/8/85	Andrew Down
16 lb	16 lb 4 oz	27/5/83	Andrew Down
20 lb	22 lb	30/8/85	Keith Winter
30 lb	Vacant		
50 lb	Vacant		
80 lb	Vacant		

Jack, Almaco (*Seriola rivoliana*)

Line test				
2 lb	Vacant		
4 lb	8 lb	13/7/90	Gene Duval
6 lb	28 lb 4 oz	5/12/77	Gary Rego
8 lb	65 lb 12 oz	20/7/90	Pete Rose
12 lb	64 lb 12 oz	10/7/78	David Lines
16 lb	Vacant		
20 lb	59 lb 4 oz	16/7/67	Wilfred Simmons
30 lb	73 lb 8 oz	19/7/75	Edmund Powell
50 lb	65 lb	30/6/63	Lester Virgil

Marlin, White (*Tetrapturus albidus*)

Line test				
2 lb	Vacant		
4 lb	Vacant		
6 lb	Vacant		
8 lb	Vacant		
12 lb	80.1 lb	27/5/90	Richard Ricca
16 lb	41 lb	30/6/91	Charles Robinson
20 lb	102 lb	29/5/60	Cmdr. C. Trumbull
30 lb	90 lb 10 oz	18/6/67	C. Robinson
50 lb	128 lb 10 oz*	23/5/48	Carl Bridges
80 lb	Vacant		

* The longest standing Bermuda record catch

Marlin, Atlantic Blue (*Makaira nigricans*)

Line test				
2 lb	Vacant		
4 lb	Vacant		
6 lb	Vacant		
8 lb	Vacant		
12 lb	Vacant		
16 lb	127 lb 4 oz	28/8/94	Maurice Shaffer
20 lb	471 lb 8 oz	18/7/89	Harold Rogers
30 lb	431 lb 8 oz	29/7/76	Gary Rego
50 lb	686 lb	28/7/88	Everard Simmons
80 lb	805 lb	19/6/89	Henry DeSilva
130 lb	1352 lb	1/8/95	Ken Danielson

Barracuda, great (*Sphyraena barracuda*)

Line test				
2 lb	Vacant		
4 lb	18 lb 8 oz	8/8/91	David Pantry
6 lb	24 lb 10 oz	2/8/73	Lawrence Maseiros
8 lb	30 lb	14/7/94	G. B. Sowers III
12 lb	40 lb	30/8/58	Edward Olander
16 lb	44.25 lb	2/2/91	Keith Winter
20 lb	44 lb 4 oz	14/9/63	Ralph Marshall
30 lb	64 lb	22/9/74	G. C. Collingwood
50 lb	57 lb 12 oz	25/11/77	Dendrick Taylor

Chub, Bermuda (*Kyphosus sectarix*)

Line test				
2 lb	3 lb 8 oz	17/6/88	J. Henry Gill
4 lb	6 lb	21/5/88	J. Henry Gill
6 lb	12 lb 11 oz	11/10/73	Joey Dawson
8 lb	Vacant		
12 lb	16 lb 10 oz	28/11/65	J. W. Rewalt
16 lb	Vacant		
20 lb	14 lb 12 oz	21/11/68	Vincent Symons
30 lb	12 lb 3 oz	28/10/69	Mrs G. Mosher

Palometa (*Trachinotus goodei*)

Line test	2 lb	Vacant		
	4 lb	Vacant		
	6 lb	4 lb	27/11/69	Clyde Adams
			7/7/72	Roy Outerbridge

Shark, Mako (*Isurus oxyrinchus*)

Line test	2 lb–20 lb	Vacant		
	30 lb	356 lb	17/2/93	Niel Jones
	50 lb	Vacant		
	80 lb	Vacant		
	130 lb	827 lb	4/8/96	Ian Card

Pompano, African (*Alectis ciliaris*)

Line test	2 lb	Vacant		
	4 lb	Vacant		
	6 lb	Vacant		
	8 lb	25 lb	19/7/90	Pete Rose
	12 lb	17 lb	13/7/90	Gene Duval
	16 lb	26 lb	18/9/96	Michael B. Leindel
	20 lb	Vacant		
	30 lb	41 lb 4 oz	13/11/93	Maurice Shaffer

Sailfish, Atlantic (*Istiophorus platypterus*)

Line test	2 lb	Vacant		
	4 lb	Vacant		
	6 lb	Vacant		
	8 lb	Vacant		
	12 lb	65 lb 8 oz	21/9/75	Allen DeSilva
	16 lb	Vacant		
	20 lb	43 lb 3 oz	19/10/69	Roland Lines
	30 lb	73 lb	19/11/72	James A. Pearman
	50 lb	Vacant		
	80 lb	Vacant		

Rainbow Runner (*Elagatis bipinnulata*)

Line test	2 lb	2.5 lb	12/7/90	Gene Duval
	4 lb	14 lb 4 oz	18/7/94	Gene Duval
	6 lb	13 lb 8 oz	6/9/75	Robert Rego
	8 lb	15 lb 4 oz	11/6/83	Linda Down
	12 lb	21 lb 8 oz	10/7/82	Grayton Greene
	16 lb	Vacant		
	20 lb	19 lb	25/7/81	Ted Whitehouse
	30 lb	24 lb 8 oz	20/6/63	J. Corrado
	50 lb	25 lb 6 oz	4/8/80	Martin Dixon

Tuna, Blackfin (*Thunnus atlanticus*)

Line test	2 lb	Vacant		
	4 lb	18.7 lb	12/11/89	R. Andrew Down
	6 lb	29 lb	6/8/72	Keith Winter
	8 lb	30 lb 4 oz	16/7/90	Gene Duval
	12 lb	39 lb 9 oz	27/6/87	Francis Patterson
	16 lb	Vacant		
	20 lb	42 lb	18/7/89	Gilbert Pearman
	30 lb	41 lb	19/9/90	James Parris
	50 lb	42 lb	2/6/78	Alan Card

Tuna, Yellowfin / Allison (*Thunnus albacares*)

Line test	2 lb	Vacant		
	4 lb	Vacant		
	6 lb	47 lb 1 oz	14/6/81	Herbert Hassell
	8 lb	63 lb 4 oz	16/9/89	David Barber
	12 lb	99.6 lb	17/9/89	Andrew Down
	16 lb	113 lb 8 oz	10/8/86	Dylis Pantry
	20 lb	136 lb 10 oz	2/5/71	Stanley Simmons
	30 lb	164 lb	4/6/78	David Fisher
	50 lb	116 lb	1/8/95	Keith Winter
	80 lb	199 lb 12 oz	9/8/85	L. Madeiros

Tuna, Skipjack (*Katsuwonus pelamis*)

Line test				
	2 lb	Vacant		
	4 lb	Vacant		
	6 lb	Vacant		
	8 lb	17 lb 2 oz	15/7/91	Pete Rose
	12 lb	32 lb 12 oz	9/7/88	Kevin Winter
	16 lb	Vacant		
	20 lb	39 lb 4 oz	13/7/78	Keith Winter
	30 lb	31 lb 8 oz	23/9/67	E. T. Sayer
	50 lb	27 lb 12 oz	31/12/57	Danny Martin

Tunny, Little (*Euthynnus alleteratus*)

Line test				
	2 lb	5 lb 8 oz	16/6/91	R. Andrew Down
	4 lb	Vacant		
	6 lb	18 lb	25/11/73	Norbert Monish
	8 lb	22 lb	31/12/89	David Barber
	12 lb	27 lb 8 oz	11/8/91	Chas O. D. Simons
	16 lb	32 lb 4 oz	23/6/90	Susan Wilson
	20 lb	28 lb 4 oz	2/7/94	Robert Charles Davies
	30 lb	29 lb	18/4/92	William Gresham

Tuna, Albacore (*Thunnus alalunga*)

Line test				
	2 lb-12 lb	Vacant		
	16 lb	59 lb	30/6/96	Robert W. Thomson
	20 lb	Vacant		
	30 lb	Vacant		
	50 lb	53 lb	30/6/96	Paul Markey

Tuna, Bluefin (*Thunnus thynnus*)

Line test				
	2 lb-50 lb	Vacant		
	80 lb	782 lb	8/6/79	William English

Wahoo (*Acanthocybium solanderi*)

Line test				
	2 lb	Vacant		
	4 lb	Vacant		
	6 lb	19 lb 3 oz	16/8/75	Tom Chasseur
	8 lb	49 lb 8 oz	4/9/89	David Pantry
	12 lb	81 lb 7 oz	27/12/84	Michael Midgett
	16 lb	65 lb	17/10/87	Mark Sidwell
	20 lb	115 lb	20/7/61	Leo Barboza
	30 lb	98 lb 10 oz	5/9/63	W. Imhauser
	50 lb	96.7 lb	27/9/91	Stephen Cabral
	80 lb	129 lb 4 oz	25/2/76	Edward Ray

Snapper, Grey (*Lutjanus griseus*)

Line test				
	2 lb (tie)	2 lb 4 oz	29/1/90	J. Henry Gill
			18/5/92	Robin Marirea
	4 lb	3 lb 4 oz	1/6/88	J. Henry Gill
	6 lb	8 lb 12 oz	27/7/80	Kenneth Henneberger
	8 lb	10.6 lb	14/7/94	Christian Sowers
	12 lb	15 lb	1/7/66	Gary Mayeaux
	16 lb	Vacant		
	20 lb	9 lb 14 oz	no date	Keith Winter

Snapper, Yellowtail (*Ocyurus chrysurus*)

Line test				
	2 lb	Vacant		
	4 lb	Vacant		
	6 lb	9 lb 4 oz	9/7/72	James A. Pearman
	8 lb	Vacant		
	12 lb	11 lb 10 oz	22/8/71	Ray Baptiste
	16 lb	Vacant		
	20 lb	11 lb 12 oz	26/7/67	Mrs T. Stock
	30 lb	Vacant		
	50 lb	13 lb 14 oz	29/8/71	James A. Pearman

Tarpon (*Megalops atlanticus*)

Line test   12 lb*   66 lb 4 oz   9/6/77   Kevin Winter

* The only line test record for this species in Bermuda

Spearfish (*Tetrapturus* spp.)

Line test   30 lb*   37 lb   25/9/88   Robert W. DeSilva

* The only line test record for this species in Bermuda

Current Bermuda Fly Tackle Records

Species	Tippet	Weight	Date	Angler
Bonefish	4 kg/8 lb	10 lb 4 oz	3/10/96	Stephen R. Gale
Bonito, Atlantic	3 kg/6 lb	6 lb 12 oz	28/6/72	Lefty Kreh
Runner, Rainbow	2 kg/4 lb	6 lb 8 oz	13/6/86	William Humes
	3 kg/6 lb	6 lb	29/6/72	Lefty Kreh
	10 kg/20 lb	2 lb 14 oz	23/7/92	William Duval
Tuna, Blackfin	6 kg/12 lb	28 lb	6/7/72	Jim Lopez
Tuna, Yellowfin	4 kg/8 lb	31 lb 8 oz	20/6/88	William Humes
	6 kg/12 lb	67 lb 8 oz	7/7/73	Jim Lopez
	8 kg/16 lb	81 lb	28/6/73	Jim Lopez
	10 kg/20 lb	37 lb 4 oz	17/7/91	Robert Trosset
Tunny, Little	1 kg/2 lb	2 lb 10 oz	28/6/86	James A. Pearman
Wahoo	10 kg/20 lb	43 lb 6 oz	17/7/91	Robert Trosset

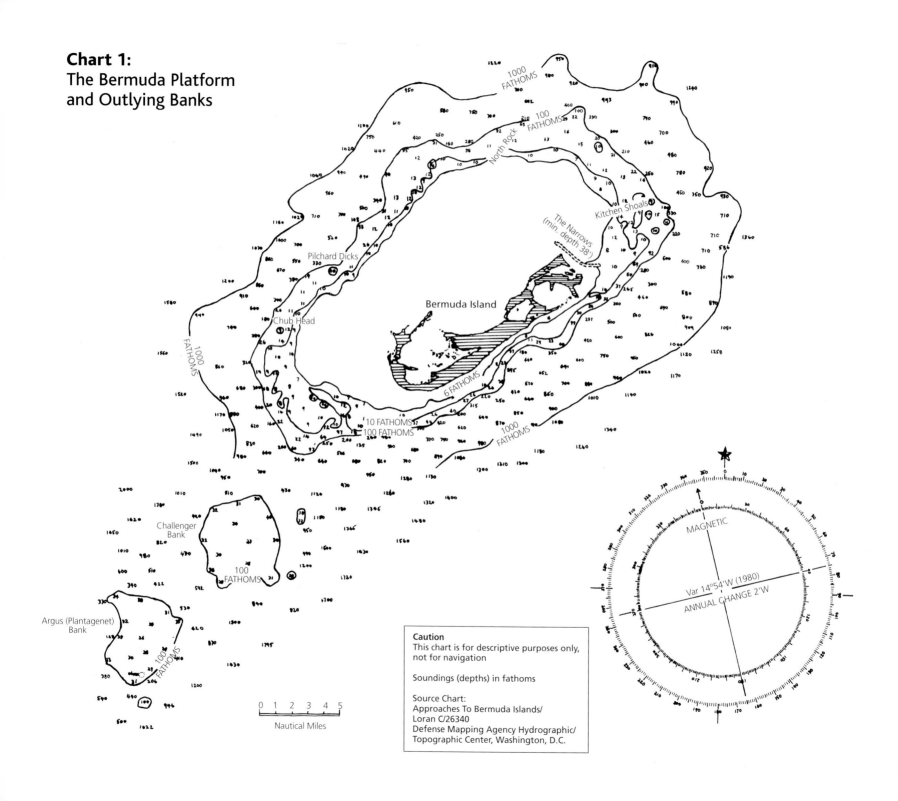

Chart 1:
The Bermuda Platform
and Outlying Banks

Bermuda Island

North Rock

Kitchen Shoals

The Narrows
(min. depth 38')

Pilchard Dicks

Chub Head

1000 FATHOMS

100 FATHOMS

6 FATHOMS

10 FATHOMS
100 FATHOMS

1000 FATHOMS

Challenger Bank

100 FATHOMS

Argus (Plantagenet) Bank

100 FATHOMS

0 1 2 3 4 5
Nautical Miles

MAGNETIC

Var 14°54'W (1980)
ANNUAL CHANGE 2'W

Caution
This chart is for descriptive purposes only,
not for navigation

Soundings (depths) in fathoms

Source Chart:
Approaches To Bermuda Islands/
Loran C/26340
Defense Mapping Agency Hydrographic/
Topographic Center, Washington, D.C.

Chart 2:
The Bermuda Platform, Reef Flats and Inshore Waters

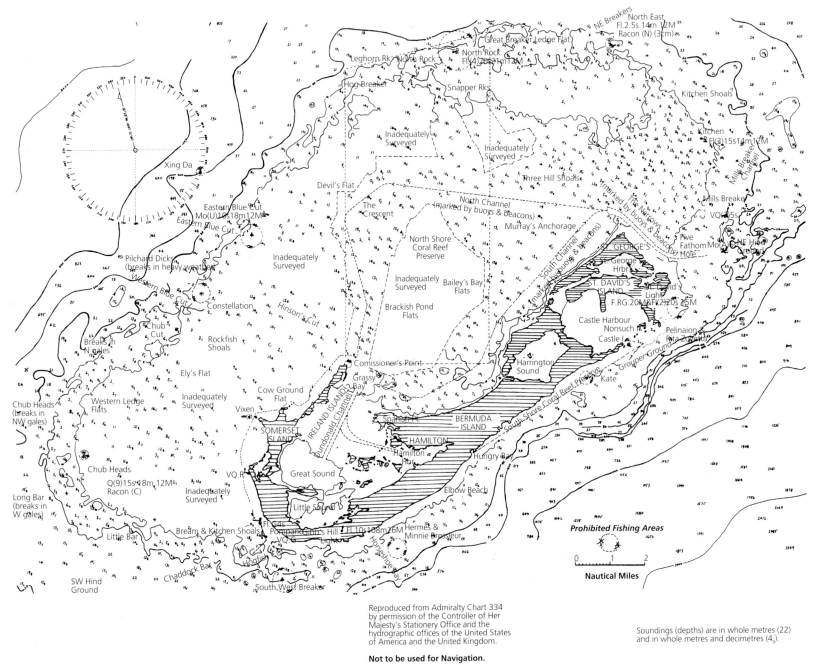

NE Breakers
North East
Fl.2.5s 14m 12M
Racon (N) (3cm)

Great Breaker Ledge Flat

Leghorn Rk · North Rock
North Rock
Fl(4)20s14m12M

Kitchen Shoals

Hog Breaker

Snapper Rks

Kitchen
Fl(3)15s14m12M

Xing Da

Inadequately
Surveyed

Inadequately
Surveyed

Three Hill Shoals

Mills Breaker
Channel

Mills Breaker

Devil's Flat

North Channel
(marked by buoys & beacons)

VQ.(3)5s

Eastern Blue Cut
Mo(U)10s18m12M

The
Crescent

Murray's Anchorage

Five
Fathom Mo(A) NE Hind
Hole Ground

Eastern Blue Cut

North Shore
Coral Reef
Preserve

ST. GEORGE'S
St. George
Hrbr.

Pilchard Dicks
(breaks in heavy weather)

Inadequately
Surveyed

Inadequately
Surveyed

Bailey's Bay
Flats

South Channel
(marked by buoys & beacons)

ST. DAVID'S
ISLAND
St. David's
Light
F.R.G.20M&Fl(2)20s 25M

Western Blue Cut

Constellation

Hinson's Cut

Brackish Pond
Flats

Castle Harbour
Nonsuch
Castle

Pelinaion
Rita Zovetta

Chub
Cut

Rockfish
Shoals

Harrington
Sound

Grouper Ground

Breaks in
N gales

Ely's Flat

Comissioner's Point

Kate

Western Ledge
Flats

Inadequately
Surveyed

Cow Ground
Flat

Grassy
Bay

South Shore Coral Reef Preserve

Chub Heads
(breaks in
NW gales)

Vixen

IRELAND ISLAND

Spanish Pt.

BERMUDA
ISLAND

Hungry Bay

SOMERSET
ISLAND

Dundonald Channel

HAMILTON

Chub Heads
Q(9)15s18m.12M
Racon (C)

VQ.R.

Great Sound

Hamilton
Hrbr.

Elbow Beach

Prohibited Fishing Areas

Long Bar
(breaks in
W gales)

Inadequately
Surveyed

Little Sound

Bream & Kitchen Shoals

Fl.4s
Pompano Gibb's Hill
VQ.G. Light

Fl.10s108m26M

Hermes &
Minnie Bresleur

Little Bar

Hogfish

Horseshoe Bay

0   1   2

Nautical Miles

SW Hind
Ground

Chaddock Bar

South West Breaker

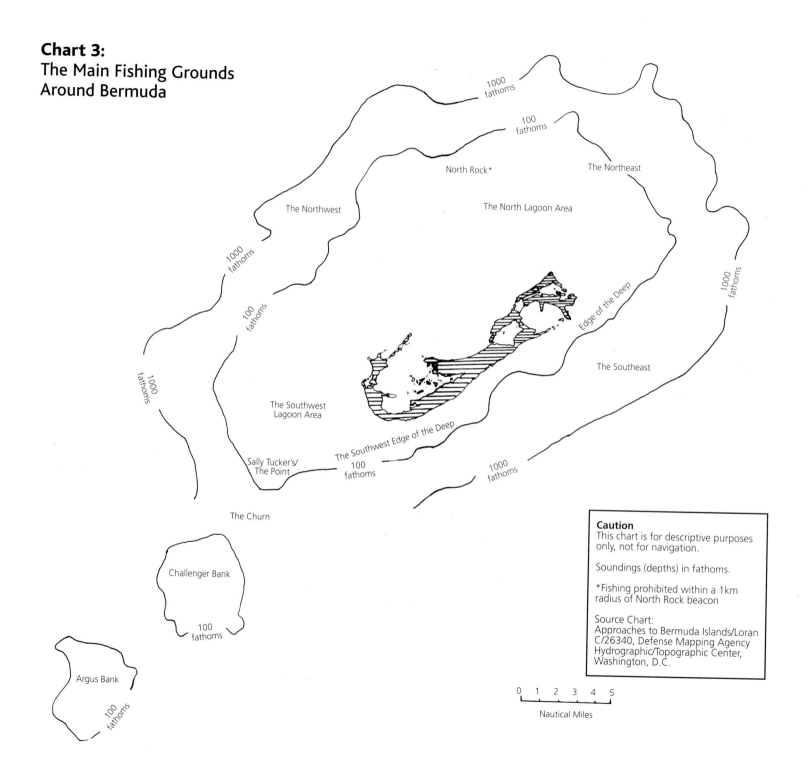

Chart 3:
The Main Fishing Grounds
Around Bermuda

1000 fathoms

100 fathoms

North Rock*

The Northeast

The Northwest

The North Lagoon Area

1000 fathoms

100 fathoms

1000 fathoms

Edge of the Deep

1000 fathoms

The Southeast

The Southwest
Lagoon Area

The Southwest Edge of the Deep

Sally Tucker's/
The Point

100 fathoms

1000 fathoms

The Churn

Challenger Bank

100 fathoms

Argus Bank

100 fathoms

Caution
This chart is for descriptive purposes
only, not for navigation.

Soundings (depths) in fathoms.

*Fishing prohibited within a 1km
radius of North Rock beacon

Source Chart:
Approaches to Bermuda Islands/Loran
C/26340, Defense Mapping Agency
Hydrographic/Topographic Center,
Washington, D.C.

0 1 2 3 4 5

Nautical Miles

Chart 4:
The Route to the Banks
(From King's Point/Mangrove Bay)

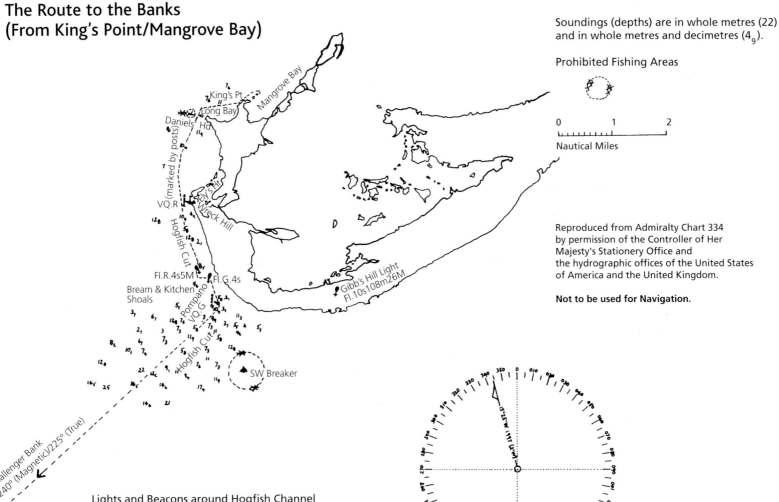

Soundings (depths) are in whole metres (22) and in whole metres and decimetres (4₉).

Prohibited Fishing Areas

0   1   2

Nautical Miles

Reproduced from Admiralty Chart 334 by permission of the Controller of Her Majesty's Stationery Office and the hydrographic offices of the United States of America and the United Kingdom.

Not to be used for Navigation.

Mangrove Bay

King's Pt

Long Bay

Daniels Hd

VQ.R

Ely's Hr

Wreck Hill

Hogfish Cut

Fl.R.4s5M

Fl.G.4s

Bream & Kitchen Shoals

Pompano VQ.G

Hogfish Cut

SW Breaker

Gibb's Hill Light
Fl.10s108m26M

Challenger Bank
240° (Magnetic)/225° (True)

Lights and Beacons around Hogfish Channel

(Buoyage Region B: *From seaward*, leave red lights/marks to starboard (right), green marks to port (left). *From shoreward*, leave red lights/marks to port (left), green marks to starboard (right).

Pompano Beacon (VQ.G): Very quick flashing green light (80 flashes/minute) – turning mark for entrance into Hogfish Channel

Hogfish Tripod (Fl.G4s): Flashing green light every 4 seconds

Hogfish Cut Beacon (Fl.R.4s): Flashing red light every 4 seconds

Wreck Hill Beacon (VQ.R): Very quick flashing red light (80 flashes/minute)

Chart 5:
Main External Parts of a Fish

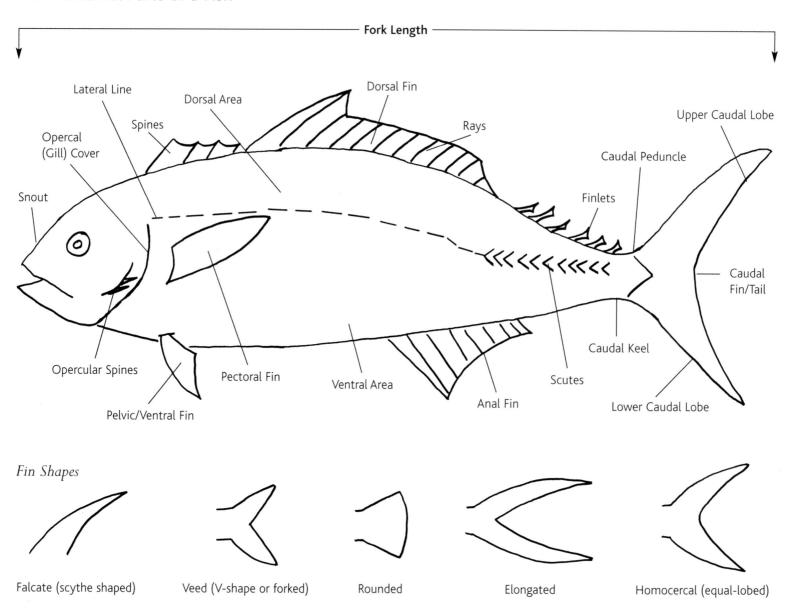

Fork Length

Lateral Line
Dorsal Area
Dorsal Fin
Rays
Upper Caudal Lobe
Spines
Opercal (Gill) Cover
Caudal Peduncle
Finlets
Snout
Caudal Fin/Tail
Opercular Spines
Pectoral Fin
Ventral Area
Scutes
Caudal Keel
Pelvic/Ventral Fin
Anal Fin
Lower Caudal Lobe

Fin Shapes

Falcate (scythe shaped)   Veed (V-shape or forked)   Rounded   Elongated   Homocercal (equal-lobed)

Graph 1: Commercial Fishing Vessel Licence Fees in Bermuda 1988/89–1999/2000

Source: Ministry of Environment Fishing Industry Green Paper, January 2000

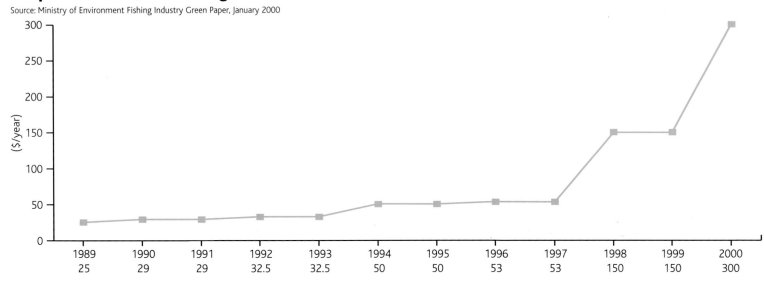

Year	1989	1990	1991	1992	1993	1994	1995	1996	1997	1998	1999	2000
($/year)	25	29	29	32.5	32.5	50	50	53	53	150	150	300

Graph 2: No. of Commercial Fishermen and Fishing Boats Licensed in Bermuda 1990–1998

Source: Dept of Agric. & Fisheries

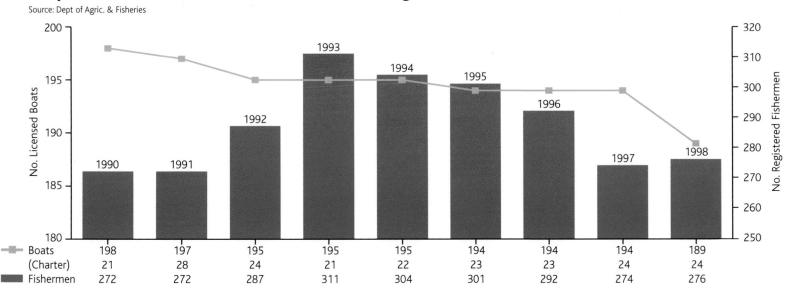

	1990	1991	1992	1993	1994	1995	1996	1997	1998
Boats	198	197	195	195	195	194	194	194	189
(Charter)	21	28	24	21	22	23	23	24	24
Fishermen	272	272	287	311	304	301	292	274	276

Graph 3: The Catch/Landings* of all Finfish in Bermuda by Main Species Groups 1986–1998

*Officially recorded by commercial fishermen; **Turbot, porgy, bream, etc. Source: Dept of Agric. & Fisheries

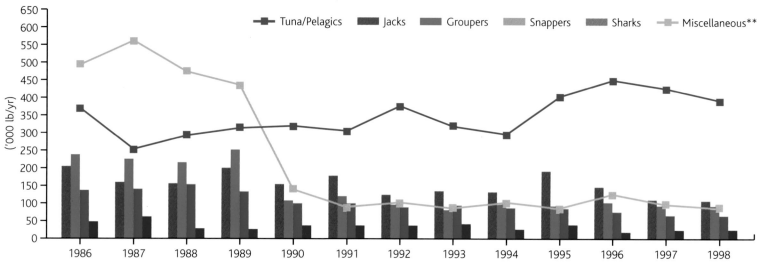

Graph 4: Composition of Foodfish Catch in Bermuda by Main Species Groups 1975–1998

*Including sharks; **Turbot, porgy, bream, chub, etc. Source: Dept of Agric. & Fisheries

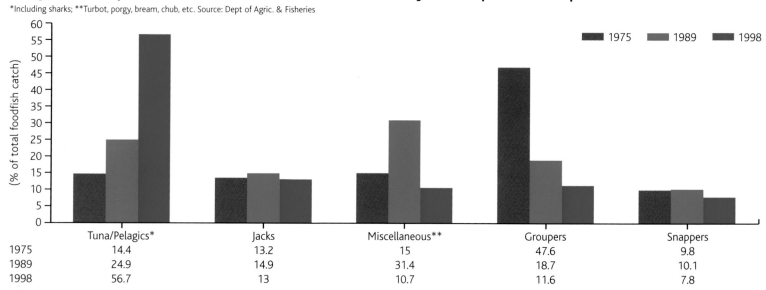

	Tuna/Pelagics*	Jacks	Miscellaneous**	Groupers	Snappers
1975	14.4	13.2	15	47.6	9.8
1989	24.9	14.9	31.4	18.7	10.1
1998	56.7	13	10.7	11.6	7.8

Graph 5: The Catch/Landings* of Groupers in Bermuda by Main Species 1986–1998

*Officially recorded by commercial fishermen. Source: Dept of Agric. & Fisheries

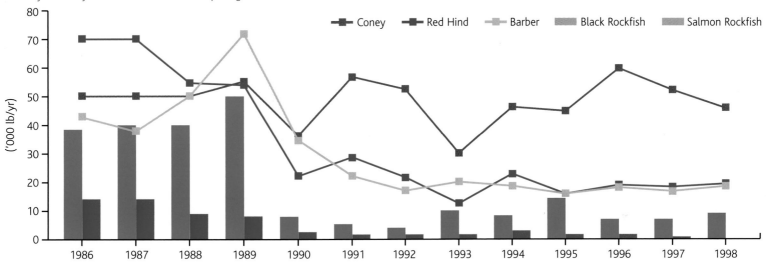

Graph 6: The Catch/Landings* of 'Rockfish' and Nassau Grouper in Bermuda by Species 1975–1998

*Officially recorded by registered commercial fishermen. Source: Dept of Agric. & Fisheries

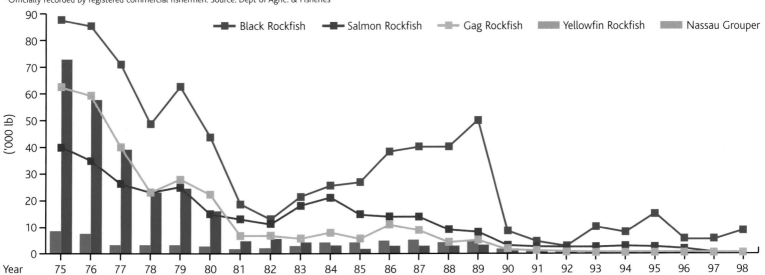

Graph 7: The Catch/Landings* of Coney, Red Hind and Barber in Bermuda 1975–1998

*Officially recorded by registered commercial fishermen. Source: Dept of Agric. & Fisheries

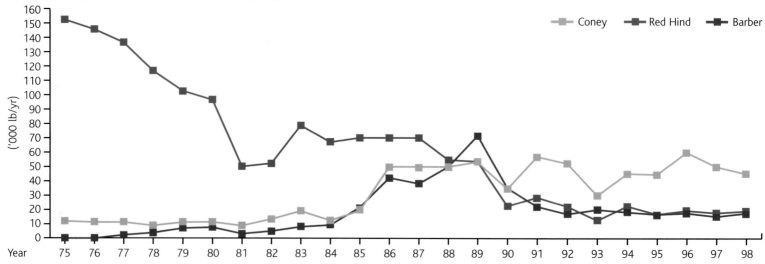

Graph 8: The Catch/Landings* of Tuna and Other Pelagic Fish in Bermuda 1986–1998

*Officially recorded/registered by commercial fishermen. Source: Dept of Agric. & Fisheries

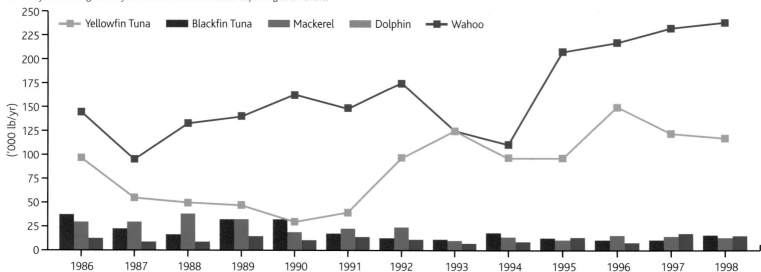

Graph 9: The Catch/Landings* of Blue/White Marlin and Barracuda in Bermuda 1986–1998

*Officially recorded/registered by commercial fishermen. Source: Dept of Agric. & Fisheries

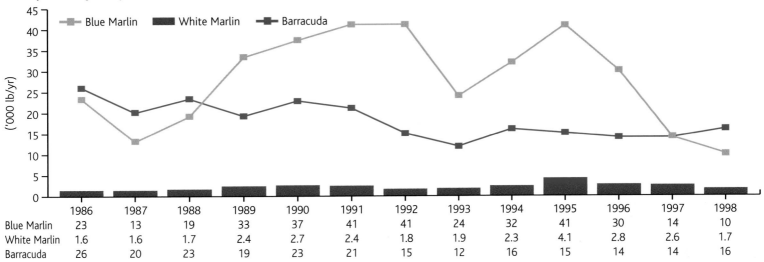

	1986	1987	1988	1989	1990	1991	1992	1993	1994	1995	1996	1997	1998
Blue Marlin	23	13	19	33	37	41	41	24	32	41	30	14	10
White Marlin	1.6	1.6	1.7	2.4	2.7	2.4	1.8	1.9	2.3	4.1	2.8	2.6	1.7
Barracuda	26	20	23	19	23	21	15	12	16	15	14	14	16

Graph 10: No. of Blue Marlin Caught and Released in Bermuda 1990–1998*

*To 1 November 1998. Source: 'Bermuda's Marlin Fishery, etc.', B. Luckhurst 1998

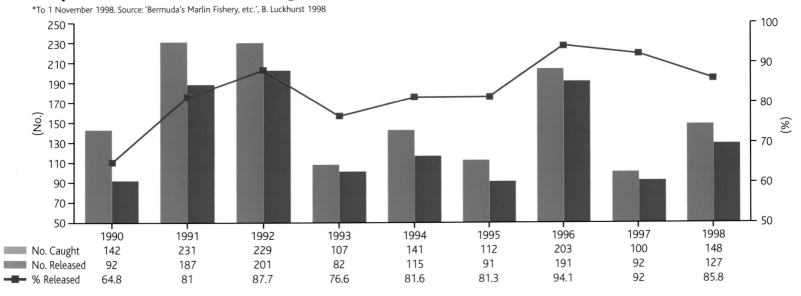

	1990	1991	1992	1993	1994	1995	1996	1997	1998
No. Caught	142	231	229	107	141	112	203	100	148
No. Released	92	187	201	82	115	91	191	92	127
% Released	64.8	81	87.7	76.6	81.6	81.3	94.1	92	85.8

Bibliography

Bermuda

Andersen, Raoul. Bermudian Handline Fishing in the Sailing Sloop Era: A Fisherman's Account. In: B. Gunda (ed.), *The Fishing Culture of the World*. Akademiai Kiado, Hungarian Academy Of Sciences, Budapest 1984.

Bardach, John E. and Mowbray, Louis S. Bermuda Fisheries Research Program. Progress Report No. 2, 7 November 1955.

Bardach, John E, Smith, C. L. and Menzel, D. W. Bermuda Fisheries Research Program: Final Report. Bermuda Trade Development Board, Hamilton, Bermuda. August 1958.

Barrett, Gene. *The Fish Pot Ban: Reef Overfishing and State Management in Bermuda. Mast*, Vol. 4(2), 1991.

Bean, T.H. *A Catalogue of the Fishes of Bermuda* (1906).

Beebe, William and Tee-Van, John. *Field Book of the Shore Fishes of Bermuda and the West Indies.* Dover Publications, Inc., 1970.

The Bermudian Magazine. Our Threatened Fish Industry. May 1990.

The Bermudian Magazine. Mind Over Mulletts. December 1997.

The Bermudian Magazine. 'Gone Fishin'. September 1989.

Brooks, Joe. *Bermuda Fishing*. The Stackpole Co., 1957.

Brooks, Joe. *A World of Fishing* (one chapter on Bermuda). D. Van Nostrand Company, Inc., New York, 1964.

Collette, Bruce B., Luckhurst, Brian A. and Smith-Vaniz, William F. *Fishes of Bermuda: History, Zoogeography, Annotated Checklist, and Identification Keys.* American Society of Ichthyologists and Herpetologists, Special Publication No. 4, 1999.

Downing, Jane. *Memories of a West End Fisherman: The Pre-War Years.* Bermuda Maritime Museum. Winter 1990.

Gammon, Clive. A Fine Kettle of Fish. *Sports Illustrated*, 5 June 1978.

Glussing, Capt. Bill. Bermuda's Triangle: A Trio of Skippers Hold Mystical Powers Over this Island's Granders: Marlin. *The International Sportfishing Magazine.* World Publications, Inc. April/May 1996.

Goode, G. Brown. *Catalogue of the Fishes of the Bermudas.* Smithsonian Institution, 1876.

Lefroy, J. H. *Memorials of the Discovery and Early Settlement of the Bermudas or Somers Islands 1515–1685.*

Luckhurst, B. E. Site Fidelity and Return Migration of Tagged Red Hinds (*Epinephelus guttatus*) to a Spawning Aggregation Site in Bermuda. Paper presented at the Gulf and Caribbean Fisheries Institute, 50th Annual Meeting, Mérida, Mexico, November 1997.

Luckhurst, B. E. Bermuda's Marlin Fishery – Catches of Blue Marlin (*Makaira nigricans*) and White Marlin (*Trapterus albidus*) with an Analysis of Recent Trends in Release Rate and Tournament Catch per Unit Effort. Paper presented at the Gulf and Caribbean Fisheries Institute, 51st Annual Meeting, St Croix, US Virgin Islands, 8–13 November 1998.

Luckhurst, B. E. Trends in Commercial Fishery Landings of Groupers and Snappers in Bermuda from 1975 to 1992 and Associated Fishery Management Issues, pp. 277–288. In F. Arreguín-Sánchez, J. L. Munro, M. C. Balgos and D. Pauly (eds), *Biology, Fisheries and Culture of Tropical Groupers and Snappers. ICLARM Conference Proceedings* **48**, 449pp.

Marine Resources and the Fishing Industry in Bermuda: A Discussion Paper. Ministry of the Environment, Government of Bermuda, Green Paper, January 2000.

McCallan, E. A. *Life on Old St David's Bermuda.* The Bermuda Historical Society, 1986. (First published 1948.)

Morris, B. *et al. The Bermuda Marine Environment.* Bermuda Biological Station, Special Publication No. 15, September 1977.

Mowbray, Louis S. *A Guide to the Reef, Shore and Game Fish of Bermuda.* Mowbray, 1965. (5th printing 1991.)

Mowbray, Louis S. The Commercial and Game Fishing Industries of Bermuda. Paper prepared for the Gulf and Caribbean Fisheries Institute held at Miami Beach, Florida, November 1949.

Mowbray, Louis S. The Modified Tuna Long-Line in Bermuda Waters. Paper presented at the 8th Annual Gulf & Caribbean Fisheries Institute, Miami Beach, Florida, 31 October–4 November 1955.

Perinchief, S. L. Bermuda: Island of Great Fishing. Pamphlet, 1965 (reprint *ca.* 1984).

Phillips, Hartie I. Bermuda – A Fisherman's Paradise. *Field and Stream Magazine*, No. 4, August 1907.

Sterrer, Wolfgang. *Bermuda's Marine Life* Bermuda Natural History Museum and Bermuda Zoological Society, 1992.

Wadson, Judith. *Traditions & Tastes.* Onion Skin Press, Portsmouth, RI, 1997.

The Fisheries Legislation of Bermuda. Legalex Bermuda, 1998.

The Mid Ocean News (various).

The Royal Gazette (various).

Report of the Commission of Inquiry: To examine and make recommendations for the future of the Fishing Industry and for the protection of the Marine Environment in Bermuda. February 1991.

Department of Agriculture and Fisheries Bermuda. *Annual Report* (various years).

Department of Agriculture, Fisheries & Parks Bermuda. *Monthly Bulletin* (various months/years).

Fisheries and Fisheries Management

Botsford, L, Castilla, J. C. and Peterson, C. H. The Management of Fisheries and Marine Ecosystems. *Science Magazine* No. 277, pp. 509–515, 25 July 1997.

Dyer, C. L. and McGoodwin, J. R. (eds). *Folk Management in the World's Fisheries.* University Press of Colorado, 1994.

Hardin, G. The Tragedy of the Commons. *Science Magazine* No. 162, pp. 1243–1248, 13 December 1968.

Hardin, G. Extensions of 'The Tragedy of the Commons'. S*cience Magazine* No. 280, pp 682–683, 1 May 1998.

Ostrom, E, Burger, J., Field, C. B., Norgaard, R. B. and Policansky, D. Revisiting The Commons: Local Lessons, Global Challenges. *Science Magazine* No. 284, pp 278–282, 9 April 1999.

Pinkerton, E. (ed). *Cooperative Management of Local Fisheries: New Directions for Improved Management & Community Development.* University of British Columbia Press, Vancouver, 1989.

Fish and Fishing

Ellis, Richard. *The Book of Sharks.* Alfred A. Knopf, 1996.

Goodson, Gar. *Fishes of the Atlantic Coast: Canada to Brazil, including the Gulf of Mexico, Florida, Bermuda, the Bahamas, and the Caribbean.* Stanford University Press, 1995.

Goadby, Peter. *Saltwater Gamefishing, Offshore and Onshore.* Angus & Robertson, 1996.

Bauer, Erwin A. *The Saltwater Fisherman's Bible.* Doubleday, 1991.

Dunaway, Vic. *Vic Dunaway's Complete Book of Baits Rigs & Tackle: Freshwater/Saltwater.* Wickstrom Publishers, Inc., 1995.

Zinzow, Jack. *Saltwater Fishing: Tackle, Rigging, How & When to Fish.* Windward Publishing, Inc., 1992.

How to Rig Baits For Trolling. Penn Fishing Tackle Manufacturing Company. Philadelphia, PA, 1987.

Sport Fishing: The Magazine of Saltwater Fishing. World Publications, Inc., FL.

Marlin: The International Sportfishing Magazine. World Publications, Inc., FL.

General / Miscellaneous

The Oceans. *Scientific American,* Autumn 1998.

The Times Atlas of the Oceans. Times Books Ltd, 1983.

Index

Page numbers in *italics* refer to illustrations